Arthur Underhill

A Practical and Concise Manual of the Procedure of the Chancery Division

Of the High Court of Justice, Both in Actions and Matters

Arthur Underhill

A Practical and Concise Manual of the Procedure of the Chancery Division
Of the High Court of Justice, Both in Actions and Matters

ISBN/EAN: 9783337159184

Printed in Europe, USA, Canada, Australia, Japan

Cover: Foto ©Suzi / pixelio.de

More available books at **www.hansebooks.com**

A

Practical and Concise Manual

OF THE

PROCEDURE

OF THE

CHANCERY DIVISION

OF THE

HIGH COURT OF JUSTICE,

BOTH IN ACTIONS AND MATTERS.

BY

ARTHUR UNDERHILL, M.A., LL.D.,

OF LINCOLN'S INN, BARRISTER-AT-LAW,

Author of " A Concise Treatise on the Law of Private Trusts and
Trustees;" and " A Summary of the Law of Torts."

LONDON:

BUTTERWORTHS, 7, FLEET STREET,

Law Publishers to the Queen's most excellent Majesty.

DUBLIN: HODGES, FIGGIS & CO.
EDINBURGH: T. & T. CLARK; BELL & BRADFUTE.
CALCUTTA: THACKER, SPINK & CO.   MELBOURNE: GEO. ROBERTSON.

1881.

TO

VICE-CHANCELLOR

The Hon. Sir CHARLES HALL, Knight,

One of the Judges of Her Majesty's High Court of Justice,

AS A HUMBLE TRIBUTE

TO HIS EMINENT JUDICIAL QUALITIES, AND TO THE UNVARYING COURTESY

WHICH HE DISPLAYS

TOWARDS ALL WHO PRACTISE BEFORE HIM,

This Work

IS,

BY PERMISSION,

MOST RESPECTFULLY INSCRIBED.

PREFACE.

Now that the old Court of Chancery has become merged in the new High Court of Justice, it may be asked why a separate account of the procedure of the Chancery Division, as distinguished from the entire court, is needed? The answer is, that although theoretically it is true, with certain limitations, that any cause of action may be tried in any division of the court, yet there is a large and important class of actions, necessarily confined to the Chancery Division, because that division alone possesses the administrative machinery, without which the complicated questions which perpetually arise in the execution of trusts, the distribution of estates, and the general administration of property, cannot be satisfactorily worked out. No fusion of Law and Equity can make the same procedure applicable to the decision of an action for goods sold and delivered, and the administration of the property of a deceased millionnaire.

In addition to this, it is found that in practice but few actions of a Common Law nature are commenced in the Chancery Division.

The procedure, therefore, in each of the several divisions of the High Court has, what may be figuratively called, an individuality of its own, as well as a common similarity; and I am led to the conclusion that a guide to the procedure of the Chancery Division, setting forth so much of the general rules of the procedure of the High Court as is applicable to this division in common with the others, adding to that general practice the procedure which is solely applicable to this division, and omitting all such rules as are solely applicable to other divisions of the court, will not be unacceptable.

Then as to the scope of this Work. In the first place, it makes no pretence to be a complete and detailed Treatise on the *minutiæ* of Chancery practice. Such a book would necessarily be some ten times the bulk of this one, and could not hope to compete with the well-known volumes of Mr. Daniell, or with the very excellent work on the subject just produced by Mr. Frank Evans. On the other hand, it is not meant as a *mere outline* for the use of persons who may wish to acquire only a general notion of Chancery practice.

In short, my aim has been to produce in relation to Chancery, a work somewhat similar to what was effected in relation to Common Law procedure, by the late John Gray, Esq., Q.C., in his well-known " Country Attorney's Practice ;" a work which shall afford to the practitioner information on all the usual points occurring in practice, and at the same time be so arranged, and so compressed, as to be a useful and complete text-book for the student.

I have entirely omitted all reference to the procedure observed in matters arising under the Companies Acts, 1862 to 1877, because such matters could not be properly considered in a small work like this, and also because they practically form a distinct and special branch of practice, to the explanation of which entire books have been devoted.

In conclusion I have to express my thanks to my friend Mr. T. M. Whitehouse, jun., of the Middle Temple, for kindly assisting me in the perusal and correction of the proof sheets.

ARTHUR UNDERHILL.

23, SOUTHAMPTON BUILDINGS, CHANCERY LANE.
July, 1881.

CONTENTS.

DIVISION I.—OF ACTIONS.

SUB-DIVISION I.— THE WRIT OF SUMMONS.

DIVISION II.—OF MATTERS.

SUB-DIVISION I.—MATTERS RELATING TO TRUSTEES.

DIVISION III.—OF PROCEEDINGS COMMON TO ACTIONS AND MATTERS.

TABLE OF CASES.

—◆—

U.

b

TABLE OF

" RULES & ORDERS OF THE SUPREME COURT, 1875."

4

U.   c

A

Practical and Concise Manual

OF THE

PROCEDURE OF THE CHANCERY DIVISION

OF THE

HIGH COURT OF JUSTICE.

———◆———

INTRODUCTORY.

BEFORE an account of the procedure which is observed in the Chancery Division of the High Court of Justice can be intelligently followed, it is necessary for the reader to have some general knowledge of the history of the several courts of law and equity which, after an interval of seven centuries, were re-united by the Judicature Act, 1873, and now form the divers divisions of one tribunal.

For this purpose we must direct our attention to times not far removed from the Norman Conquest, and taking the reign of the first Henry as our point of departure, sketch roughly the rise of English jurisprudence from the establishment of the first formal Court of Imperial jurisdiction dispensing justice throughout the realm, and exercising authority over all local courts, to the latest reconstruction of our system of judicature in the year 1875.

U.   B

4

Henry I. introduced into England, what I may perhaps be permitted to call a new and improved civil service.

An official was appointed of great dignity and power, who bore the title of "Justiciar," and whose office, shorn of its political attributes, still survives in that of the Lord Chief Justice of England. The Justiciar acted as lieutenant-general of the kingdom and regent of the realm in the king's absence, and his staff of assistants, chosen from the barons connected with the royal household, formed a court in the broadest sense, not a court merely for the administration of justice, but a court having three distinct functions :—As a royal council it exercised (it is true by a merely formal consent to the king's will) legislative and consultative functions ; in this character it subsists to this day in the Privy Council. As a council of finance, it saw to and regulated the assessment and collection of the revenue ; and as a court of justice it exercised both civil and criminal jurisdiction, and, by a process which still survives in the Queen's Bench Division in the writ of *certiorari*, it could call up suits from all lower tribunals (*a*), and, by its writ of *mandamus*, could compel them to do their duty.

Parvis componere magna, the bureaucracy introduced by Henry I., bore some likeness to the lower ranks of the civil service of British India at the present date, the same individual acting at once as a judge, a collector of revenue, and an administrative official.

In the reign of Henry II., however, this union of functions ceased, and the king's court or council was

(*a*) See Green's Hist. of the English People, vol. i. p. 145.

broken up by the severance of the purely legal members. These members became simply judges, and formed a court which still continued to bear the name of the *Aula Regis*, or King's Court (b). This separation of the *Aula Regis* from the king's council had a very important bearing on the future of English jurisprudence.

So long as justice was dispensed by the king in council, by a body possessing legislative as well as judicial functions, the court was not fettered by the strict letter of the law, nor bound to follow precedent and custom to the verge of injustice. To some extent such a court could *make law* for the redress of a wrong. But the new court possessed no such powers. It was merely the exponent of the law. However hardly the application of the law might bear upon particular persons, the new court was still bound to apply it. If Shylock demanded his pound of flesh according to law, such a court was bound to give him judgment. But "*jus summum sæpe summa est malitia*," and however valuable the new tribunal might be (and it was most valuable) for building up a fixed and certain rule of civil conduct, in place of the arbitrary moral code of successive monarchs, it is obvious that such a court, fenced round with precedents, and restricting itself in a way which we must now pronounce to be somewhat pedantic and narrow, must frequently not only have failed to redress a wrong, but, in many cases, have actually aided an unconscientious but acute suitor in the commission of gross injustice.

To give an instance of this, the *Aula Regis* presumed

(b) Ib. vol. i. p. 326.

B 2

that every kind of civil injury must fall within the limits of some particular form of action, (*ex. gr.* trespass, replevin, debt, and so on), and this presumption was so rigidly acted upon, that unless an injury could be referred to some established form of action, the injured party was left without remedy.

This narrowness of the *Aula Regis* led to Henry II. reserving to himself and the royal council the cognizance of all cases in which the judges failed to do justice, and it is in this reservation that we see the first seeds of the appellate jurisdiction of the House of Lords, the Privy Council, and the equitable jurisdiction of the Lord Chancellor (*c*).

Putting aside the provision of the Great Charter, that the court for hearing suits between subject and subject should remain in one place, the scheme of judicature commenced in the reign of Henry II. lasted until the time of Edward I. That monarch greatly modified and improved it. By him the *Aula Regis* was divided into three distinct courts. To the Court of King's Bench was assigned the cognizance of all suits (including criminal cases), affecting the king or government; to the Court of Exchequer was assigned all cases affecting the royal revenue; and to the Court of Common Pleas jurisdiction was given in all suits between subject and subject.

It is no part of this Work to trace the causes which led to the first two of these courts acquiring a concurrent jurisdiction with the last; it is sufficient to state, that by a series of acute legal fictions and quibbles, both Queen's Bench and Exchequer eventually succeeded in obtaining cognizance of all civil suits.

(*c*) Green's Hist. of the English People, vol. i. p. 180.

In the same reign that this separation of the courts took place, an attempt was made to render the procedure of these courts more elastic, and to give them jurisdiction to afford relief in cases which would not fall under any existing form of action, by an act by which it was enacted, that " whensoever from henceforth it shall fortune in the Chancery, that in one case a writ is found, and in like case falling under like law and requiring like remedy is found none, the clerks of the Chancery (who were the writ issuing officials of the time), shall agree in making the writ, or the plaintiff may adjourn it until the next parliament; and let the cases be written in which they cannot agree, and let them refer them unto the next parliament, and by agreement of men learned in the law, let a writ be made, lest it should happen that the court should long time fail to minister justice unto complainants " (d).

New forms of action created under the provisions of this statute were called " actions on the case," but partly owing to the jealousy of the judges (who disallowed many of the new writs), partly to the fact that although new *complaints* were allowed, new and just *defences* were left unprovided for, and partly to the fact that the new writs being limited to " *like* cases falling under *like* law, and requiring *like* remedy," did not apply to *dissimilar* cases requiring *dissimilar* remedies, there still remained, and as civilization increased there arose from time to time civil injuries, which were either not susceptible of any, or at least not adequate, relief at common law, and defences to common law actions, which, although founded on principles of equity and

(d) 13 Edw. 1, c. 24.

good conscience, were not capable of being pleaded in the common law courts.

The old jurisdiction of the king's council, therefore, remained in force, and, indeed, under Edward I. it was greatly developed. As has been truly said by an eminent historian, "his assembly of the ministers and higher permanent officials, and the law officers of the Crown, for the first time reserved to itself, in its judicial capacity, the correction of all branches of the law which the lower courts had failed to repress, whether from weakness, partiality or corruption, and especially of those lawless outbreaks of the more powerful baronage, which defied the common authority of the judges" (c). This jurisdiction of the council for the correction of all breaches of the law, which the lower courts failed to repress, later on took the form of the notorious Star Chamber, and is long since obsolete. The jurisdiction of the council, however, still subsists in the case of appeals from the colonies.

But besides the jurisdiction of the council itself, the same necessity of tempering the hard and fast rules of the law with equity, led to the equitable jurisdiction of the Lord Chancellor, who at a very early date acquired a separate jurisdiction of his own. It is difficult, if not impossible, to say how this jurisdiction, apart from the council, first arose, or how far it was concurrent with the jurisdiction of the council; but it seems to have been thoroughly established under Edward I. In the words of the historian above referred to, the equitable jurisdiction of the Chancellor "sprang from the defective nature and the technical and unbending rules

(r) Green's Hist. of the English People, vol. i. p. 327.

of the common law. As the council had given redress in cases where law became injustice, so the Court of Chancery interfered without regard to the rules of procedure adopted by the common law courts, on the petition of a party for whose grievance the common law provided no adequate remedy. An analogous extension of his powers enabled the Chancellor to afford relief in cases of fraud, accident or abuse of trust, and this side of the jurisdiction was largely extended at a later time by the results of legislation on the tenure of land by ecclesiastical bodies (*f*).

Thus arose the High Court of Chancery, which, from the time of Edward I. down to the end of the year 1875 existed as a court of justice, separate and distinct from the ordinary courts of common law, exercising (1) *exclusive* jurisdiction over those cases in which the common law gave no relief, or in which, if relief were given to a plaintiff, injustice would be done to the defendant; (2) *concurrent* jurisdiction in cases where the law did not afford adequate relief, at least without great delay or circuity; and (3) *auxiliary* jurisdiction in cases where its peculiar procedure enabled it to obtain evidence not capable of being obtained by the courts of common law.

The court, however, had no jurisdiction over cases where the courts of law could afford full and adequate relief.

The Court of Chancery differed also very materially from the courts of common law in its method of enforcing its judgments. The common law courts could enforce their judgments against the *property* of a suitor

(*f*) Ib. vol. i. p. 328.

or defendant. The Court of Chancery always enforced its orders upon his *person*. If he refused compliance with its decree, it imprisoned him for contempt until he obeyed its order.

It need scarcely be pointed out that this isolation from the ordinary tribunals caused, at times, much inconvenience, more particularly in those cases in which proceedings in the courts of common law, to which a defendant had no *legal* defence, were stopped by an injunction from the Court of Chancery. Such conflicts of jurisdiction were a grave source of scandal, and it is obvious that when public attention was once earnestly directed to the fact, that two distinct and in some cases conflicting systems of law were being administered concurrently in the same kingdom, the destruction of such an anomaly was only a question of time.

Accordingly, by the Common Law Procedure Act, 1854, an attempt was made to give the common law courts an equitable jurisdiction, by empowering them to entertain equitable pleas in cases where such pleas would have been good ground for an *unconditional* injunction in Chancery, restraining the plaintiff from prosecuting the action.

This act, however, only partially remedied the evil, inasmuch as the common law courts could not entertain equitable pleas which would have been sufficient to induce the Court of Chancery to grant a *conditional* injunction, and it was generally such an injunction, and not an unconditional one, that the court granted in such cases.

At last, by the Judicature Acts, 1873 and 1875, the old courts of common law and the old Court of Chancery, together with the Probate, Admiralty and Divorce

Courts, were united and consolidated into one court, called " the Supreme Court of Judicature," possessing the jurisdiction formerly exercised by all the old courts collectively, and administering both law and equity. This new court was divided into two main parts, viz. : (1) the Court of Appeal and (2) the High Court of Justice, the latter being the court in which proceedings were commenced, and the former the court in which appeals from the latter were heard and determined.

By the Act of 1873, s. 5, it was enacted that all the judges of the High Court should " have in all respects, save as in this act is otherwise provided, equal power, authority and jurisdiction ; " and by the 25th section, after various provisions assimilating in particular cases the law to be administered by the new court to that prevailing in the old Court of Chancery, it was enacted that, " generally in all matters not hereinbefore mentioned, in which there is any conflict or variance between the rules of equity and the rules of the common law with reference to the same matter, the rules of equity shall prevail."

In consequence of these provisions, one of the most useful purposes of the old Court of Chancery became no longer necessary. Formerly, as has been above pointed out, when a defendant in a common law action possessed a defence consistent with " equity and good conscience," but unavailable in a court of law, either because of the harshness of the common law or because the common law courts could only say yea or nay, and could not, like the Court of Chancery, nicely adjust the rival claims and rights of the parties, he could apply to the Court of Chancery for an injunction restraining the plaintiff from continuing his action upon certain conditions, and if in spite of this injunction the latter persisted in doing so, then (although the Court of Chancery could not stop the action, for that was beyond its powers) it could and did seize the plaintiff's person and keep him in prison until he purged his contempt by abandoning his action and submitting to the jurisdiction of the Chancellor.

This branch of the jurisdiction is now of course at an end, as the new High Court is not only a court of common law, but also a court of equity; and by the 24th section of the Act of 1873, after providing for equitable claims and defences to have effect in all branches of the new court, it was enacted that the new court, and every judge thereof, " shall recognize and take notice of all equitable estates, titles and rights, and all equitable duties and liabilities appearing incidentally in the course of any cause or matter, in the same manner in which the Court of Chancery would have recognized and taken notice of the same in any suit or proceeding duly instituted therein before the passing of this act;" and also, that " no cause or other proceeding at any time pending in the High Court of Justice or before the Court of Appeal, shall be restrained by prohibition or injunction, but every matter of equity on which an injunction against the prosecution of any such cause or proceeding might have been obtained if this act had not passed, either unconditionally or on any terms or conditions, may be relied on by way of defence thereto."

But although all the judges of the High Court were given equal jurisdiction in law and in equity, yet for the more convenient despatch of business the High Court was divided into five divisions (g), viz. :—

(1) The Chancery Division ;
(2) The Queen's Bench Division ;

(g) Jud. Act, 1873, s. 31.

(3) The Common Pleas Division;

(4) The Exchequer Division, and

(5) The Probate, Divorce and Admiralty Division.

These divisions have, however, been since reduced to three by the amalgamation of the Queen's Bench, Common Pleas and Exchequer Divisions into one division, called the Queen's Bench Division (h). To each division certain specified judges of the High Court are attached, but this does not prevent any judge from sitting whenever required in a different division, or for any judge of a different division from his own; and any judge may be transferred by her Majesty under the sign manual from one division to another (i). All ordinary actions may be commenced in any division of the court; so that the Chancery Division has now cognizance of many matters which formerly belonged exclusively to the courts of common law, and the Queen's Bench Division has cognizance of many matters which formerly belonged exclusively to the old Court of Chancery. The old exclusive and auxiliary jurisdiction has, in fact, been abolished, and the concurrent alone remains.

As however certain administrative machinery is requisite in certain peculiar classes of actions and not in others, such actions are still distributed among the three divisions in the way most convenient. To the Chancery Division there are assigned (k)—

(1) All causes and matters which were pending in the old Court of Chancery on the 1st day of November, 1875.

(2) All causes and matters which have been or shall be

(h) Order in Council of Dec. 1880.

(i) Jud. Act, 1873, s. 31.

(k) Ib. s. 34.

commenced since the 1st day of November, 1875, under *any Act of Parliament whereby exclusive jurisdiction*, in respect of such causes or matters has been given to the old Court of Chancery or to any judges or judge thereof, except appeals from county courts.

(3) All causes and matters for any of the following purposes :

    (a) The administration of the estates of deceased persons ;

    (b) The dissolution of partnerships or the taking of partnership or other accounts ;

    (c) The redemption or foreclosure of mortgages ;

    (d) The raising of portions or other charges on land ;

    (e) The sale and distribution of the proceeds of property, subject to any lien or charge ;

    (f) The execution of trusts, charitable or private ;

    (g) The rectification or setting aside or cancellation of deeds or other written instruments ;

    (h) The specific performance of contracts between vendors and purchasers of real estates, including contracts for leases ;

    (i) The partition or sale of real estates ;

    (j) The wardship of infants and the care of infants' estates.

To the other divisions of the court are assigned all causes pending in them on the 1st day of November, 1875, and all causes which would have been within their respective jurisdictions if the new court had not been created. There is, however, full power, as will be seen hereafter, of transferring proceedings wrongly commenced in one division, to the right one, and of transferring proceedings rightly commenced in one division, to another division, when on account of special circumstances it is desirable to do so.

The business of the Chancery Division is carried on by a staff of officers consisting of judges, masters of the Supreme Court, registrars, and chief clerks.

The judges consist at present of the Lord Chancellor (who is president of the division), the Master of the Rolls, two Vice-Chancellors, and two Justices. Although these judges have such divers titles, that is only because the present Master of the Rolls and the two present Vice-Chancellors were appointed before the coming into operation of the Judicature Acts. All future judges of the division (except the president and possibly the M. R.) will be simply designated "Justices" (*l*).

The duties of the other officers will fully appear hereafter, and it is sufficient to state in this place, that each of the four senior ordinary judges (*i. e.*, exclusive of the president) of the division has three chief clerks attached to him, to aid in the administrative business of his court, and to exercise certain minor judicial functions. The fifth or junior judge has no chief clerks, and his functions are limited to hearing in court cases which have been transferred to him from the courts of the four senior judges.

Owing to the complex nature of the causes assigned to the Chancery Division, and to the rule laid down by the Judicature Act, 1875, that where no other provision

(*l*) While this work is passing through the press the Lord Justice James has died, and there is a rumour that the Master of the Rolls will be made president of the Court of Appeal, and cease to be one of the judges of the Chancery Division. If, however, this should be so, it will make no difference to the practice.

was made by that act, or the rules and orders annexed thereto, the then present practice should remain in force, the procedure of the Chancery Division, although assimilated to that of the other divisions of the High Court, still differs from it in many important particulars; and, possessing an administrative machinery which is altogether unknown in the other divisions, that machinery is of course carried on according to a procedure peculiar to the Chancery Division, and consequently a separate and distinct account of the practice in that division of the court seems to be required, and is intended to be furnished in the following pages.

Before, however, commencing to detail the procedure, it is desirable that I should here point out the authorities by which that procedure is regulated, which are contained—

1. In certain statutes, particularly the Judicature Acts, 1873 and 1875, and the Chancery Procedure Act, 1852.

2. In certain rules and orders which parliament has from time to time empowered the judges to make or alter. The most important of these are the Consolidated General Orders of 1860 (hereafter referred to as Cons. Ords.) and the Rules of the Supreme Court, 1875 (hereafter referred to as R. S. C.).

3. In judicial decisions evidenced by the reports which record them. These decisions sometimes relate to the interpretation of statutes, rules, or orders, and sometimes to points of practice left untouched by any written authority. In the latter case, the judge frequently takes the opinion of the officers of his court most conversant with the particular procedure to which the point relates by sending a written question to them,

which they answer in the form of a certificate. This certificate has no binding effect on the judge, and is merely for his guidance.

Having now sketched very lightly the present relation of the Chancery Division to the other branches of the court, I will pass on to the main object of this Work, viz., a concise, but at the same time a practical, account of the procedure observed in that division, premising that all proceedings in it are divided into two principal classes, viz. (1) Actions and (2) Matters; the former being proceedings commenced by writ, and—*in form*, at least,—necessarily contentious, and seeking relief against a third party; and the latter being proceedings other than actions, or proceedings in actions, and not necessarily contentious, either in form or fact.

An action is the *ordinary* mode of obtaining relief in the High Court. A matter is an *extraordinary* proceeding, and is almost invariably instituted under the provisions of some statute.

DIVISION I.

—◆—

OF ACTIONS.

c

PRELIMINARY SYNOPSIS.

EVERY action is commenced by a writ of summons, prepared by the plaintiff, and calling, in the Queen's name, on the defendant, to "enter an appearance" to it. This writ is "issued," by being sealed either at the London central office or a district registry, and must then be served on the defendant, or, where he cannot be found or is out of the jurisdiction, service may be dispensed with, and certain notices or advertisements substituted in its stead (*a*).

On service of the writ, the defendant either enters an appearance by leaving a memorandum to that effect at the central office or district registry, or neglects to appear; and in the latter case, in actions specially assigned to the Chancery Division, the action goes on as if he had appeared. If he appears, the defendant may in certain cases bring in third parties, and may sometimes interplead, which is practically allowing the plaintiff and a third party to fight the matter out between them (*b*).

The next step is the delivery of the pleadings (*c*), which are written, or (where over ten folios in length) printed statements of, (1) claim by the plaintiff, (2) defence by the defendant, and (3) reply by the plaintiff. By these pleadings, an "issue," or disagreement of some material question or questions of fact, or of the law applicable to the facts, is arrived at, or sometimes the disagreement is

(*a*) Sub-div. I. (*c*) Sub-div. III.
(*b*) Sub-div. II.

both as to the facts alleged, and also to the law applicable to them.

If either the plaintiff or defendant disagrees with his adversary's view of the law, that is to say, if, admitting the truth of the facts alleged by his adversary, he still contends that these facts do not show a good case in law —he "demurs," and in that case the objection—or "demurrer," as it is called,—is argued in open court before the judge, who either gives his decision in favour of the demurrer or overrules it. If there is no real dispute as to the facts, the question of law raised by the demurrer really decides the dispute between the parties, and, judgment being moved *pro formá*, the action is finished with the decision on the demurrer; but very often the facts are also disputed, and in that case, if the demurrer is overruled, the case goes on as before, but if it is upheld, leave must be obtained to amend the condemned pleading, by the addition of new facts sufficient to make it a good statement of claim or defence. The issues of fact are set down for "trial," either before a judge alone, which is the most usual course, or before a judge and jury, or before a judge and assessors, or before an official or special referee, the counsel of each party stating and arguing his case, and producing evidence in support of it, either by means of witnesses examined *vivá voce*, or (by consent), by affidavit, and also producing and reading his documentary evidence if any (*d*).

Where the trial is before a judge alone, or a judge and assessors, the judge usually delivers judgment at once, or reserves it until a subsequent day. When the

(*d*) Sub-divs. IV. and V.

trial is before a judge and jury, the latter return a verdict as to the facts, and the judge either then delivers
judgment, or leaves the party in whose favour the issues
of fact have been found, to "move the court" for judgment subsequently.

Where the trial is before a referee, he makes a report
to the court, which is in the nature of the verdict of a
jury, stating in whose favour he finds the facts in dispute, and upon this report, the party in whose favour it
is made, subsequently moves for judgment (e).

Judgments are of two distinct classes in the Chancery
Division (f). In one the whole matter in dispute is
decided and finally disposed of, either in favour of the
plaintiff or the defendant. Such judgments are those
arising out of claims for injunctions, specific performance of contracts, or other simple claims.

In the other class the judgment is merely preliminary
to certain other, more or less complicated, proceedings,
upon which the real litigation takes place. Such are
judgments in administration actions, partnership actions,
and the like. In these cases the pleadings rarely show
any issue of fact or law, and the judgment is seldom
opposed, as it merely consists of a declaration that an
estate ought to be administered or a partnership wound
up, or the like, together with directions that the judges'
chief clerk shall, in chambers, examine the accounts of
the trustees, or of the partners, make enquiries as to who
are interested in the estate as creditors, mortgagees,
legatees, or otherwise, and generally find out the exact
state of facts relating to the property in question in the
action. Such actions are really only brought into court

(e) Sub-div. VI.   (f) Sub-div. VII.

in order that the judge may see that proper directions are contained in the judgment, and as there are seldom any issues of fact involved, there is seldom a trial of such actions, but merely a motion for judgment, either for default in delivering of a statement of defence, or on admissions contained in the defence, if one be delivered. In such cases evidence is rarely taken, both parties admitting that an administration must be had, or a dissolution of partnership decreed, and consequently they are called "short actions," and one day in every week is appropriated to them by each of the four senior judges. Such actions usually consume only a few minutes each.

When, however, the accounts and enquiries come to be taken in chambers (g), a good deal of ligitation may be anticipated, and this is usually conducted by the solicitors of the respective parties, (indeed in some of the judges' chambers counsel are not heard before the chief clerks,) unless the point is of importance, and then it is adjourned before the judge himself in his chambers, in most of which counsel may appear, if thought necessary.

Frequently in the course of an action money or stock or securities have to be paid or transferred into or deposited in court, and this is done through the medium of an official called the paymaster-general (h).

When the chief clerk has examined all the accounts, and made all the enquiries directed by the judgment, he makes a certificate of the result to the judge, and if any question of law arises on that certificate, the case is again set down to come before the court on " further consideration " (i).

Sometimes the chief clerk's certificate is such that no

(g) Sub-div. VIII.   (i) Sub-div. X.
(h) Sub-div. IX.

point of law arises, but frequently (particularly in actions for the administration of the estates of deceased persons) such points do arise. For instance, from the chief clerk's certificate that the deceased did not leave sufficient personal estate to pay his debts, but left plenty of real estate, a question may at once arise whether in the particular construction of his will some part of that real estate is not exempt from contributing towards payment of the debts; and such a point would have to be decided on further consideration, and the question as to the incidence of the costs is also dealt with at this stage.

But in addition to these ordinary steps in an action, there are certain other proceedings called interlocutory applications (*k*), which are sometimes resorted to between the issue of the writ and the delivery of the judgment. Such are made either (1) by motion in open court, (2) by petition heard in open court, or (3) by summons in the judges' chambers. A motion is an application made to the court, either by counsel or by the suitor in person; and where it is interlocutory, is made for the purpose of obtaining some temporary but immediate protection, pending the trial of the action. Thus, in cases where an injunction is sought to protect property from injury, it is obvious that before the trial of the action the property might be irretrievably damaged, and therefore the plaintiff in such a case may "move" for an interlocutory injunction directly he commences his action. And so a receiver may be moved for, where property is likely to be made away with, or requires to be managed. Motions are either brought on *ex parte* without notice to the other side, or after two days' notice given to the other side.

(*k*) Sub-div. XI.

Petitions are usually made use of in administration actions pending the enquiries in chambers, and are for the purpose of obtaining allowances, investment of funds, and the like. They are written statements of facts, and are heard within a week or ten days of being filed.

Summonses are perhaps the commonest form of interlocutory applications, being used for the purpose of raising all kinds of minor and incidental points. For instance, the amendment of pleadings, the question whether a pleading is embarrassing or not, applications for further time to deliver a pleading or to strike out interrogatories, and the like. They are heard before one of the judges' chief clerks in chambers in the first instance, but may be adjourned at the request of either party before the judge himself in chambers, and he may adjourn them into court for formal argument if they raise points of importance.

There are also certain motions and petitions called "motions and petitions of course." These are never argued, but are merely formal documents, requiring either counsel's signature or that of the judge.

All these matters will be found treated of in detail in the first division of this Work. The method of enforcing a judgment or an order (which is carried out in various ways, from imprisonment and sequestration of property down to a distraint of goods), and the mode of taxing the costs incurred by a successful litigant, and which have been ordered to be borne by his opponent, and the procedure on appeal from a judgment or order, are treated of in the third division of this Book.

SUB-DIVISION I.

The Writ of Summons.

CHAPTER I.

THE GENERAL FORM AND NATURE OF A WRIT OF SUMMONS.

As I said before, every action in the High Court of Justice must be commenced by the issue of a writ of summons (*a*), which is in form a command by the sovereign to the defendant, to appear and answer the plaintiff's claim on pain of judgment being given against

(*a*) R. S. C., Ord. II. r. 1.

him in his absence. The following is an example of a writ of summons, from a perusal of which its nature will be at once understood.

1880. J. No. 100.

In the High Court of Justice.
   Chancery Division.
      Birmingham District Registry.
         V.-C. Hall.
    Between Thomas Jones . . . . Plaintiff,
and
         William Smith . . . . Defendant.

Victoria, by the grace of God of Great Britain and Ireland Queen, Defender of the Faith, To William Smith, of No. 1100, New Street, Birmingham, in the county of Warwick.

We command you that within eight days after service of this writ on you, inclusive of the day of such service, you do cause an appearance to be entered for you in the Chancery Division of our High Court of Justice in an action at the suit of Thomas Jones ; and take notice, that in default of your doing so, the plaintiff may proceed therein, and judgment may be given in your absence. Witness, &c.

N.B.—This writ is to be served within twelve calendar months from the date thereof, or, if renewed, from the date of such renewal, including the day of such date and not afterwards.

The defendant may appear hereto by entering an appearance either personally, or by solicitor, at the Central Office, Royal Courts of Justice, [*or at the* office at *where issued out of a District Registry.*]

On the back of this writ is indorsed a short statement of the plaintiff's claim, as, for example, the following :—

The plaintiff's claim is to have an account taken of the partnership dealings between the plaintiff and defendant, under articles of partnership dated the 1st day of January, 1875, and to have the affairs of the partnership wound up. And for an injunction and (if necessary) a receiver.

If any party sues or is sued in a representative capacity, this indorsement must state the fact (*b*), for instance, thus :—

The plaintiff sues as executor of A. B., and the defendant is sued as administrator of C. D.

(*b*) R. S. C., Ord. III. r. 4.

Beneath this claim must be indorsed the following statement :—

This writ was issued by Charles Roberts, of No. 500, New Street, Birmingham, in the county of Warwick, solicitor for the said plaintiff, who resides at No. 610, Temple Row, Birmingham, aforesaid.

If the defendant resides outside the district registry, an address for service must be added within three miles of Temple Bar.

From a careful perusal of this model writ, it will be seen that a great portion of it is purely formal. The first line consists of the year in which the writ is issued, the first letter of the plaintiff's name, and a number which is attached to it by the officer who seals it (as we shall see hereafter in Chapter IV. of this sub-division).

Then comes the name of the court and division ; and if the writ be issued in the country, and not in London, the name of the district registry out of which it is issued. The name of the judge, to whose court the plaintiff wishes the action to be assigned, comes next; but owing to there being no administrative staff of chief clerks attached to the junior Chancery judge for the time being, it is not permitted to assign an action to his court, and he only takes actions for hearing in court, which the other judges cannot hear on account of press of work. The junior judge at present is Mr. Justice Kay. Next comes a statement of the parties to the action, of which I shall treat separately in the next chapter.

The parties are followed by the sovereign's command, which is tested or witnessed in form (but of course not in reality) by the Lord Chancellor for the time being, or, in default of a Lord Chancellor, by the Lord Chief Justice of England for the time being.

The memoranda as to service and appearance describe

themselves, but will be further alluded to hereafter under the chapters relating to " issuing of the writ" and " entering an appearance" respectively.

We now come to the indorsements. The indorsement of claim being an essential part of the writ, and varying according to the special circumstances of each case, requires to be considered somewhat minutely, and will be treated of in Chapter III.

With regard to the indorsement of the statement by whom the writ was issued, the example shows the simplest form of it; but where an agent as well as a solicitor is employed, the names and addresses of both must be given; and where the office of the agent or solicitor, or abode of the plaintiff, is not within three miles of the central office, or within the district registry, as the case may be, an "address for service" must be also given within those limits (c). It should also be observed, that the defendant may make demand in writing calling on the solicitor, whose name is indorsed, to declare forthwith whether the writ has been issued with his authority, and if he declares that it has not, all proceedings will be stayed until leave be obtained from a judge to pursue the action (d).

It should be here observed that if the writ is to be served out of the jurisdiction of the court, the form is slightly different to that given above, in the commanding part, the form being—

We command you William Smith that within [*here insert the number of days directed by the court or judge ordering the service or notice*] after service of this writ [*or* notice of this writ, *as the case may be*], on you, &c., as in the form already given.

Having described the form of the writ, it only remains to say that it must be prepared by the plaintiff or his

(c) R. S. C., Ord. IV.   (d) R. S. C., Ord. VII. r. 1.

solicitor, and may be written or printed, or partly written and partly printed, on cream wove machine drawing foolscap folio paper, 19 lbs. per mill ream or thereabouts, with an inner margin about three quarters of an inch wide, and an outer margin about two inches and a half wide (e).

In practice, the plaintiff's solicitor buys from a law stationer the formal parts of the writ printed on proper paper, and fills this form up in writing, with the names of the plaintiff and defendant, the claim, &c. This writ when prepared is sealed by the proper officer as described in Chapter IV., and is then said to be issued, and then and not till then becomes an authoritative summons.

With regard to mistakes appearing in the parties or indorsement of claim after issue of the writ, the practice is treated of in the chapters on those subjects respectively. With regard to other mistakes it may be here mentioned that at any stage of the proceedings the court or a judge may allow the plaintiff to amend the writ in such manner and upon such terms as may seem just (f). Before the defence is delivered, the application is made by motion or petition of course; but after defence, if the defendants oppose the amendment, the application must be by summons (g). Where notice of trial has been given or notice of an interlocutory motion, the application should be by summons, which should state that it is without prejudice to the notice, otherwise the notice will be taken as waived (h).

(e) R. S. C., Ord. V. r. 5; Ord. LVI. r. 2.

(f) R.S.C., Ord. XXVII. r. 2; *Caldwell* v. *Pagham Harbour Co.*,

L. R., 2 Ch. D. 221.

(g) *Marriott* v. *Marriott*, 26 W. R. 416.

(h) Daniell's Forms, 3rd ed. 127.

CHAPTER II.

THE PARTIES.

General rule. It may be stated as a general rule, subject, however, to considerable exceptions, that (1) all persons, whatever their sort or condition, may sue and be sued in any division of the High Court, and (2) that all persons who may have in the object of an action in the Chancery Division an apparent interest, or against whom the decree sought for will establish a right, or upon whom it will impose a duty, ought to be made parties.

Let us first enquire whether there are any and what sorts or conditions of persons with regard to whom the *right of suing,* or the *liability of being sued,* is subject to modification, and afterwards we can proceed to the more general consideration of what persons *ought to be joined* as parties to an action.

SECTION 1.

Particular Persons with regard to whom the General Rule is modified.

SUBSEC. 1.—*The Crown.*

It is a rule that the sovereign may be a plaintiff in a Chancery action, either in her private capacity as an individual (*a*), or in her capacity as representing the public generally (*b*); but (except by petition of right the consideration of which does not come within the scope of this Work), the sovereign can only be made a defendant to an action where her rights are merely incidentally

(*a*) *Du Plessis* v. *Att.-Gen.,* 1   (*b*) Dan. 13.
Bro. P. C. ed. Toml. 415.

involved, and no direct relief is claimed against her (c). Whenever the sovereign is either plaintiff or defendant, she never sues or is sued in person but by her Attorney-General, or, when that office is vacant, by her Solicitor-General (d)

Thus, in the case of land claimed by the sovereign by reason of forfeiture, an action will lie by her for discovery of facts material for enforcing the forfeiture (e). Or, again, as head of the Church, or as *parens patriæ* in matters affecting charities, and in certain cases respecting the property of idiots and lunatics, or where property is entrusted to trustees for public purposes, or in cases of public nuisance, and also under certain Acts of Parliament (f), it is a privilege of the sovereign by her Attorney-General to intervene for the purpose of asserting the right and interest of the public. It is impossible in a small Work of this description to go fully into the cases in which the sovereign has the right to be a plaintiff, and indeed they rather concern the general rules of equity than the rules which govern procedure.

As an instance of the sovereign being joined as defendant, may be mentioned the case where there is no heir-at-law of a deceased intestate, whose real property is in litigation (g).

A suit by the sovereign was formerly called an information, and the Attorney-General was termed the informant, because he was supposed to have been informed of the wrong complained of by some third party. This third party was called a relator. The terms information

---

(c) Dau. 125 ; *Reeve* v. *Att.-Gen.*, 2 Atk. 223.

(d) Dan. 125.

(e) *Du Plessis* v. *Att.-Gen.*, sup.; but query whether such an action would lie now.

(f) As, for instance, the Marriage Acts, 4 Geo. 4, c. 76, and 19 & 20 Vict. c. 119.

(g) Dan. 125.

or informant are, however, now done away with, the suit being now called an action, and the Attorney-General plaintiff, as in any other cause (h).

Where, as is usually the case, the action concerns the sovereign only in her representative capacity, the Attorney-General is really set in motion by a relator, and in that case the relator must be named in the writ for the purpose of answering costs in case the sovereign should be defeated (i), the crown being never liable for costs.

Sometimes when the relator has also a private interest, beyond and above that of the public generally, he may be joined not only as relator but as plaintiff.

A relator, as such, has no right to take any step in an information without the sanction of the Attorney-General, but where he is also plaintiff, he may of course conduct his own case as plaintiff.

Where an action by the Attorney-General immediately affects the rights of the crown he may proceed *mero motu* without any relator (k); but even in such cases a relator is frequently named *ex gratiâ*, and to give the defendant a security for his costs. Even in charity and other public cases, it would seem to be doubtful whether a relator is absolutely necessary (l).

As the relator is named for the purpose of answering costs, it follows that he must be a person of substance and reasonably capable of paying them, and unless he be so all further proceedings will be stayed upon the application of the defendant (which may be made by

(h) R. S. C., Ord. I. r. 1; *Att.-Gen.* v. *Shrewsbury Bridge Co.*, W. N. 1880, p. 23.

(i) *Att.-Gen.* v. *Smart*, 1 Ves. sen. 72; *Att.-Gen.* v. *Parker*, 3 Atk. 579.

(k) Dan. 13.

(l) *Re Bedford Charity*, 2 Sw. 520; but see *Att.-Gen.* v. *Oglander*, 1 Ves. jun. 246; and *Att.-Gen.* v. *Middleton*, 2 Ves. sen. 327.

summons in chambers), until a responsible relator is appointed (*m*). For the same reason neither a *feme covert*, an infant, nor an idiot, can be a relator.

Before getting the writ sealed and issued in an action in the nature of an information, a written authority, signed by the person named as relator, must be produced to the officer sealing the same, and the consent of the Attorney-General must also be obtained. This is done by leaving at his chambers a copy of the proposed writ and of the proposed statement of claim, together with a certificate of the counsel who has settled the statement of claim, that the action is one which is proper for the sanction of the Attorney-General, and also a certificate of the solicitor for the relator, that the latter is a proper person to be relator, and is able to pay costs, and also a certificate that the copy statement of claim is a true copy of the draft as settled by counsel. Although a relator is named for the purpose of being answerable to the defendant for costs, yet where property is in question (as in cases regarding charities), he will be allowed his costs out of the property as between solicitor and client, where he has acted properly and for the benefit of the property in question (*n*).

SUBSEC. 2.—*Foreign Governments.*

The sovereign power of a foreign state (whether emperor, king or republic) may sue, either on his own behalf or on behalf of his subjects (*o*), in respect of his or their private rights; but he cannot sue in respect of

(*m*) *Att.-Gen.* v. *Tyler*, 2 Ed. 230; *Att.-Gen.* v. *Knight*, 3 M. & C. 154.

(*n*) *Att.-Gen.* v. *Kerr*, 5 Bea. 303; *Moggridge* v. *Thackwell*, 13 Ves. 416.

(*o*) *Hullett* v. *King of Spain*, 2 Bli., N. S. 60.

his own prerogatives (b). Unlike the British sovereign, such persons must sue in their recognized official names, and not by an attorney, ambassador, or other officer.

The government of a colony is in the same position with regard to suing as a foreign government (c).

Like the British sovereign, foreign sovereigns or states cannot be made original defendants to an action where relief is sought against them, as the court has no jurisdiction over them (d); but if they themselves commence an action, they *ipso facto* submit themselves to the jurisdiction, and are liable to be made defendants to a counter-claim or cross action (e), and are then liable to answer interrogatories on oath (f).

Where, however, the king of a foreign state is also an English subject, he may be sued in the latter character (g).

Where no active relief is sought against a foreign sovereign, but he is interested in the subject-matter of a suit, he may (as in the case of the British sovereign) be made a defendant, but this of course does not compel him to come in, but only enables him to do so and be heard if he likes (h).

Subsec. 3.—*Corporations.*

The power to sue and the liability to be sued in the corporate name is inseparable from all corporations,

---

(b) *Emperor of Austria* v. *Day*, 3 De G., F. & J. 217.

(c) *Penn* v. *Lord Baltimore*, 1 Ves. S. 444.

(d) *Duke of Bedford* v. *King of Hanover*, 2 H. L. C. 1; *Strousberg* v. *Republic of Costa Rica*, Times Report, Nov. 16th, 1880.

(e) *Hullett* v. *King of Spain*, sup.

(f) Ib. and *King of Spain* v. *Hullett*, 7 Bli., N. S. 359; *Duke of Bedford* v. *King of Hanover*, sup.; *Prioleau* v. *United States of America*, L. R., 2 Eq. 659.

(g) *Duke of Bedford* v. *King of Hanover*, sup.

(h) *Gladstone* v. *Musurus Bey*, 9 Jur., N. S. 71; *Smith* v. *Weguelin*, L. R., 8 Eq. 198.

whether sole or aggregate (*i*) ; but a corporation sole must say in the writ in what capacity he sues (*k*).

A foreign corporation is in the same position as an English one, but must (if it be disputed) prove its incorporation (*l*).

Closely allied to corporations are certain companies created by act of parliament or charter, who, although not incorporated, are thereby allowed to sue and be sued by their public officer (*m*).

The officers of a corporation might formerly be joined as defendants for the purpose of obtaining discovery on oath (a corporation answering interrogatories only under their seal), but it is now permissible to interrogate an officer without making him a party (*n*).

Subsec. 4.—*Partnership Firms.*

Although not corporate bodies, any two or more persons claiming or being liable as partners may sue and be sued in the name of their firm ; but any other party may in that case apply, by summons, to a judge for a statement of the names of the persons who constitute the firm, to be furnished in such manner, and verified on oath or otherwise as the judge may direct (*o*). And any *one* person carrying on business in the name of a firm, *apparently* consisting of more than one person, may *be sued* in the firm's name (*p*).

Where the firm are plaintiffs, they or their solicitors must on demand in writing, by or on behalf of any defendant, forthwith declare the names and places of

(*i*) Dan. 23, 132.

(*k*) Ib. 24.

(*l*) *Dutch W. I. Co.* v. *Van Moyses*, 2 Ld. Ray. 1335.

(*m*) Dan. 26.

(*n*) R. S. C., Ord. XXXI. r. 4.

(*o*) R. S. C., Ord. XVI. r. 10.

(*p*) Ib. r. 10a.

residence of all the persons constituting the firm, and in default, the action may be stayed by a judge on application by summons in chambers (q).

It must, however, be borne in mind in suing a firm, that it can only be sued *when at the time of the action it consists of the same individual partners as it did at the date when the cause of action first arose* (r).

Subsec. 5.—*Aliens.*

An alien friend may sue and be sued like an English subject (s), but is liable, like every plaintiff who resides out of the jurisdiction, to be called upon to give security for costs (t). An alien enemy, or a person residing in the country of an enemy without the Queen's licence, cannot sue during hostilities (u), nor afterwards in respect of any contract entered into during the continuance of the war, as such contracts are void (x). Where, however, one foreigner sues another foreigner, the court is very chary of granting a writ of *ne exeat regno* (y).

Subsec. 6.—*Married Women.*

As a general rule, where a husband and wife have a common interest in a property (as, for instance, where the action is in respect of fee simple property devised to the wife), the husband must be joined with her in whatever character she appears (z). But where she appears

---

(q) R. S. C., Ord. VII. r. 2.

(r) *Ex parte Blaine*, L. R., 12 Ch. Div. 522.

(s) Dan. 28.

(t) *Fox* v. *Blew*, 5 Mad. 147; *Kerr* v. *Gillespie*, 7 Bea. 267; *Partington* v. *Reynolds*, 6 W. R. 307.

(u) Dan. 49.

(x) *Ex parte Boussmaker*, 13 Ves. 71.

(y) *De Carriere* v. *De Colonne*, 4 Ves. 58.

(z) *Beardmore* v. *Gregory*, 2 H. & M. 491.

as plaintiff, and has an interest in the subject-matter of the suit conflicting with that of her husband, or where she institutes proceedings to recover property settled to her separate use, in which her husband has no interest, she must sue by the intervention of a person called " her next friend," who, like the relator in actions at the suit of the Crown, undertakes the responsibility of answering costs in case of her defeat (a married woman being unable to bind herself to answer costs personally), and the husband must then be made a defendant (*a*). ✗

Suing without a next Friend. The above general rule is, however, subject to certain exceptions; viz., that the wife may sue in her own name and without either a next friend and without joinder of her husband with her as co-plaintiff, or may be sued without joinder of her husband as co-defendant ; (1) where the husband is civilly dead; or (2) is undergoing sentence of penal servitude or transportation; or (3) after she is judicially separated; or (4) after she has obtained a protection order under 20 & 21 Vict. c. 85 ; or (5) where her husband is an alien enemy ; or (6) where she sues for property belonging to her by virtue of the Married Women's Property Act, 1870, or is sued for debts contracted before marriage, and for which under the same act, and the Amending Act of 1874, the husband is not liable; or (7) in any case where she is able to obtain the leave of the court or a judge to sue or defend by herself and without a next friend, and either with or without giving such security for costs as the court or judge may require (*b*); or (8) where she is named as defendant, and

(*a*) *Roberts* v. *Evans*, L. R., 7 Ch. D. 830.

(*b*) R. S. C., Ord. XVI. r. 8; *Martana* v. *Mann*, W. N. 1880, p. 80.

✗ But see 45 & 46 Vict c 75 s 12. (The M. W. P. Act/82

her husband is plaintiff, in which case, of course, he cannot be a co-defendant.

Next Friend. Although when a married woman sues without joinder of her husband as co-plaintiff, she usually sues by her next friend, the latter cannot commence the action without her consent; and in case he does so, she may apply to the court by motion, to have the action dismissed with costs against him.

As the next friend is a kind of surety for costs, he must (like a relator) be a person of substance, and if he should be a "man of straw," the court will at any stage of the action stay all proceedings until security for costs is given (c).

For similar reasons, and to prevent a woman using the name of a next friend without authority, the latter must sign a written authority to the solicitor to use his name, which must be filed when the writ is issued (d).

A next friend may (in the discretion of the court or a judge) be changed during a suit, proper provisions being made with regard to the defendant's costs (e); and on the death of a next friend, a new one will be appointed; and in case the plaintiff neglects to apply, the defendant may get an order calling on her to do so within a certain time, in default of which the action will be dismissed (f).

SUBSEC. 7.—*Infants.*

The cases in which an infant can claim relief, or be a party against whom relief can be claimed, will be found

---

(c) Dan. 104; *Martana* v. *Mann*, L. R., 14 Ch. D. 419.

(d) 15 & 16 Vict. c. 86, s. 11; and R. S. C., Ord. XVI. r. 13.

(e) *Jones* v. *Fawcett*, 2 Phil. 278; *Payne* v. *Little*, 14 Beav. 647; and 16 ib. 563.

(f) *Barlee* v. *Barlee*, 1 S. & S. 100.

discussed in the various works treating of *the law* administered by the court. In a work treating of the *procedure* of the court, it suffices to say that an infant plaintiff cannot sue in person, but only by his next friend (*f*), and he defends by his guardian *ad litem* (*g*).

Next Friend. With regard to the next friend of an infant, the rule of the court is very different to that which prevails in reference to the next friend of a married woman, for, as we have seen, the latter cannot commence an action in the name of a married woman without her authority, whereas, in the case of an infant, any person can commence an action in his name as his next friend, even though he be no relative, and the action is commenced against the wish of the infant's parents (*h*).

Actions improperly brought in the Names of Infants. Such a power as this of course requires to be carefully watched, in order to prevent its abuse by unscrupulous practitioners who might commence actions in the names of infants merely in order to make business for themselves; and, accordingly, the court will, on the application of the defendant (*i*), or of a third person acting *pro tem.* as a next friend of an infant plaintiff (*k*), order the removal of a next friend whose interest appears to be adverse to that of the infant (*l*), or who is a relative, clerk or nominee of the solicitor for the plaintiff (*m*), and will substitute a new one; and, on the

---

(*f*) R. S. C., Ord. XVI. r. 8.

(*g*) Ib.

(*h*) *Andrews* v. *Cradock*, Prec. Ch. 376; *Lewis* v. *Nobbs*, L. R., 8 Ch. D. 591.

(*i*) *Fox* v. *Suwerkrop*, 1 Bea.

583; *Sale* v. *Sale*, ib. 586.

(*k*) *Guy* v. *Guy*, 2 Bea. 460; *Towsey* v. *Groves*, 11 W. R. 252.

(*l*) *Gee* v. *Gee*, 12 W. R. 187.

(*m*) *Sandford* v. *Sandford*, 9 Jur. 398.

like application, will order an inquiry in chambers whether it is for the benefit of the infant that such an action should be proceeded with, or whether it has been instituted from improper motives; and if the result of such inquiry is unfavourable to the next friend, the action will be dismissed against him with costs, or stayed as may seem desirable (*n*).

Next Friend of Infant need not be a Person of Substance. The office of next friend to an infant differs in another respect from that of the next friend to a married woman, viz., that the court does not insist on his being a person of substance; for otherwise, where the infant or his relatives were poor, he might be deprived of his rights (*o*).

Several Actions for same Cause. It occasionally happens that more than one action is brought in an infant's name for the same relief by different next friends. In such a case an inquiry will be directed as to which should be proceeded with, and the others will be stayed (*p*); but if it is obvious which action is the most beneficial without the necessity of an inquiry, the action may be stayed at once (*q*). In general, other things being equal, the action first commenced will be the one allowed to be continued, and the others will be stayed (*r*).

Removal of next Friend. A next friend may be removed (on summons or motion supported by affidavit, notice being of course given to the defendant)

(*n*) *Fox* v. *Suwerkrop*, sup.; *Sale* v. *Sale*, sup.; *Guy* v. *Guy*, sup.

(*o*) Dan. 73.

(*p*) *Mortimer* v. *West*, 1 Sw. 358; *Virtue* v. *Miller*, 19 W. R. 406.

(*q*) *Staniland* v. *Staniland*, M. R., 21st January, 1864; *Harris* v. *Harris*, 10 W. R. 31; *Kenyon* v. *Kenyon*, 35 Bea. 300.

(*r*) *Campbell* v. *Campbell*, 2 M. & C. 30.

where it is desirable to substitute a nearer relative (*s*), and à *fortiori* where the next friend has been guilty of misconduct (*t*). A next friend may also by leave of the court (but not otherwise) retire, but he will generally be ordered to give security for costs already incurred (*u*).

No next Friend. Where an action is brought in an infant's name without a next friend (*v*), the defendant may move to dismiss it with costs against the solicitor, and where the next friend dies or is removed, the defendant may move to have a new one appointed (*x*).

When an infant plaintiff comes of age *pendente lite*, he may abandon the action and either have it dismissed with costs against himself, or may refrain from taking any step, in which case the defendant may have it dismissed _without costs_; or the infant may adopt and continue it, in which case he becomes liable for costs *ab initio* (*y*).

Infant Defendants. Infants are made defendants in their own names, and therefore no more need be said here concerning the appointment of guardians *ad litem*, which will come more fitly under consideration when we come to treat of the defendant's appearance to the writ.

SUBSEC. 8.—*Lunatics and Persons of Unsound Mind.*

Lunatics may be divided into two classes; (1) lunatics so found by inquisition, and (2) imbeciles who without being lunatics so found by inquisition, are yet in reality unable to manage their own affairs.

(*s*) *Woolf* v. *Pemberton*, L. R., 6 Ch. D. 19.

(*t*) *Russell* v. *Sharp*, 1 J. & W. 482; *Towsey* v. *Groves*, 11 W. R. 252; *Lander* v. *Ingersoll*, 4 Ha.

596.

(*u*) Haynes' Ch. P. 368.

(*v*) *Cox* v. *Wright*, 9 Jur. 981.

(*x*) Dan. Ch. Pr. 76.

(*y*) Ib.

Lunatic so found. A lunatic so found by inquisition becomes thereby a kind of ward, and under the protection of the Lord Chancellor, who as keeper of the sovereign's conscience performs his office of *parens patriæ;* and although the Chancellor appoints in every such case persons called committees to manage the estate, and look after the person, of the lunatic, yet the committees cannot act in extraordinary matters without the leave of the Chancellor or the Lords Justices of Appeal. It follows, therefore, that before a lunatic so found can commence an action, such leave must be obtained, which is done by laying a proposal before one of the Masters in lunacy, who makes his report to the Chancellor or Justices, upon which an order is made. If the order is favourable the committee commences the action in the name of the lunatic " by A. B. his committee," and the committee then stands in the same position as the next friend of an infant. So also, as in the case of an infant, if an action is commenced by a lunatic so found without his committee, the defendant may move or take out a summons to dismiss or stay it (*z*).

With regard to imbeciles who have not been found lunatics by inquisition, they can commence and carry on actions by their next friends like infants (*a*).

With regard to defendant lunatics, whether so found or not, they are made defendants in the writ in their own names, and appear by guardian *ad litem*, as will be seen hereafter.

SUBSEC. 9.—*Paupers.*

Taking into consideration the fees payable at every step in an action to the court, and the fact that few persons are sufficiently conversant with the practice of the

---

(*z*) Dan. Ch. Pr. 81.   (*a*) *Light* v. *Light*, 25 Bea. 250.

court and the doctrines of equity to commence and carry
on an action without the aid of solicitor and counsel, it is
obvious that if some special provision were not made on
their behalf, poor persons would be unable to obtain
justice, or to defend themselves against unjust claims.
A person, therefore, who can make an affidavit stating
that he is not worth 5*l.* in the world except his wearing
apparel and the matters in dispute in the action, is
allowed to sue or defend, as the case may be, *in formâ
pauperis.* It certainly seems at this date somewhat
ludicrous to fix the poverty at 5*l.*, as it is only too certain
that a man only worth 50*l.* or even 100*l.*, would soon
exhaust his means in prosecuting or defending an ordinary suit, and that to deny the right of suing *in formâ
pauperis* to a man who has only 10*l.* in the world, is a
practical denial of justice.

A person desiring to sue *in formâ pauperis* must present a petition to the High Court praying to be admitted
to sue or defend *in formâ pauperis*, and that a solicitor
and counsel may be assigned him. This petition must
concisely state his case, and what proceedings (if any)
have been taken. In the case of plaintiff paupers a
certificate of counsel must be written at the foot, stating
that the petitioner has just cause to be relieved (*h*).
This petition and the above-mentioned affidavit of
pauperism must be left with the secretary of causes at
the Rolls, who if he sees no objection to it will draw up
the order as of course. By virtue of this order, the
pauper is excused from paying court fees, or solicitors
or counsel's fees, and the latter are bound to act, and to
act gratuitously, whether they like it or not, unless they
can satisfy the judge that they have good reason for

(*h*) Cons. Ord. VII. r. 8.

being excused (c). Indeed, so strict is the court in enforcing this duty, that if such a solicitor or counsel
accepts any reward from the pauper, or agrees to accept
any such, he will be held guilty of contempt, and the
pauper will be promptly dispaupered (d).

A person who has wrongly procured permission to sue
in formâ pauperis will be dispaupered on motion (e).

SECTION 2.
The Persons who ought to be made Parties.

As already stated at the commencement of this chapter, it is a general rule that all persons who may have
in the object of an action in the Chancery Division an
apparent interest, or against whom the decree sought for
will establish a right, or upon whom it will impose a
duty, ought to be made parties either as plaintiffs or
defendants.

This rule, however, is not now of such vital importance as formerly, because by Order XVI. r. 1, of the
R. S. C., it is ordered, that "all persons may be joined
as plaintiffs in whom the right to any relief claimed is
alleged to exist, whether jointly or severally, or in the
alternative. And judgment may be given for such one
or more of the plaintiffs, as may be found to be entitled
to relief, for such relief as he or they may be entitled to
without any amendment." And by rr. 3 and 5 of the
same Order, it is ordered, that all persons may be joined
as defendants, against whom the right to any relief
claimed is alleged to exist, whether jointly, severally, or
in the alternative, and judgment may be given against
such one or more of the defendants as may be found to

(c) Cons. Ord. VII. r. 10.
(d) Ib. r. 9.
(e) *Newell* v. *Whitaker*, 6 Bea. 407.

be liable, according to their respective liabilities, without any amendment. And by r. 13 of the same Order, it is ordered, that "no action shall be defeated by reason of the misjoinder of parties, and the court may in every action deal with the matter in controversy, as far as regards the rights and interests of the parties actually before it. The court or a judge may, at any stage of the proceedings either upon or without the application of either party, and on such terms as may appear to the court or judge to be just, order that the name or names of any party or parties, whether as plaintiffs or as defendants improperly joined, be struck out, and that the name or names of any party or parties, whether plaintiffs or defendants, who ought to have been joined, or whose presence before the court may be necessary in order to enable the court effectually and completely to adjudicate upon and settle all the questions involved in the action, be added." And by r. 2, a new plaintiff, even, may be substituted, where there has been a *bonâ fide* mistake. All such applications should, by r. 14, be made by motion or summons before trial, or at the trial itself, and should not be *ex parte*. Still, although the above rule takes away the former importance of joining the right parties to an action, yet it is still desirable that the proper parties should be ascertained in the first instance, because the plaintiff will have to bear all costs occasioned by not having done so (*f*).

The above general rule must therefore still be observed, and in carrying it out, care must be taken not to join as plaintiffs any persons who have interests ad-

(*f*) R. S. C., Ord. XVI. rr. 1, 3; and see *Child* v. *Stenning*, L. R., 7 Ch. D. 413. As to new plaintiffs, see *New Westminster Brewery* v. *Hannah*, W. N. 1877, p. 35; *Duckett* v. *Gorer*, L. R., 6 Ch. D. 8; *Clowes* v. *Hilliard*, 4 ib. 413.

verse to one another. *All persons having such adverse interest should be made defendants.* For example, a husband and wife, in respect of the wife's property *not settled to her separate use,* have a common interest, and therefore they may properly be joined together as coplaintiffs. But where a woman has property settled to her separate use, her interest is adverse to that of her husband's *legal* right, and therefore he should be made a defendant, even though the action may be commenced at his desire (*g*).

Numerous Class. Where there is a numerous class of persons having the same interest in the subject-matter of the suit (as, for example, creditors of a deceased insolvent, the inhabitants of an unincorporated town or village, &c.), it would obviously be very costly and inconvenient, if not impossible, to join all of them; and in this case it is permissible to name one or more of such persons to represent the rest, either as plaintiffs or (by leave of the court) as defendants (*h*). This is very frequently seen in the case of an administration action, commenced by one creditor " on behalf of himself and all other creditors of" a deceased insolvent against the executors of the latter. If a member of the class dissents from the course taken by the plaintiff in such a case, he should apply to the court by motion either to take the conduct of the action out of the plaintiff's hands and to substitute another, or to have the applicant added to the action as a defendant (*i*).

Parties to Administration Actions. This principle was considerably extended in certain specified

---

(*g*) *Roberts* v. *Evans,* L. R., 7 Ch. D. 830.

(*h*) R. S. C., Ord. XVI. r. 9. For instances, see L. R., 2 Ch.

D. 109; 5 ib. 540; and 24 W. R. 317.

(*i*) *Watson* v. *Cave,* L. R., 17 Ch. D. 19, per Cotton, L. J.

cases by the act 15 & 16 Vict. c. 86, s. 42, which laid
down certain rules, of which the following is a summary, viz. :—Any residuary legatee or next of kin (as
to personal estate), and any person interested in any
legacy charged on real estate, or in the proceeds of
real estate directed to be sold, or any residuary devisee or heir (as to real estate), or any *cestui que trust*
(as to settled, real or personal property), may have
a decree for administration of such property without
making any other person beneficially interested a party.
And in all suits for the protection of property pending
litigation, or in cases of waste, one person may sue on
behalf of himself and all other persons having the same
interest ; and an executor, administrator or trustee may
obtain a decree against any one person beneficially interested for the administration of the estate. And in
actions concerning property vested in trustees, they are
to represent the persons beneficially interested to the
same extent and in the same manner as executors or
administrators represent the persons interested in the
personal estate of their testator or intestate (*j*). But in all
these cases (except the last) the other persons interested
have to be served with notice of the decree, and are
afterwards as much bound as if they had been made
parties ; and by an order, obtained on petition of course,
they may obtain leave to attend all subsequent proceedings, and may also obtain leave to add to the original
judgment or order. In the case of trustees representing
their *cestuis que trust*, the court may, if it think fit, order
the latter to be made parties.

Parties to Partition Actions. In addition to
the foregoing enactment, it is enacted by the Partition

(*j*) And see R. S. C., Ord. XVI. r. 7 ; and *Mills* v. *Jennings*,
L. R., 13 Ch. D. 639.

Act (j), that any person entitled to sue for a partition may bring an action for such partition against *one or more* of the parties interested, without making the others parties; but such other parties are to be served with notice of the judgment, after which they become to all intents and purposes parties, and may have liberty to attend subsequent proceedings, and may apply to the court to add to the decree. This enactment has been added to by the Partition Act, 1876 (k), which enacts, that where it appears to the court that the above-mentioned notice of the judgment cannot be served, or at least without expense disproportionate to the property involved, the court may dispense therewith, and direct advertisements to be published instead, calling on all persons interested to come in and establish their claims by a certain date, in default of which they will be as fully bound by the proceedings as if served with the judgment.

Construction of certain Instruments. Again, by R. S. C., Ord. XVI. r. 9a, it has been ordered, that in any case in which the right of an heir, next of kin or class shall depend on the construction of any instrument, and it shall not be known, or difficult to ascertain who is or are such heir, next of kin or class, and the court shall consider that, to save expense or some other reason, it will be desirable to have such question of construction forthwith tried, the court may appoint some person or persons to represent such heir, next of kin or class, and the judgment of the court shall be binding on the persons so represented.

Doubtful Cases. Where a plaintiff has reasonable ground for doubting from whom he is entitled to obtain

---

(j) 31 & 32 Vict. c. 10, s. 9.   (k) 39 & 40 Vict. c. 17, s. 3.

redress, he may join all persons against whom he may
reasonably suppose himself to have ground of complaint (*l*), and may even claim inconsistent alternative
relief from them, and in that case the costs of any
against whom he fails may have to be paid by those
against whom he succeeds. The case of *Child* v. *Sten-*
ning (*m*) will illustrate this new and important rule. In
that case the plaintiff, a lessee of land, brought an
action against the lessor and other lessees who claimed
a right of way over the plaintiff's land under a grant
from the same lessor, claiming an injunction, or if the
court should hold that the defendant lessees had a right
of way, then, instead of an injunction, claiming damages
against that lessor. This latter relief was given, and
the lessor being the cause of the whole litigation, was
ordered to pay the costs both of the plaintiff and the
other lessees.

Misjoinder. If the plaintiff should issue the writ,
with the wrong parties, the court or a judge may, at
any time before trial, allow him to add or strike out, or
substitute a plaintiff or defendant (*n*). Such application
should be by summons or motion, or made at the trial,
and will not be granted *ex parte* (*o*). It should be
remembered, that if notice of trial or of interlocutory
motion has been given, the application to amend should
be by summons, which should state that it is without
prejudice to the notice (*p*).

(*l*) R. S. C., Ord. XVI. r. 6.
(*m*) L. R., 11 Ch. D. 82; 5 Ch.
D. 695; and see also *Honduras*
Rail. Co. v. *Lefevre*, L. R., 2
Ex. D. 301.
(*n*) R. S. C., Ord. XVI. rr. 13

and 14.
(*o*) Ib. ; and see *Tildesley* v.
Harper, L. R., 3 Ch. D. 77. For
form of order, see *Edwards* v.
Lowther, 24 W. R. 437.
(*p*) Ante, p. 29.

SECTION 3.

Change of Parties by Death, &c.

In case of the death, marriage or bankruptcy, or devolution of estate by operation of law of any party to an action, the court or a judge may, if he deems it necessary for the complete settlement of all the questions involved in the action, order that the personal representative, husband, trustee or other successor in interest (if any) of such party, be made a party to the action, or be served with notice of it (*q*).

In case of an assignment, creation, or devolution, of an estate *pendente lite*, the action may be continued by or against the person to, or upon, whom such estate has come or devolved (*r*).

It would seem that an order for a change of parties, or for joining a person already a party, in another capacity, ought in general to be obtained on petition of course (*s*), although, in cases of nicety, the application may be made by *ex parte* motion (*t*).

The order, when obtained, must be served on all the old and new parties, and the order is binding on them from the time of such service, and the new parties must enter an appearance as if the order were a writ of summons (*u*); but any person under no disability other than coverture, or who, being under disability, nevertheless has a guardian *ad litem* in the action, may apply to discharge or vary the order within twelve days from the service; and any party under disability (save as

(*q*) R. S. C., Ord. L. r. 2.
(*r*) Ib. r. 3.
(*s*) Ib. r. 4 ; and *Roffey* v. *Miller*, W. N. 1875, p. 225.

(*t*) *Haldane* v. *Eckford*, W. N. 1879, p. 80.
(*u*) R. S. C., Ord. L. r. 5.

above) may apply for that purpose within twelve days from the appointment of a guardian *ad litem* to him or her (*x*).

———◆———

CHAPTER III.

INDORSEMENT OF CLAIM.

THE writ, as we have seen before, must be endorsed with a statement of the nature of the claim made, or relief or remedy required by the plaintiff.

If the claim is for a liquidated demand (*i.e.*, a demand for a sum certain), the plaintiff must state how much such demand is, and also how much he claims for costs, and must state that if the amount be paid within four days after service (or where the writ is to be served out of the jurisdiction, within the time allowed for appearance) further proceedings will be stayed (*a*). In such cases, also, the plaintiff may, what is called, " specially indorse " the writ with particulars of the liquidated sum which he claims, with dates and amounts (*b*), in which case the plaintiff may apply for leave to sign judgment, and the defendant will have to satisfy a judge that he ought to be allowed to defend the action, before being permitted to do so (*c*). However, these special indorsements are rarely used in the Chancery Division, because a Chancery action is not the appropriate tribunal in which to recover a liquidated

---

(*x*) Ib. rr. 6, 7.

(*a*) R. S. C., Ord. III. r. 7.

(*b*) *Parpaite* v. *Dickenson*, 38 L. T. 178.

(*c*) R. S. C., Ord. XIV. r. 1a.

sum, the Queen's Bench Division of the High Court being the tribunal more usually appealed to for that purpose.

Misjoinder of Causes of Action. In indorsing the writ, the chief danger to be avoided is the joinder of several causes of action which ought not to be joined. Before the passing of the Judicature Acts, the right of the plaintiff to join several causes of action in one suit, was very much restricted, and an attempt to do so frequently gave rise to a " demurrer for multifariousness," which in effect was an objection, that even granting the truth of all the plaintiff's allegations, yet they were too numerous and too complex to be dealt with in one suit.

Such an objection, however, is now in a great measure removed, and subject to some exceptions, which will be presently noticed, the plaintiff may unite in the same action several causes of action; and joint claims by several plaintiffs may be joined with claims by one or more of them against the same defendant; and claims by or against a husband and wife may be joined with claims by or against either of them separately (d).

The rule is subject to the following exceptions, which can, however, for sufficient cause, be abrogated in particular cases by the court or a judge.

(1) No cause of action unless by leave of a judge or the court can be joined with an action for the recovery of land, except claims for mesne profits or rent of such land, or damages for breach of any contract under which such land is held (e). It would seem, however, that leave is not required to join any other cause of action which arises out of or is incident to the claim to the

<hr>

(d) R. S. C., Ord. XVII. rr. 1, 6, 4.   (e) Ib. r. 2.

land in question (as for the appointment of a receiver, or an injunction (*f*), or the cancellation of a deed relating to the property (*g*)). Where the recovery of the land forms part and parcel of a general claim to have property administered leave will be granted (*h*). A foreclosure action is <u>not an</u> action for recovery of land within this rule (*i*).

(2) Claims by a trustee in bankruptcy as such, cannot be joined with claims by him in any other capacity (*k*).

(3) Claims by or against an executor or administrator, as such, cannot be joined with claims by or against him in his private capacity, unless the latter are alleged to arise with reference to the estate of his testator or intestate, as the case may be (*l*).

In order to get leave to transgress any of the above exceptions, the plaintiff should, before the writ is served (*m*), apply to the court by *ex parte* motion for the required leave (*n*). It is not necessary to produce any evidence in support of such an application.

If, without obtaining leave, a plaintiff joins any of

(*f*) *Gledhill* v. *Hunter*, L. R., 14 Ch. D. 492; but see *Allen* v. *Kennett*, 24 W. R. 845; *Cook* v. *Enchmarsh*, L. R., 2 Ch. D. 111.

(*g*) *Cook* v. *Enchmarsh*, sup.

(*h*) *Gledhill* v. *Hunter*, sup.; but see *Kitching* v. *Kitching*, 24 W. R. 901; *Manisty* v. *Kenealy*, ib. 919; *Whetstone* v. *Dewis*, L. R., 1 Ch. D. 99.

(*i*) *Tawell* v. *Slate Co.*, L. R., 3 Ch. D. 629.

(*k*) R. S. C., Ord. XVII. r. 3.

(*l*) It is assumed that this is the correct interpretation of R. S. C., Ord. XVII. r. 5.

(*m*) *Pilcher* v. *Hinds*, L. R., 11 Ch. D. 905.

(*n*) See cases cited, notes (*f*) and (*h*), sup. As to mode of making an ex parte motion, see infra, Sub-div. XI. Chap. II. Sect. 1.

the prohibited causes of action, a summons to strike out the claim objected to should be taken out.

Inconvenient Joinder of Claims. If, although not transgressing the above-mentioned rule, the plaintiff should join several causes of action which cannot *conveniently* be *tried* together, the court or a judge may order them to be *tried* separately (o); and if a plaintiff should join several causes of action which cannot be conveniently *disposed of in one action*, the court or a judge may, on application by summons, order any of such causes of action to be excluded, and may direct the statement of claim and writ to be amended accordingly, and may make such order as to costs as may be just (p).

If the plaintiff finds that he has made a mistake in his indorsement of claim, he may, it is believed, before service of the writ, amend the statement without leave; but it is safer to get leave.

If, however, the writ has been served, he *must* get leave to amend, which (if the statement of defence has not been delivered) will be granted on motion or petition of course (q), but if the defence has been delivered, then, unless the defendant consents, the application must be by summons (r).

It has been said, however, by the Master of the Rolls that the indorsement of claim need not be amended if the statement of claim has been delivered (that document superseding the indorsement of claim) (s), and as it is very unusual not to deliver a statement of claim in

---

(o) R. S. C., Ord. XVII. r. 1.

(p) Ib. rr. 8, 9.

(q) Ib., Ord. III. r. 2; *Matthias* v. *Matthias*, W. N. 1876, p. 214.

(r) *Marriott* v. *Marriott*, 26 W. R. 416.

(s) *Lange* v. *Lange*, W. N. 1877, p. 198; *Eyre* v. *Cox*, 24 W. R. 316.

a Chancery action, it would seem that it can scarcely ever be necessary to amend the indorsement after the defence has been delivered.

It is nevertheless humbly conceived, that the observations of the Master of the Rolls can only be taken to extend to cases where the variance between the writ and the statement of claim consists in the latter claiming merely some additional relief by way of *supplement* to the former, and not altogether differing from it in point of substance. For instance, a writ for dissolution of partnership would not require to be amended, in order to admit of the statement of claim containing a claim for an injunction and a receiver; but, on the other hand, a writ for foreclosure could scarcely support, without amendment, a statement of claim, praying damages against the defendant for inducing the plaintiff to advance money on the mortgage by fraudulent representations.

It must not be forgotten that if notice of trial, or of an interlocutory application, has been given, the application to amend should be by summons, *which should state that it is without prejudice to the notice* (t).

CHAPTER IV.

ISSUING THE WRIT.

Solicitor's Retainer. Before issuing the writ, the solicitor for an intended plaintiff should take care to be

(t) Ante, p. 29.

provided with sufficient evidence of his authority to commence and prosecute the action; for if the plaintiff afterwards denies that he gave such authority, and there is nothing but assertion against assertion, the court will say that the solicitor ought to have secured himself by having an authority in writing, and that not having done so, he must abide the consequences of his neglect, and the action will be dismissed, and the solicitor ordered to reimburse the plaintiff all the expenses caused by its having been commenced (*u*).

When a solicitor has commenced an action without the plaintiff's authority, the proper course is for the latter to serve notice of motion on the defendant and on the solicitor, that the action may be dismissed, and that the solicitor may pay the costs of the plaintiff as between solicitor and client, and the costs of the defendant as between party and party (*v*).

Sealing. After the writ has been duly prepared, and the proper parties determined, and the proper claim indorsed, the next step is to "issue" it, by which is meant getting it made an authoritative summons of the court. This is done by getting it sealed, either at the London central office by a master of the High Court, or, at one of the various district registries which have been established in various parts of the country, by the registrar (*x*). The plaintiff or his solicitor must, on presenting the writ for sealing, leave with the officer who seals the same, a copy of the writ (including indorsements) on the proper kind of paper, and such copy

(*u*) *Wright* v. *Castle*, 3 Mer. 12; *Bird* v. *Harris*, W. N. 1880, p. 166; and see *Re Savage*, L. R., 16 Ch. D. 557.

(*v*) *Newbiggin, &c. Gas Co.* v. *Armstrong*, L. R., 13 Ch. D. 310.

(*x*) R. S. C., Ord. V. rr. 1, 1a, 6.

must be signed by or for the solicitor (if one be employed), or by the plaintiff himself (if he sue in person) (y).

The officer who seals the writ, at the same time files the copy, and enters a memorandum of such filing in a book called "the cause book," distinguishing the action by the date of the year, the initial letter of the first plaintiff's name, and a number (z) thus:—"1881. B. No. 102," and this distinguishing mark is placed at the head of the writ, and all pleadings and other documents filed in the action.

If the writ is issued out of a district registry, the name of the registry is also added to the writ beneath the words Chancery Division (a) thus:—

1880. B. No. 102.

In the High Court of Justice.

Chancery Division.

Birmingham District Registry.

Master of the Rolls.

Sealing for Service out of the Jurisdiction.

If the writ is intended to be served out of the jurisdiction the leave of a judge must be obtained before it can be sealed (b). This is done by leaving the unsealed writ at the chambers of the judge, with an affidavit, and the judge marks the order or the writ itself, without hearing counsel or solicitor, and a copy of this order must be written on the copy for filing. The affidavit must state (1) the value or amount of the property in dispute (c) ; (2) the place or county where the

(y) Ib. r. 7.
(z) Ib. r. 8.
(a) Ib., Addition of June, 1876.
(b) R. S. C., Ord. II. r. 4.
(c) R. S. C., Ord. XI. r. 1a.

defendant is probably to be found; (3) whether the
defendant is a British subject or not (*d*); (4) whether
or not there is at the place where the defendant resides,
a local court which has jurisdiction in the matter (*c*),
and also that the plaintiff is informed and believes that
he has a good cause of action within the jurisdiction (*f*),
and also the special reasons for suing in the High
Court (*g*).

Concurrent Writs. Where it is doubtful where
the defendant is to be found, it is permissible to issue
concurrent writs after the issue of the original writ.
Such writs are marked "concurrent," and bear the
same date as the original writ, and are sealed in the
same manner (*h*). The original writ may be issued for
service within the jurisdiction, and the concurrent writs,
or some or one of them, for service out of it, or *vice
versâ* (*i*); but, of course, before a concurrent writ can be
marked for service outside the jurisdiction, leave must
be obtained.

New Defendants added after Issue. Where
a writ is amended after issue by the addition of a defendant, the plaintiff must (unless otherwise ordered by
the court or a judge) file an amended copy of, and sue
out a writ of summons, and serve such new defendant
with such writ or notice in lieu of service thereof, as the
case may be, in the same manner as original defendants
are served (*k*).

(*d*) R. S. C., Ord. XI. r. 3.

(*c*) Ib. r. 1a; *Wood* v. *MacInnes,*
L. R., 4 C. P. D. 67.

(*f*) *Great Aust. Gold Co.* v.
Martin, L. R., 5 Ch. D. 1.

(*g*) R. S. C., Ord. XI. r. 3.

(*h*) R. S. C., Ord. VI. r. 1.

(*i*) Ib. r. 2.

(*k*) R. S. C., Ord. XVI. rr. 15,
13.

CHAPTER V.

SERVICE OF THE WRIT.

THE writ being issued, it has next to be served on the defendant, and this must be done by the plaintiff or his solicitor, and not by the officers of the court.

If, however, the defendant, by his solicitor, agrees to accept service, no personal service is necessary (*a*).

If the defendant does not agree to accept service, the writ must (subject to what is said hereafter in regard to substituted service) be personally served on the defendant, by tendering him a copy of the writ and producing the original, if required (*b*).

But although personal service on a defendant is generally necessary where his solicitor does not consent to accept service for him, yet there are certain exceptions to the general rule which arise out of the exceptional status of particular classes of defendants.

Husband and Wife. When a husband and wife are both defendants, service on the husband is sufficient unless a judge or the court directs otherwise (*c*).

Infants. Service on the father or guardian of an infant defendant, or if he has neither, then upon the person with whom he resides or under whose care he is, is sufficient, unless a judge or the court directs otherwise (*d*).

Lunatics. If a defendant be a lunatic so found, service on his committee is sufficient; and in the case of a person of unsound mind not so found, service on the

(*a*) R. S. C., Ord. IX. r. 1.   (*c*) Ib. r. 3.
(*b*) Ib. r. 2.   (*d*) Ib. r. 4.

person with whom he resides, or under whose care he is, is sufficient, unless in either case a judge or the court directs otherwise (*e*).

Partnership Firm. Where a firm is sued in the firm name, whether such firm actually consists of more than one person or only of one person, the writ may be served on any one or more members of the firm, *or* at the principal place of business within the jurisdiction upon any person having at the time of service the management of the firm business (*f*).

Foreigners living out of the Jurisdiction. A foreign defendant living out of the jurisdiction should not be served with the writ, but with notice that the writ is issued (*g*), such notice being indorsed as to address of parties, &c. like a writ of summons.

Companies. Companies chartered under the act 7 Will. 4 & 1 Vict. c. 73, may be served by service on the clerk of the company, or if he be not known, or cannot be found, then on any agent or officer of the company, or by leaving it at the usual abode of such agent or officer (*h*).

Companies incorporated under the Companies Clauses Consolidation Act, 1845, may be served by sending the writ through the post to the principal office of the company, or to one of the principal offices where there is more than one, or by giving it personally to the secretary, or, where there is no secretary, by giving it to a director (*i*).

(*e*) R. S. C., Ord. IX. r. 5.
(*f*) Ib. rr. 6, 6a.
(*g*) *Re Howard*, L. R., 10 Ch. D. 550.

(*h*) R. S. C., Ord. IX. r. 7; and 7 Will. 4 & 1 Vict. c. 73, s. 26.
(*i*) R. S. C., Ord. IX. r. 7; and 8 Vict. c. 16, s. 135.

Companies incorporated under the Lands Clauses Consolidation Act, 1845, may be served by sending the writ by post to the principal office, or one of the principal offices, of the promoters, or by posting it to the secretary, or, where there is no secretary, to the solicitor (k).

Companies incorporated under the Railways Clauses Consolidation Act, 1845, may be served, by sending the writ by post to the principal office, or one of the principal offices, of the company, or by giving it personally to the secretary, or, where there is no secretary, to one of the directors (l).

Companies incorporated under the Companies Act, 1862, may be served, by leaving the writ, or sending it through the post in a prepaid letter addressed to the company, at their registered office (m).

Inhabitants of Counties, Towns, &c. Service may be effected on a municipal corporation, by serving the mayor or other head officer, or the town clerk, secretary, or treasurer (n).

The inhabitants of a hundred, or other like district, may be served, by serving the high constable, or one of them, if more than one (o).

The inhabitants of a county, city, town, or of any franchise, liberty, city, town or place, not being part of a hundred or other like place, may be served, by serving some peace officer thereof (o).

(k) R. S. C., Ord. IX. r. 7; and 8 Vict. c. 18, s. 134.

(l) R. S. C., Ord. IX. r. 7; and 8 Vict. c. 20, s. 138.

(m) R. S. C., Ord. IX. r. 7; and 25 & 26 Vict. c. 189, s. 62.

(n) R. S. C., Ord. IX. r. 7; and C. L. P. Act, 1852, s. 16.

(o) Ib.

Ejectment. Ejectment actions are not usual in the Chancery Division, but it may be remarked that in case of vacant possession, and when the defendant cannot otherwise be served, it is sufficient to post a copy of the writ on the door, or any other conspicuous part of the property.

Substituted Service. Where service cannot be promptly made in accordance with the foregoing rules, the plaintiff may apply to the court by a motion *ex parte*, supported by an affidavit, stating the issue of the writ, that the cause books at the offices where the defendant might have entered an appearance have been searched, but no appearance has been entered, and showing what efforts have been made to serve the defendant, and that all practicable means of doing so have been exhausted, and proposing some method of bringing the writ to the defendant's knowledge (*q*); and thereupon the court may make such order for substituted or other service, or for the substitution of notice for service, as may seem just (*r*). Thus the writ has been ordered to be left at the defendant's place of business, and a copy to be posted to him (*s*); and so where the defendant had absconded, the writ was ordered to be left at his premises, and advertisements to be inserted in the Times and Gazette (*t*). Where the order is for substituted service, the order for it and the writ should be served together in manner prescribed by the order.

(*q*) R. S. C., Ord. X.; and see Dan. Ch. Pr., 4th ed. vol. i. p. 404.

(*r*) R. S. C., Ord. IX., r. 2.

(*s*) *Capes* v. *Brewer*, 24 W. R. 40.

(*t*) *Cook* v. *Day*, L. R., 2 Ch. D. 220; and see *Crane* v. *Jullion*, ib. 220; *Rafael* v. *Ongley*, 34 L. T. 124.

Indorsement of Service. The person who serves a writ must, within three days afterwards, indorse on the writ the day of the month and week on which such service was effected, otherwise the plaintiff cannot proceed by default (*u*); but of course this rule is inapplicable to cases of substituted service (*x*); and the time may be extended by the court on motion (*y*).

(*u*) R. S. C., Ord. IX. r. 13.   (*y*) *Hastings* v. *Hurley*, L. R.,
(*x*) *Dymond* v. *Croft*, L. R., 3   16 Ch. D. 734.
Ch. D. 512.

Sub-division II.

Defendant's Proceedings on Service of Writ.

UPON the writ being served, or notice in lieu of service being given, the defendant has to consider what
course he should pursue.   He may either enter an appearance, enter a conditional appearance and apply to
set the writ aside for irregularity, or omit to enter any
appearance; or he may enter an appearance and interplead; or he may take proceedings to bind a third party
who is bound to indemnify him.

CHAPTER I.

APPEARANCE.

SECTION 1.
General Practice.

BY appearing in obedience to a writ of summons, a
defendant formally submits himself to the jurisdiction

of the court; and formerly it was considered essential that the defendant should either appear himself, or that under the orders of the court the plaintiff should enter an appearance for him, and until one of these courses was adopted the court had no jurisdiction over the matter in dispute. This theory is, however, now in a great measure done away with, and as we shall see hereafter in the third chapter of this sub-division, judgment may now be had in default of appearance.

An appearance is entered by delivering to the proper officer (who in London is the master of the High Court and in a district registry the registrar), a memorandum in writing, in duplicate, dated on the day of delivering the same, and containing the name and place of business of the defendant's solicitor, or stating that the defendant defends in person, and giving an address for service within three miles of Temple Bar if appearance is entered in London, or within the district of the District Registry where appearance is entered in a district registry (a). If the defendant requires a statement of claim to be filed and delivered, the memorandum should state so. If the memorandum does not contain the addresses above referred to, it will not be received; and if such addresses are false or illusory, the appearance will be set aside on the plaintiff applying by summons in chambers (b).

The following is the form of a memorandum of appearance (c); and it may be here conveniently stated that all defendants who are represented by the same solicitor appear together and in one memorandum (d).

(a) R. S. C., Ord. XII. rr. 6b, 7. (c) Ib. r. 10.
(b) Ib. r. 9. (d) Ib. r. 13.

U. F

1881. S. No. 300.

High Court of Justice.
 Chancery Division.
  Vice-Chancellor Hall.

    Smith *v.* Jones.

Enter an appearance for Thomas Jones in this action.
Dated this 3rd day of May, 1881.

      JAMES BROWN,
       Solicitor for the Defendant.

The place of business of the said James Brown is 500, Strand, in the county of Middlesex.

His address for service is at 500, Strand aforesaid.

The said defendant requires a Statement of Complaint to be filed and delivered.

Place of Appearance.

With regard to the *place* of appearance, if the writ is issued out of the London office, the defendant *must* appear there (*e*); if out of a district registry, then, (1) if the defendant resides or carries on business there, he *must* appear there (*f*); but (2) if he neither resides nor carries on business there, he may appear either in London or the District Registry (*g*).

If the defendant enters appearance in the wrong place, the plaintiff may proceed as in default of appearance.

Removal of Action from District Registry.

Although, however, a defendant *must* in the cases above mentioned appear in a district registry, yet any defendant may except where the writ is "specially indorsed" (which is very rare in Chancery actions), and even when it is specially indorsed, may, subject to certain

---

(*e*) R. S. C., Ord. XII. rr. 1, (*f*) Ib. r. 2.
1a, 3.   (*g*) Ib. r. 3.

limitations, as of right after appearance, and before
delivering his statement of defence, remove the action
to the London office (*h*), by serving on the other parties
to the action, and delivering to the district registrar, a
notice signed by himself or his solicitor, to the effect
that he desires the action to be removed to London.
If, however, a judge or the court is satisfied that the
defendant giving such notice is merely a formal defendant, or has no substantial cause to interfere in the
conduct of the action, it may be ordered to proceed in
the district registry notwithstanding the notice (*i*).

Notice of Appearance. The officer who receives
the memorandum of appearance enters it in the cause
book (*k*), and seals the duplicate, which thereupon becomes a certificate of due entry of appearance. The
defendant's solicitor must, *on the same day*, give or post
to the plaintiff's solicitor, notice of entry of appearance,
accompanied by the sealed memorandum (*l*).

Although the writ names a time within which appearance must be entered, yet in reality the defendant
may appear at any time before judgment is obtained,
or even afterwards by leave of the court; but in case he
appears after the expiration of the time limited in the
writ, he must *on the same day* give notice thereof to
the plaintiff or his solicitor, but he does not gain any
further time for delivering his defence by appearing
late (*m*).

Notice of appearance must also be given *forthwith* by
a person who not being named defendant in an action

(*h*) Ib. r. 4 ; and Ord. XXXV.
r. 11.

(*i*) Ord. XXXV. r. 12.

(*k*) Ord. XII. r. 11.

(*l*) Ib. r. 6b (1880).

(*m*) Ib. r. 15.

for the recovery of land, obtains leave to appear and defend *n* .

Appearance after Judgment. A defendant who wishes to appear after judgment and in administration and other like actions it may sometimes be for a defendant's advantage to do so) may obtain leave to do so by petition of course, if the plaintiff consents; but if not, the application must be by summons or motion, upon which no order will be made, unless the defendant submits to be bound by all prior proceedings, including the judgment *o* .

Appearance of Partners. An individual or partners sued in the firm name must appear in his or their individual names, but the title of the action nevertheless remains the same as before *p*).

Attaching Solicitor who breaks undertaking to appear. Lastly, a solicitor who has given an undertaking to accept service of writ and to enter an appearance, and who omits to do so, is liable to be attached for contempt *q*).

Section 2.

Appearance of Infant or Lunatic Defendants.

An appearance should be entered for a defendant who is an infant or lunatic whether so found or not), by the person on whom the writ is properly served, or the

---

n R. S C., Ord. XII. r. 20.
o Dan. Ch. Pr. 139.

(*p* R. S. C., Ord. XII. rr. 12, 12a.
q Ib. r. 14.

person to whom notice in lieu of service has been properly given, as prescribed on page 59.

In the case of infants and lunatics *not so found*. no further step in the action can be taken on their behalf, until a guardian *ad litem* is appointed (r) ; but in the case of a lunatic *so found by inquisition*, the action is defended by the committee of his estate, if he has one, and if such committee has no interest in the subject-matter of the action adverse to the lunatic. If, however, there is no committee, or the interest of the committee is adverse, then the lunatic must have a guardian *ad litem* appointed.

Appointment of Guardian. Where a guardian *ad litem* is necessary, the friends of the infant or lunatic should apply for the appointment forthwith after his appearance, which is done by petition of course in the infant's, or lunatic's, name by his next friend, supported by affidavit of his solicitor, that the proposed guardian has no adverse interest to the infant or lunatic in the subject-matter of the action, and that the proposed guardian is a fit and proper person for the office.

Neither the plaintiff, nor any person not *sui juris*, nor a person out of the jurisdiction. will be appointed (s). An order appointing a guardian *ad litem* must be left at the central office or district registry for entry.

Removal of Guardian. A guardian *ad litem* may be removed for good cause on application by summons or motion, made by any person acting as next friend, for that purpose, of the infant or lunatic ; and in that case, or in case of the death of a guardian *pendente lite*,

(r) *Lushington* v. *Sewell*, 6 Mad. 28 ; R. S. C., Ord. XVI. r. 8.

(s) *Banfield* v. *Grant*, 11 W. R.

275; *Newman* v. *Self.*, ib. 764; and see 9 Ha. Append. 27, and 18 Jur. 776.

a new one must be appointed, who (in a case of removal) is appointed by the same order which removes
the old one (z).

———◆———

CHAPTER II.

CONDITIONAL APPEARANCE.

WHERE a defendant wishes to test the legality or regu-
larity of the writ, or service thereof or notice in lieu of
service, he can only do so by application to the court (a);
and before he can apply to the court he must submit to
its jurisdiction. But if he submits to the jurisdiction
by an ordinary appearance, he will be taken to have
waived all such objections (b). The proper course,
therefore, is for the defendant in such a case to enter a
conditional appearance (c), but this is only allowed by
leave of the court, which may be obtained either by
petition of course or *ex parte* motion, on the defendant
consenting to submit to any process which may be
issued against him on such appearance. As soon as
possible after entering a conditional appearance, the
defendant should take steps to test his objection to the
writ, or the service of it, as the case may be, or he will
be taken to have waived such objection (d).

(z) Dan. 146.

(a) R. S. C., Ord. LIX.

(b) *Preston* v. *Lamont*, L. R., 1 Ex. D. 361.

(c) Dan. Ch. Pr. 459.

(d) *Westman* v. *Aktiebolaget Snickfabrik*, L. R., 1 Ex. D. 237; *Re Howard*, L. R., 10 Ch. D. 550; *Beddington* v. *Beddington*, L. R., 1 P. D. 126.

CHAPTER III.

DEFAULT OF APPEARANCE.

The consequences of non-appearance by the defendant vary according to the nature of the action ; but as debts or liquidated demands, actions for damages, or actions in the nature of trover or detinue, or actions of eject-ment, are not generally brought in the Chancery Divi-sion, being more appropriately cognizable by the Queen's Bench Division of the Court, I shall confine my re-marks to those actions which are usually, or under the Judicature Act, 1873, assigned to the Chancery Division.

General Practice on Default of Appearance. In the Chancery Division then, where the defendant does not appear within the time limited for appearance, the plaintiff may, unless the defendant is an infant or a person of unsound mind not so found by inquisition, file an affidavit of service of the writ, and the action then proceeds as if the defendant had appeared (e). If the defaulting defendant does not appear within the time allowed for delivering his statement of defence, the plaintiff may forthwith set the case down on motion for judgment (f); or if some of the defendants appear, and some do not, he may set it down on motion for judg-ment against those making default, or may wait until the hearing (g).

Infants and Lunatics. Where, however, the de-fendant is an infant or person of unsound mind not so found, the plaintiff should apply by motion (h) for an

(e) R. S. C., Ord. XIII. r. 9.
(f) R. S. C., Ord. XXIX. r. 10.
(g) Ib. r. 11.

(h) Dan. Ch. Pr. 147 ; Evans' Pr. Ch. D. 586. Nevertheless, in a recent case in which the

order that some proper person be assigned guardian of
such defendant, by whom he may appear and defend
the action. No such order will be made unless it appears that the writ was duly served, and that notice of
the summons was, after the time limited for entry of
appearance, and at least six days before the date named
for the hearing of the summons, served upon or left at
the dwelling-house of the person with whom or under
whose care such defendant was at the time of serving
such writ; and also (in case of such defendant being an
infant not residing with or under the care of his father
or guardian) served upon or left at the dwelling-house
of such father or guardian, if any, unless the judge at
the hearing of the summons dispense with such last-
mentioned service (e).

Upon appearance being entered for such defendant
by the guardian *ad litem* so appointed, the action proceeds in the ordinary course.

Service of subsequent Proceedings. In actions set down on motion for judgment in default of
appearance, the statement of claim (if any) and notice
of motion for judgment should be filed with the master
of the court at the central office or with the district
registrar, according as the action is proceeding in
London or the district registry (*f*), or where the defendant has been duly served with the writ, they may
be served on him without being filed (*g*).

---

author applied, V.-C. Hall expressed an opinion that such applications should be by summons.

(e) R. S. C., Ord. XIII. r. 1.

(*f*) R. S. C., Ord. XIX. rr. 6,
29.

(*g*) R. S. C., Ord. LIII. r. 7;
Whitaker v. *Thurston*, W. N. 1876,
232; *Dymond* v. *Croft*, L. R., 3
Ch. D. 512; *Morton* v. *Miller*, ib.
516.

Setting aside Judgment obtained for Default.

Where, however, judgment has been obtained in default of appearance, it may be set aside by the court or a judge on such terms as to costs or otherwise as may seem just (h). The application is usually made by summons, supported by affidavit, satisfactorily explaining why judgment was allowed to go by default, and should be made as quickly as possible. Such applications are seldom granted, except on condition of the defaulting defendant paying all the plaintiff's costs up to, and of, the application, in addition to other terms.

It will be carefully remembered, that where the writ is irregular, or has been irregularly issued or served, the proper course is not to apply to set aside the judgment, but to set aside the writ.

CHAPTER IV.

INTERPLEADER.

INTERPLEADER is the right of a defendant who is in possession of property in respect of which the action is brought, but who does not claim any interest in it, and believes that it belongs to some third person who has sued or is expected to sue for it, to insist that the plaintiff and such third person shall fight the matter out between them, the defendant being ready to bring into court, or to pay, or dispose of the subject-matter of the action in such manner as the court or a judge may order or direct.

(h) R. S. C., Ord. XXIX. r. 14.

Interpleader is seldom resorted to except in actions which are more conveniently assigned to the common law divisions, and, therefore, in a treatise on the practice of the Chancery Division it is sufficient to say, that the practice is for the defendant to take out a summons returnable in chambers, supported by an affidavit, and served on the plaintiff. Upon such summons the judge may make an order calling on the third party to appear and to state the nature and particulars of his claim, and to maintain or relinquish his claim, and may hear the allegations as well of such third party as of the plaintiff, and in the meantime may stay the proceedings in such action, and may finally order the third party to make himself defendant in the same or some other action, or to proceed to trial on one or more issue or issues, and may also direct which of the parties shall be plaintiff or defendant in such trial. With the consent of the plaintiff and such third party, their counsel or attorneys (*or*, where the subject-matter in dispute is of small value, *or*, the question is one merely of law, and not of fact, then without any such consent), the judge may dispose of the merits of their claims, and determine the same in a summary manner, and make such other orders therein as to costs and all other matters as may appear to be just and reasonable (*a*).

The judge may, if the third party refuses or neglects to comply with any order, declare his rights to be barred, except as against the plaintiff (*b*), and may, at any stage, refer the matter into court instead of chambers (*c*); and where there is a question of law too important to be

---

(*a*) 1 & 2 Will. 4, c. 58, s. 1, applied to Chancery Division by R. S. C., Ord. I. r. 2; and 23 & 24 Vict. c. 126, ss. 14, 15.

(*b*) Ib. sect. 3.

(*c*) Ib. sect. 5.

decided summarily, and no dispute as to facts, may order a special case to be stated (*d*).

———◆———

CHAPTER V.

PROCEEDINGS TO BIND A PERSON NOT A PARTY TO AN ACTION.

WHERE a defendant claims to be entitled to contribution or indemnity, or any other remedy or relief over against any other person, or where from any other cause it appears that a question in the action should be determined, not only as between the plaintiff and the defendant, but as between the plaintiff, defendant, and any other person, or between any or either of them, the court or a judge may, on notice being given to such last-named person, make such order as may be proper for having the question determined (*e*).

Effect of bringing in a Third Party. The bringing in of a third party under this rule does not alter the rights of the plaintiff against the defendant, nor give the plaintiff any rights against the third party, nor the third party any rights against him (*f*); nor does it enable a defendant to obtain actual present relief. The sole effect is to bind the third party not to dispute the validity of the proceedings, with a view to obtaining future relief against him (*g*).

(*d*) 23 & 24 Vict. c. 126, s. 15.
(*e*) R. S. C., Ord. XVI. r. 17.
(*f*) *Williams* v. *S. E. Rail. Co.*, L. R., 26 W. R. 352.

(*g*) *Padwick* v. *Scott*, L. R., 2 Ch. D. 736 ; *Warner* v. *Twining*, 24 W. R. 536.

Method of bringing in Third Party. A defendant wishing to bring in a third party under this rule should get the leave of the court (obtained on motion, of which notice must be given to the plaintiff (d)) to serve the third party with a notice, sealed by the proper officer with the seal with which writs of summons are sealed. A copy of such notice must be filed with the proper officer, and the notice served (together with a copy of the statement of claim, or where none has been delivered, with a copy of the writ) on the third party, in like manner as a writ of summons is served (e).

If the person so served, desires to dispute the plaintiff's claim in the action as against the defendant on whose behalf the notice has been given, he must enter an appearance in the action within eight days from the service of the notice. In default of his doing so, he will be deemed to admit the validity of the judgment obtained against such defendant, whether obtained by consent or otherwise; but a person making such default may still apply to the court or a judge for leave to appear (f).

If, however, he does appear, the defendant may apply to the court or a judge for directions as to the mode of having the question in the action decided, and the court or judge may, upon the hearing of such application, if it appear desirable, give the third party liberty to defend the action, upon such terms as may seem just, and may direct such pleadings to be delivered (g) or amended, and generally direct such proceedings and give such directions as shall seem proper

(d) *Wye Valley Rail. Co.* v. *Hawes*, L. R., 16 Ch. D. 489.

(e) R. S. C., Ord. XVI. r. 18.

(f) Ib. r. 20.

(g) See *Witham* v. *Vane*, 28 W. R. 276.

for having the question most conveniently determined, and as to the mode and extent in or to which the third party shall be bound or made liable by the decision of the question (*h*).

At present it does not seem to be well settled whether or not a third party brought in can in his turn bring in a fourth (*i*); but where a defendant claims contribution, indemnity, or the like, against a *co-defendant*, it is not necessary to get leave to serve him with the notice above mentioned. In such a case it is sufficient to serve him with a copy of the defence (*k*).

(*h*) R. S. C., Ord. XVI. r. 21.

(*i*) Compare *Walker* v. *Balfour*, 26 W. R. 511; and *Fowler* v.

Knoop, 36 L. T. 219.

(*k*) *Furness* v. *Booth*, L. R., 4 Ch. D. 586.

The Pleadings.

———◆———

CHAPTER I.

PRELIMINARY.

A PLEADING is the written or printed statement of a litigant's demand or claim, or of his defence or answer thereto, or of the reply to such defence or answer.

Pleadings formerly consisted of a bill and answer, and sometimes a replication; but since the Judicature Acts came into operation they consist of—(1) A statement of claim by the plaintiff; (2) A statement of defence or a demurrer by the defendant; and (3), A reply or demurrer by the plaintiff. No pleading subsequent to a reply is allowed except by special leave of the court or a judge obtained on summons (*a*). The

(*a*) R. S. C., Ord. XXIV. r. 2.

object of pleadings is to arrive at an issue, either of fact or law, or both; that is to say, to arrive at some point at which one party affirms a proposition of fact or a proposition of law which the other denies. When the denial is a denial of fact, it is called a statement of defence or reply, as the case may be. When it is a denial of law, it is called a demurrer.

Printing of Pleadings. Every pleading which contains less than ten folios of seventy-two words each, (every figure being counted as one word) may be either printed or written, or partly printed or partly written, and every other pleading must be printed (*b*). Pleadings must be printed upon cream wove machine drawing foolscap folio paper, 19 lbs. per mill ream or thereabouts, in pica type, leaded, with an inner margin about three-quarters of an inch wide and an outer margin about two and a half inches wide (*c*).

Counsel's Signature. It is usual, but not now compulsory (*d*), for pleadings in the Chancery Division to be signed by the counsel by whom they have been settled, where they have (as is almost universally the case) been settled by counsel. It is very desirable that this custom should be observed, as not only do some of the judges object to its non-observance, but it gives the other side notice of the counsel by whom their opponents will be represented, and thus often renders it possible for the opposing counsel to settle between themselves trifling matters of procedure which might otherwise be the occasion of expensive wrangling.

Delivery of Pleadings. Every pleading is delivered by the pleading party to the solicitor of every

(*b*) R. S. C., Ord. XIX. r. 5.   (*d*) R. S. C., Ord. XIX. r. 4.
(*c*) R. S. C., Ord. LVI. r. 2.

other party who appears by a solicitor, or to the party personally if he does not appear by a solicitor; but if no appearance has been entered by any party, then such pleading is filed with the proper officer at the central office or district registry, as the case may be (e).

Let us now examine the different pleadings in detail.

<hr>

CHAPTER II.

SPECIFIC PLEADINGS OF FACT.

<hr>

SECTION 1.

Statement of Claim.

Rule as to Delivery of Claim. The plaintiff *may*, if he think fit, at the same time as, or at any time after, the service of the writ of summons, and he *must* within six weeks from the time of the defendant's entry of appearance (unless the defendant, upon entering appearance, states that he does *not* require it) deliver to the defendant a statement of his complaint, and of the relief or remedy to which he claims to be entitled (*f*). But where a plaintiff delivers a statement of claim without being required so to do, and such delivery is unnecessary or improper, he may have to pay the costs occasioned thereby (*g*).

With regard to this, it may be laid down as a general rule, that where there is no question of fact or law to

(e) R. S. C., Ord. XIX. r. 6.

(*f*) Ib. r. 1; and Ord. XXI. r. 1.

(*g*) R. S. C., Ord. XXI. r. 1. This rule appears to be self-contradictory.

be determined (as, for instance, in a creditor's administration action, where the only thing to be done is to
ascertain the debts and distribute the assets), a statement of claim is improper; for the object of pleadings
being to raise some issue or dispute of fact or law, it is
obviously useless to employ them where no such dispute
can arise. But where the rights of parties under an
instrument have to be ascertained, or any question of
construction arises, or where trusts have to be carried
out, a statement of claim is desirable, because it brings
clearly before the court the points of law on which the
opinion of the court is desired (h).

Form. The following is the form of a statement of
claim :—

1876. B. No. 233.

In the High Court of Justice.
Chancery Division.
V.-C. Hall.

Writ issued 22nd December, 1876.

Between John Briggs . . . . Plaintiff,

and

Thomas Jones . . . . Defendant.

STATEMENT OF CLAIM.

Delivered the   day of   , 1876, by Charles Smith, of No. 500,
Southampton Row, in the county of Middlesex, agent for Alfred
Robinson, of No. 300, High Street, in the city of Exeter, solici-
tor for the above-named plaintiff.

1. By indenture dated the 25th of March, 1873, and made between
the defendant of the one part, and the plaintiff of the other part, in
consideration of the sum of 500l. lent by the plaintiff to the defendant, the defendant granted to the plaintiff and his heirs, a messuage
or dwelling-house, with its appurtenances, situate in High Street,
in the city of Exeter, and being No. 200 in the said street, subject to
a proviso for redemption of the same premises on payment by the

(h) *Breton* v. *Mackett*, W. N.
1875, p. 255; *Boyes* v. *Cook*, W. N.
1876, p. 28; and see *Green* v.

Coleby, L. R., 1 Ch. D. 693; *Taylor* v. *Duckett*, W. N. 1875, p.
193.

U.   G

defendant, his heirs, executors, administrators or assigns to the plaintiff, his executors, administrators or assigns of the sum of 500*l.*, with interest for the same in the meantime at the rate of 5*l.* per cent. per annum on the 29th day of September then next.

2. The whole of the said principal sum of 500*l.* with an arrear of interest thereon remains due to the plaintiff on his said security.

The plaintiff claims as follows :—

    (1) That an account may be taken of what is due to the plaintiff for principal money and interest on his said security, and that the defendant may be decreed to pay to the plaintiff what shall be found due to him on taking such account, together with his costs of this action, by a short day to be appointed by the court, the plaintiff being ready and willing, and hereby offering, upon being paid his principal money, interest and costs at such appointed time, to convey the said mortgaged premises as the court shall direct.

    (2) That in default of such payment the defendant may be fore-closed of the equity of redemption in the said mortgaged premises.

    (3) Such further or other relief as the nature of the case may require.

ARTHUR UNDERHILL.

It will be seen from the above simple example, that a statement of claim consists of (1) the "title" or formal heading, (2) the "stating part" or statement of facts upon which the plaintiff relies, and (3) the "claiming part" or statement of the relief which he claims.

1. The Title. As to the formal parts, they are like those of the writ, viz., the reference to the cause book, the name of the court, division, district registry (where the writ was issued out of one), and judge, to which the action is attached, the date of the issue of the writ, and the names of the parties. If the action is for the administration of the estate of a deceased person, the words "In the matter of the estate of A. B. deceased" must be inserted immediately above the names of the parties, both in the writ and in the pleadings. The description of the pleading (*i. e.* " statement of claim "), and the name and place of business of the solicitor and agent (if any) delivering the same, or the name and address of the plaintiff if appearing in person, and the date of delivery, must also appear (*d*).

2. Stating part. As to the stating part, it should be as concise as possible, and should consist of a statement of the material facts upon which the plaintiff relies, but not the evidence by which they are to be proved (*e*). For instance, if a party sues in respect of a trespass, which the defendant has admitted in a letter to the plaintiff, the fact of the trespass should be stated in the statement of claim, and not the letter which is the evidence of the trespass (*f*).

The stating part should be divided into paragraphs, each paragraph containing as nearly as may be a separate allegation. Dates, sums and numbers must be expressed in figures and not in words (*g*).

Where a plaintiff seeks relief in respect of several *distinct causes* of action *founded on separate and distinct facts*, these separate and distinct facts should be stated separately and distinctly, and not mixed up altogether (*h*). Of course, where there are several distinct kinds of *relief* claimed, all arising out of the same facts (as, for instance, in a patent action where an injunction, and also an account of profits, or, in the alternative, damages are all claimed), there is no necessity to state the same facts separately.

(*d*) R. S. C., Ord. XIX. r. 7.
(*e*) Ib. r. 4.
(*f*) *Davy* v. *Garrett*, L. R., 7 Ch. D. 485 ; and see *Williamson* v. *L. & N. W. Rail. Co.*, L. R., 12 Ch. D. 787.
(*g*) R. S. C., Ord. XIX. r. 4.
(*h*) Ib. r. 9.

Whenever the contents of a document are material, it is sufficient to state the effect thereof as briefly as possible, without setting out the whole or any part of the document, *unless the precise words of the document or any part thereof are material* (*i*). However, where the rights of parties under a deed or will have to be determined, the precise words are almost always material, and it is usual, and certainly convenient, to set forth the document or will (except the merely formal parts) thus: "A. B. late of   in the county of   duly made and executed his last will dated the   day of   , 18 , which, omitting formal parts, was in the words and figures following, that is to say, 'I devise,' &c."

Where any contract or relation between persons does not arise from express agreement, but is to be implied from a series of letters or conversations, or otherwise from a number of circumstances, it is *sufficient* to allege such contract or relation as a matter of fact, and to refer generally to such letters, conversations, or circumstances without setting them out in detail; and if in such case the plaintiff desires to rely in the alternative upon more contracts or relations than are to be implied from such circumstances, he may state the same in the alternative (*k*).

Where, however, the language of letters is material, it is usual and proper to set them out.

Wherever it is material to allege malice, fraudulent intention, knowledge, or other condition of mind, it is sufficient to allege the same as a fact, without setting out the circumstances from which it is to be inferred (*l*), for that would be pleading evidence. And so, again, where it is material to allege notice of a fact, it is sufficient to allege such notice *as a fact,* and not to set forth

(*i*) R. S. C., Ord. XIX. r. 24.   (*l*) Ib. r. 25 : *Herring* v. *Bis-*
(*k*) Ib. r. 27.   *choffsheim*, W. N. 1876, p. 77.

the form or terms of notice, *unless the precise terms of such notice are material* (*m*).

And it would seem that this rule applies, even in cases of implied notice, as such notice is in reality nothing more than knowledge inferred from circumstances, which circumstances (as we have already seen) need not be specified.

In spite, however, of these principles, it has been (as is submitted somewhat inconsistently) held, that a pleading should not contain conclusions of law drawn from facts (*n*). It certainly seems that allegations of malice, notice, or fraud, or an allegation that a series of letters constitute a legal contract, are statements of conclusions of law, and if so, it is difficult to reconcile this decision with the rules of court.

It is not necessary to allege any matter of fact which the law presumes in the plaintiff's favour, or as to which the burden of proof lies upon the other side (*o*), as, for instance, consideration for a deed, or that the husband of a married woman married since 1874, received assets with her sufficient to satisfy the plaintiff's demand (*p*).

3. Claiming part. The claiming part must state specifically the relief which the plaintiff claims, either simply or in the alternative (*q*), and may also ask for general relief (*i.e.*, "such further or other relief as the nature of the case may require"); under which latter claim, any omission in the specific claims (which is consistent with them (*r*)) may be rectified (*s*). If it is

(*m*) R. S. C., Ord. XIX. r. 26.
(*n*) Per Mellish, L. J., *Watson* v. *Rodwell*, 45 L. J., Ch. 716; *Williamson* v. *L. & N. W. Rail. Co.*, L. R., 12 Ch. D. 787.
(*o*) R. S. C., Ord. XIX. r. 28.
(*p*) See *Matthews* v. *Whittle*,

L. R., 13 Ch. D. 811.
(*q*) Ib. r. 8.
(*r*) *Cargill* v. *Bower*, L. R., 10 Ch. D. 502.
(*s*) *Breslauer* v. *Barwick*, 21 W. R. 901.

proposed that the action should be tried at the assizes instead of in London, a note to that effect must be appended at the foot of the claim (*t*).

Section 2.

Statement of Defence and Counter-claim.

Time for Delivery. Where a statement of claim is delivered, the defendant *must* deliver a statement of defence within eight days from the delivery of the statement of claim, or from the time limited for appearance, whichever shall be last, unless such time is extended by the court or a judge. And where a defendant has appeared, and stated that he does not require any statement of claim, and to whom no statement of claim has been delivered, he *may*, but is not bound to, deliver a statement of defence at any time within eight days after appearance, unless such time is extended by the court or a judge (*u*).

Title. The formal parts of the statement of defence are exactly like those of the statement of claim, with the exception that the date of the issue of the writ is not stated.

The stating part is also subject to the same rules as the stating part of the statement of claim.

· **Denial of Facts alleged in Claim.** It is not sufficient for a defendant to deny *generally*, or to refuse to admit generally, the facts alleged in the plaintiff's statement of claim, but he must deal *specifically* with each allegation of fact of which he does not admit the truth (*v*); and where he denies an allegation of fact, he must not do

(*t*) R. S. C., Ord. XXXVI. r. 1; *Redmayne* v. *Vaughan*, 24 W. R. 983.

(*u*) R. S. C., Ord. XXII. rr. 1, 2.

(*v*) R. S. C., Ord. XIX. r. 20; and see *Jones* v. *Quinn*, 40 L. T., N. S. 135; *Rutter* v. *Regent*, L. R., 12 Ch. D. 758.

so evasively (*w*); in fact, he must not use what the old pleaders call "a negative pregnant." Thus, if it is alleged that the defendant received 1,000*l.*, it is not sufficient for him to deny that he received 1,000*l.*, but he must deny that he received that sum "or any other sum," or else he must set out how much of it he did receive.

And so, when a matter of fact is alleged, with divers circumstances, it is not sufficient to deny it as alleged along with those circumstances, but a fair and substantial answer must be given.

Every allegation of fact in a statement of claim which is not denied specifically or by necessary implication in the statement of defence, or stated to be "not admitted," is taken to be admitted, except as against an infant, lunatic or person of unsound mind not so found, and it is not sufficient merely to "put the plaintiff to proof" (*x*). It should, however, be borne in mind that the defendant will have to pay the costs of unnecessary denials (*y*).

Where the plaintiff alleges a contract, a bare denial of the contract by the defendant is construed only as a denial of the making of the contract in fact, and not of its legality or sufficiency in point of law, whether with reference to the Statute of Frauds, or otherwise (*z*); and, indeed, it would seem that where the Statute of Frauds is pleaded, the facts must be stated which are alleged to bring the case within the statute (*a*).

And so, a defence founded on fraud, the Statute of Limitations, a release, or any other plea "in confession and avoidance," must be specifically pleaded, and will not be proveable under a mere denial of liability, unless, of course, such facts appear by the statement of claim,

(*w*) Ib. r. 22; *Tildesly* v. *Harper*, L. R., 10 Ch. D. 393.

(*x*) R. S. C., Ord. XIX. r. 17; *Harris* v. *Gamble*, L. R., 7 Ch. D. 877.

(*y*) R. S. C., Ord. XXII. r. 4.

(*z*) R. S. C., Ord. XIX. r. 23.

(*a*) *Pullen* v. *Snelus*, 48 L. J. 394; *Clarke* v. *Callow*, 46 L. J. 53; *Wakelee* v. *Davis*, 25 W. R. 60.

in which case there is no need for the defendant to allege
them (*b*).

Several grounds of Defence. It is competent
for a defendant to plead any number of distinct defences,
so long as they are not actually inconsistent with one
another (*c*).

Denial of Plaintiff's representative capacity.
If a defendant wishes to deny the right of the plaintiff
to claim as an executor, or as a trustee, or in any representative, or other alleged, capacity, or wishes to deny
the constitution of any partnership firm, he must do so
specifically (*d*).

Defence arising after Action brought. Lastly,
any ground of defence which has arisen after the commencement of the action, may be pleaded either alone or
with any other ground of defence; and if it has arisen
after the defence has been delivered, or the time for delivering a defence has expired, the defendant may, within
eight days after such new matter has arisen, by leave of the
court or a judge (obtained on summons), deliver a further
defence setting it up (*e*). But, in such case, the plaintiff,
if he confesses that such defence is a bar to him, may
abandon his action by delivering a confession in the following form, and may thereupon sign judgment for his
costs up to that date (*f*):—

In the High Court of Justice.　　1881.　B.　No. 300.
　　Chancery Division.
　　　V.-C. Hall.
　　　　Between John Brown . . . . Plaintiff,
　　　　　　　　　　　and
　　　　　Thomas Jones . . . . Defendant.
　　The plaintiff confesses the defence stated in the　　paragraph of
the defendant's statement [*or* further statement] of defence.

(*b*) R. S. C., Ord. XIX. r. 18;　6 Q. B. D. 302.
Dawkins v. *Lord Penrhyn*, L. R.,　　(*d*) R. S. C., Ord. XIX. r. 11.
4 App. Ca. 59.　　　　　　　　　(*e*) R. S. C., Ord. XX. rr. 1, 2.
　(*c*) R. S. C., Ord. XIX. r. 9;　(*f*) Ib. r. 3.
and *Hawkesly* v. *Bradshaw*, L. R.,

Counter-claim. In addition to or substitution for
a statement of defence, a defendant may deliver a
" counter-claim," claiming relief against the plaintiff in
respect of some right or claim of the defendant, whether
sounding in damages or not, and such counter-claim has
the same effect as a statement of claim in a cross-action,
so as to enable the court to pronounce a final judgment
in the same action both on the original and on the
cross-claim. But the court or a judge may, on the application of the plaintiff, before trial, if the counter-
claim cannot be conveniently disposed of in the action,
or ought to be made the subject of a separate action, or
ought not to be allowed, refuse to allow the defendant
to use it (g).

This application should, it would seem, be by motion.
A counter-claim will not be allowed to stand if quite
unconnected with the original action (h).

The counter-claim and statement of defence form one
document, but it is essential that the defendant should
separate the statements intended as defences from the
statements upon which it is intended to rely by way of
counter-claim, and to state specifically which facts are
intended to be used by way of counter-claim (i).

In fact the counter-claim must be as specific and self-
contained as a statement of claim (k). It is, therefore,
proper to finish the statement of defence, and then to
add, " and by way of counter-claim the defendant states
as follows."

(g) Ib. r. 3, and Ord. XXII.
r. 9 ; *Huggens* v. *Tweed*, L. R., 10
Ch. D. 359.

(h) *Naylor* v. *Farrer*, W. N.
1878, p. 187 ; *McLay* v. *Sharp*,
W. N. 1877 ; p. 216.

(i) R. S. C., Ord. XIX. r. 10 ;
Crave v. *Barnicot*, L. R., 6 Ch. D.
753 ; *Lees* v. *Patterson*, L. R., 7
Ch. D. 868.

(k) *Holloway* v. *York*, W. N.
1877, p. 112.

Where the same facts have to be alleged for the counter-claim as for the defence, it is not necessary to set them out anew, but is sufficient to state that by way of counter-claim " the defendant repeats the statements contained in paragraphs 1, 2," &c. (*l*).

The rules in relation to the statements in statements of claim are equally applicable to those in counter-claims.

The question has arisen more than once whether a counter-claim has the effect of an independent action, or whether it is not entirely subsidiary to the action in which it is pleaded. For instance, if the original action is dropped, does the counter-claim fall with it, and is a counter-claim pleadable in respect of matters which have arisen subsequent to the issue of the writ of summons? On this point the law is at present far from clear: the Master of the Rolls holding that the counter-claim is part of the original action and falls with it, and can only be pleaded to facts occurring before the writ was issued (*m*). Mr. Justice Fry, on the other hand, and some of the common law judges, taking the contrary view (*n*). The argument for either view is of considerable weight, and it is difficult to express any opinion as to which the Court of Appeal may eventually hold to be correct; but it would seem that the words of the act and rules favour the contention of the Master of the Rolls, whereas the view of Mr. Justice Fry is more consistent with convenience and with that desire to prevent mul-

(*l*) *Birmingham Estates Co.* v. *Smith,* L. R., 13 Ch. D. 507 ; *Green* v. *Sevin,* ib. 589.

(*m*) *Vavaseur* v. *Krupp,* L. R., 15 Ch. D. 474 ; *Original Hartle-* *pool, &c. Co.* v. *Gibb,* 5 ib. 713.

(*n*) *Beddall* v. *Maitland,* L. R., 17 Ch. D. 174 ; *Winterfield* v. *Bradnum,* L. R., 3 Q. B. D. 324 ; *Stooke* v. *Taylor,* 5 ib. 569.

tiplicity of suits and unnecessary litigation which is a distinguishing feature of the Judicature Acts.

Third Parties brought in by Counter-claim.

Where a defendant by his defence sets up any counter-claim which raises questions between himself and the plaintiff along with any third person, he must add to the title of his defence a further title, similar to the title in a statement of claim, setting forth the names of all persons who, if such counter-claim were to be enforced by cross action, would be defendants to it, and must deliver his defence to such of them as are parties to the action, within the period within which he is required to deliver it to the plaintiff (o).

Where any such third person is not a party to the action, he must be summoned to appear, by being served with a copy of the statement of defence and counter-claim; and such service is regulated by the same rules as exist with respect to writs of summons. The copy of the statement of defence and counter-claim so served, must be indorsed with a notice to such third party, thus (p) :—

"To the within-named Arthur Hill.

"Take notice, that if you do not appear to the within counter-claim of the within-named Thomas Jones within 8 days from the service of this defence and counter-claim upon you, you will be liable to have judgment given against you in your absence.

"Appearances are to be entered at the Central Office, Royal Courts of Justice, W.C."

Any person, not being a defendant to an action, who is served with a defence and counter-claim, must

(o) R. S. C., Ord. XXII. r. 5; *Dear* v. *Sworder*, L. R., 4 Ch. D. 476; *Padwick* v. *Scott*, L. R., 2

Ch. D. 736.

(p) R. S. C., Ord. XXII. r. 6.

appear thereto as if he had been served with a writ of summons (*q*).

This right of the defendant to bring in a third party by way of counter-claim must not be confounded with the right of bringing in a third party *who is bound to indemnify* the defendant against the claim of the plaintiff. The latter case has been already treated of at p. 75.

———

SECTION 3.

The Reply and subsequent Pleadings.

Time. A plaintiff must deliver his reply (if any) within three weeks after the statement of defence, or the last of the statements of defence shall have been delivered, unless the time is extended by a judge or the court (*r*). The formal parts of the reply are like those of the statement of defence.

Joinder of Issue. Where the plaintiff denies all the material facts alleged by the defendant by way of defence (and not by way of counter-claim), he is allowed to deny them *generally*, and this general denial is called "joining issue;" the form being, "the plaintiff joins issue on the defendant's statement of defence" (*s*). Where, however, the plaintiff does not deny all of the defendant's facts, but wishes to admit them and explain away their *primâ facie* effect, he only joins issue on so much as he denies, and pleads the explanatory facts as to the rest (*t*), and it is then for the defendant to join issue on these.

(*q*) R. S. C., Ord. XXII. r. 7.   (*s*) R. S. C., Ord. XIX. r. 21.
(*r*) R. S. C., Ord. XXIV. r. 1.   (*t*) *Hall* v. *Eve*, L. R., 4 Ch. D. 341.

Departure. The plaintiff must, however, in doing so, be careful not to commit what is known as " a departure;" that is to say, he must not raise any new ground of claim, or allege any new fact inconsistent with his statement of claim (*u*). In fact a reply (not being a joinder of issue) must add some fact to those contained in the statement of claim, in support of, and not in contradiction, to them (*x*). For instance, plaintiff sues for breach of a contract; defendant retorts that the breach has been released by deed. It would be a departure for the plaintiff to reply that, although this was so, the release was upon the terms that the defendant should pay a sum of money equivalent to the amount claimed in the action. For such would be an admission that the claim for the breach of the original contract, the subject of the action, was bad; and that the plaintiff was in reality trying to enforce another contract altogether (*y*). The proper course to be taken by a plaintiff who should find that he had made a mistake in claiming on the original and released agreement, would be to amend his claim.

Reply to Counter-claim. Where the defendant has delivered a counter-claim, it is not open to the plaintiff to join issue on it, or to deny generally the facts contained in it; for a counter-claim has the same incidents as an original statement of claim, and must be replied to specifically (*z*).

In fact, a reply to a counter-claim has all the incidents

(*u*) R. S. C., Ord. XIX. r. 19.

(*x*) *Breslauer* v. *Barwick*, 24 W. R. 901.

(*y*) See *Collambell* v. *Flight*, W. N. 1877, p. 125.

(*z*) R. S. C., Ord. XIX. r. 20 ; *Benbow* v. *Low*, L. R., 13 Ch. D. 553 ; and it is not sufficient to repeat, by way of reference, the statement of claim. *Green* v. *Sevin*, ib. 589.

of a defence to an original statement of claim, including the pleading of new matter which has arisen subsequently to the commencement of the action (*a*), and instead of the plaintiff joining issue on it, it is for the defendant to join issue on his reply.

Pleadings subsequent to Reply. No pleading is allowed subsequent to a reply without special leave, except a joinder of issue, and such leave is usually only granted on terms (*b*).

Every pleading subsequent to a reply must be delivered within four days after the delivery of the previous pleading, unless the court or a judge extend the time (*c*).

Close of Pleadings. So soon as either party has joined issue upon any pleading of the opposite party simply, without adding any further or other pleading thereto, the pleadings as between such parties is considered to be "closed" (*d*); and they are also considered to be closed by default of pleading (*e*).

CHAPTER III.

DEMURRERS.

A DEFENDANT instead of delivering a statement of defence or subsequent pleading, and a plaintiff instead of a reply, or subsequent pleading, may "demur" to his opponent's previous pleading, or to any part of it (*f*).

(*a*) R. S. C., Ord. XX. rr. 1, 2.　　(*e*) R. S. C., Ord. XXIX. r. 12.
(*b*) R. S. C., Ord. XXIV. r. 2.　　(*f*) R. S. C., Ord. XXVIII.
(*c*) Ib. r. 3.　　　　　　　　　　　　r. 1.
(*d*) R. S. C., Ord. XXV.

The "demurrer" is derived from the Latin *demorari*, and signifies a stoppage in pleading, and is in the nature of an allegation that, admitting the facts in the previous pleading to be true, yet they do not show any cause of action or ground of defence (as the case may be) to which effect can be given as against the party demurring.

A demurrer must state specifically whether it is to the whole, or to a part only, and, if so, to what part, of the pleading demurred to, and must state some ground in law for the demurrer; but the party demurring is not limited to such ground on the hearing of the demurrer (*g*).

The following example shows the form of a demurrer:—

1876. No. .

In the High Court of Justice.

Chancery Division.

V.-C. Hall.

Smith *v.* Jones.

The plaintiff demurs to so much of the defendant's statement of defence as alleges that the matters mentioned in paragraph 17 thereof constitute a release, and the plaintiff says that the same is bad in law, on the ground that such alleged release is not under seal, and on other grounds sufficient in law to sustain his demurrer.

Where, however, a party wishes to demur to part of a pleading, and to answer or deny or join issue on the *residue* of the pleading, he must combine both demurrer and answer, denial or joinder of issue, in one document (*h*).

Demurring and Pleading together. Where a party wishes not merely to demur to part, and plead in answer or denial to the *residue*, but wishes to both demur

(*g*) Ib. r. 2. (*h*) Ib. r. 4.

and plead to the *whole* or the *same part* of a pleading, he must obtain special leave on summons to do so (*d*). If the judge thinks the demurrer reasonable, this leave will be granted, or leave will be reserved to plead if the demurrer shall be overruled (*e*).

Time. A demurrer is delivered in the same way and within the same time as any other pleading (*f*), and, if frivolous, a summons may be taken out to set it aside with costs (*g*).

Entry for Argument. A demurrer is what is called "a dilatory proceeding," that is, it has a tendency to delay matters, and, consequently, in order to prevent this as much as possible, all demurrers are heard as quickly as may be, and do not wait until the hearing of the action. Thus either party may enter a demurrer for argument immediately (which is done by leaving a memorandum of entry with the registrar), and must on the day of such entry give notice of it to the other party; and if a demurrer is not entered and notice given within ten days after delivery, and if the party whose pleading is demurred to does not obtain and serve on the other party within such time leave to amend his pleading, the demurrer is held to be allowed without argument (*h*).

Briefs and Argument. When the demurrer has been set down, both sides instruct their counsel with copies of the pleadings and the demurrer and counsel's opinion (if any). A copy of the pleadings and demurrer

---

(*d*) R.S.C., Ord. XXVIII. r. 5.

(*e*) Ib.; and see *Bell* v. *Wilkinson*, 26 W. R. 275.

(*f*) R. S. C., Ord. XXVIII. r. 3; *Hodges* v. *Hodges*, L. R., 2 Ch. D. 112.

(*g*) R. S. C., Ord. XXVIII. r. 2.

(*h*) Ib. r. 6.

is also left with the officer of the court who sits beneath the judge, for the use of the judge.

When the day arrives for the argument the demurrer is called on, and the counsel for the demurring party urge their objections to, and the counsel for the other party defend the pleading demurred to, and one of the counsel for the demurring party replies, and the judge then delivers his decision.

In the argument of a demurrer all allegations of fact are taken to be admitted, but not, it would seem, allegations of fraud or other intention (*i*).

Demurrer allowed. If the judge allows the demurrer to *the whole of a statement of claim*, then, unless the plaintiff sees his way to make out a materially different case, and obtains leave to amend his pleading accordingly (which is rarely refused where there is any reasonable ground), the action is practically at an end, and, unless the court orders otherwise, the plaintiff must pay to the demurring defendant the costs of the action (*k*). This is often the case where an action is brought to test the validity of a claim founded on the disputed construction of a document, or where all the facts on both sides are admitted, but the legal result of those facts is in dispute. For it is obvious that when the disputed construction or the legal result of the facts is determined, as it is determined on the hearing of the demurrer, it is useless to go to trial for the purpose of proving facts which were never in dispute, and which when proved would avail nothing. It is, however, necessary, even in that case, to move *pro formâ* for judgment, as the decision of the demurrer is technically

(*i*) *Nesbitt v. Berridge*, 9 Jur.,   (*k*) R. S. C., Ord. XXVIII.
N. S. 1014.   r. 9.

only like the verdict of a jury, *i. e.*, a decision as to the issues or points in dispute, and it still remains for the court to give judgment just as it does where no points are disputed at all.

Where a demurrer is allowed to a *part only of a statement of claim*, or to the whole or a part only of a defence, reply or other pleading, then (subject to the court allowing an amendment of the pleading or part of the pleading demurred to) the matter demurred to is taken to be struck out of the pleading, and the rights of the parties continue the same as if it had never been pleaded (*l*); but the unsuccessful party (unless the court orders otherwise) has to pay to the successful one the costs of the demurrer (*m*).

The practical result is, that where *the whole* of a defence or other subsequent pleading is demurred to successfully, and no leave to amend it is given, the pleading party stands in the position of never having pleaded a defence or subsequent pleading, as the case may be, at all; and, as we shall see hereafter, the plaintiff is at liberty to move for judgment for default of pleading (*n*).

And, similarly, if the whole of a reply is demurred to successfully, the statements of the defence are taken to be admitted, and the pleadings to be closed, the effect of which will be seen hereafter.

Where, however, only *part* of a pleading is demurred to successfully, that part only is struck out, and the residue of the pleading remains as before.

Demurrer overruled. Where a demurrer is overruled, the demurring party must pay to the opposite

(*l*) R. S. C., Ord. XXVIII.   (*m*) Ib. r. 8.
r. 10.   (*n*) R. S. C., Ord. XXIX. r. 10.

party the costs occasioned by the demurrer, unless the court directs otherwise (o); but the court may make such order, upon such terms as shall seem right for allowing the demurring party to raise by pleading any case he may be desirous of setting up in opposition to the matter unsuccessfully demurred to (p); and it would seem that, subject to compensating the opposite party, and doing his best to press the action on, he is *entitled* to this indulgence (q).

Where, however, no such leave is asked for or granted, the result of a demurrer being overruled is, that there is no denial of the facts contained in the previous pleading of the opposite party; and such party may move for judgment for default of pleading, or he may use the admissions when the action comes to trial in ordinary course.

Where the demurrer overruled is only to part of a pleading, that part is taken to be admitted ; and, as we shall see hereafter, the opposite party may either move for judgment on that part, or may wait till the trial of the action in ordinary course, and then take the facts demurred to as admitted without further proof.

CHAPTER IV.

MOVING ON ADMISSIONS IN AN ADVERSARY'S PLEADING.

CLOSELY allied to demurrer is the right of moving on admissions of fact in the pleadings, for an order for relief in respect of such admissions.

Any party to an action may, at any stage, apply to

(o) R. S. C., Ord. XXVIII. r. 11.

(p) Ib. r. 12.

(q) *Bell* v. *Wilkinson*, 26 W. R. 275.

H 2

the court or a judge for such order as he may be entitled to, upon *any admissions of fact in the pleadings*, without waiting for the determination of any other question (if any (*a*)) between the parties (*b*).

Such application is made by motion on notice in the ordinary way, and may be made so soon as the right of the party applying, to the relief claimed, has *appeared from the* pleadings; and the court may on such motion give such relief subject to such terms (if any), as it may think fit (*c*).

The object of this rule has been explained by Sir George Jessel, M. R., in the following words: "The 11th rule of Order XL. enables the plaintiff or defendant to get rid of so much of the action as to which there is no controversy. That is the meaning of it. It may be that the whole issue may not be in controversy, and thereupon either party may be entitled to more on admissions of fact in the pleadings. What amounts to admissions of fact in a pleading is defined by the 17th rule of Order XIX; 'every allegation of fact in any pleading . . . . if not denied specifically or by necessary implication, or stated to be not admitted in the pleading of the opposite party, shall be taken to be admitted.' Consequently all you have to find is no specific denial, or no specific refusal to admit" (*d*).

Thus, where a defendant pleads evasively, and makes no specific denial of the claim, judgment may be obtained against him under this rule (*e*).

(*a*) *Clutton* v. *Lee*, 21 W. R. 607.

(*b*) R. S. C., Ord. XL. r. 11.

(*c*) Ib.; and *Hetherington* v. *Longrigg*, L. R., 10 Ch. D. 162. If, on the motion being made, it appears that there must be an argument, it will be ordered to go into the general paper (Ch. Reg. Notice, Ap. 1877).

(*d*) *Thorp* v. *Holdsworth*, L. R., 3 Ch. D. 610.

(*e*) Ib.

So, where in a suit to take the accounts of a partnership, the defendants admitted the partnership, and that they had not accounted, but alleged that the plaintiff had not accounted and owed money to the firm, an account was ordered to be taken of the partnership dealings under this rule (*f*).

Indeed, where the right to the relief claimed is admitted, an order may be made under this rule dispensing with any further hearing, and, if necessary, reserving further consideration or liberty to apply in chambers (*g*).

Default in Pleading not sufficient. The admission, however, must be an admission *on the pleadings*, and therefore default in delivering a pleading is not sufficient (*h*); although, as we have seen, where a pleading *is* delivered, default of a specific denial in it is a sufficient admission. The proper course when no pleading is delivered, is to set down the case on *motion for judgment* for default of pleading (see p. 105).

The exercise of the power given to the court to make orders or admissions is discretionary, and cannot be demanded as of right (*i*); but wherever it appears to be just and proper on the face of the pleadings that the expense and delay of a formal trial of the whole or any part of the action should be dispensed with, the court exercises the power.

(*f*) *Turquand* v. *Wilson*, L. R., 1 Ch. D. 85; *Rumsey* v. *Reade*, ib. 643; *Gilbert* v. *Smith* (partition action), L. R., 2 Ch. D. 626; *Burnell* v. *Burnell*, L. R., 11 Ch. D. 213.

(*g*) *Bennett* v. *Moore*, ib. 692.

(*h*) *Litton* v. *Litton*, L. R., 3 Ch. D. 793; *Gillott* v. *Kerr*, 21 W. R. 428.

(*i*) *Mellor* v. *Sidebottom*, 25 W. R. 401; *Pike* v. *Fitzgibbon*, 41 L. T., N. S. 118.

CHAPTER V.

AMENDMENT OF PLEADINGS.

If a party finds that he has made any mistake in a pleading, or wishes to add anything to it, or otherwise wishes to alter it, he may, if plaintiff, do so without any leave *once* at any time before the expiration of the time limited for reply, and before replying, or (when no defence is delivered) at any time before the expiration of four weeks from the appearance of the defendant, or where there is more than one defendant, from the appearance of the last who shall have appeared (*a*).

Similarly a defendant may amend a counter-claim or set-off (but not a defence), at any time before the expiration of the time allowed him for pleading to the reply, and before pleading thereto; or in case there be no reply, then at any time before the expiration of twenty-eight days from the filing of his defence (*b*).

The above powers of amendment are subject to this, that the opposite party may within eight days after the amended pleading has been delivered, apply to the court or a judge to disallow the amendment which may be done upon terms or otherwise, and also that no amendment can be made without leave during the pendency of a demurrer (*c*).

But, in addition to the above-mentioned powers of amendment without leave, any party may *by leave of the*

(*a*) R. S. C., Ord. XXVII. r. 2.   (*c*) Ib. r. 4, and Ord. XXVIII.
(*b*) Ib. r. 3.   r. 7.

court or a judge amend at any stage of the action (*d*). This leave should be applied for by summons in chambers (*e*), otherwise the applicant will have to bear his extra costs.

Compulsory Amendment of Scandalous or Embarrassing Pleading. In addition to these powers given to a party to amend his own pleading, he may at any stage take out a summons to strike out or amend any matter in his adversary's pleadings which may be scandalous, or which may prejudice, embarrass or delay the fair trial of the action, and, on such an application, all such amendments will be made as may be necessary for the purpose of determining the real questions or question in controversy (*f*).

By "scandalous matter" is meant any matter immaterial to the action, which is contrary to good manners, or which charges another with any offence against morals or law.

Where statements of immorality, or dishonesty, and so on, are material to the issue, they are of course not scandalous; but in such case they must not be loose and general, but particular acts of immorality or dishonesty must be charged; for a person cannot well defend himself against general and hazy charges (*g*). A pleading is embarrassing where it pleads evidence (*h*), or raises immaterial issues, or otherwise offends against the rules of pleading (*i*).

(*d*) R. S. C., Ord. XXVII. rr. 1, 6, and see Ord. LIX.

(*e*) *Marriott* v. *Marriott*, 26 W. R. 416.

(*f*) R. S. C., Ord. XXVII. r. 1.

(*g*) *Mozley* v. *Cowie*, 47 L. J., Ch. 271; *Harbord* v. *Monk*, 38

L. T. 411.

(*h*) *Davy* v. *Garrett*, L. R., 7 Ch. D. 473; *Askew* v. *N. E. Rail. Co.*, W. N. 1875, p. 238.

(*i*) *Heugh* v. *Chamberlain*, 25 W. R. 742.

However, leave will always be given to amend, unless it will work some injustice to the other side (*k*).

Time. A party who has obtained leave to amend forfeits the order, unless he amends and delivers the amended pleading within the time named in the order, or if no time is named, then within fourteen days (*l*), unless the time is extended.

How made. The amendment is made in writing in the pleading already delivered, unless the amendment requires more than two folios to be inserted in any one place, or unless the amendments are too numerous to make it convenient to have them made in writing, in either of which cases the pleading as amended must be reprinted (*m*). And whenever a pleading is amended, it must be marked with the date of the order, and of the day when the amendment is made (*n*).

Effect of Amendment on Pleadings already delivered. Where a plaintiff has amended his claim after delivery of the defence, the defendant may either deliver a new defence or obtain leave to amend his former one, or rely on his original one, but in the latter case the amendments will be taken to be admitted, and the defence will stand as an answer *pro tanto* (*o*).

Of course the same practice will obtain where a defendant amends his defence after the delivery of the reply, the plaintiff having the option of delivering a new reply, of obtaining leave to amend the old one, or of relying upon the old one.

(*k*) *Tildesley* v. *Harper*, L. R., 10 Ch. D. 393.

(*l*) R. S. C., Ord. XXVII. rr. 7, 10.

(*m*) Ib. r. 8.

(*n*) Ib. r. 9.

(*o*) *Boddy* v. *Wall*, L. R., 7 Ch. D. 164.

CHAPTER VI.

DEFAULT OF PLEADING.

CLAIMS for debts, detention of goods, or damages, or some or all combined, or for ejectment, are not the proper subjects of Chancery actions, the Queen's Bench Division of the court being more suitable for adjudicating upon them; and, as with regard to such claims, the procedure on default by a defendant in pleading is different to that which obtains in other actions (*a*), I shall not touch upon that procedure in this work.

By Defendant. In a Chancery action then (not being brought in respect of any of the above matters), if a defendant, or one of several defendants, who ought to deliver a defence makes default in delivering one, or in delivering a demurrer, the plaintiff may set the action down at once on motion for judgment against such defaulting defendant, or, where there are several defendants, he may set it down at the time when it is entered for trial against the other defendants (*b*).

The effect of this is, that there is no *trial* of the action at all. The action, however, goes into the ordinary list of actions for trial, and comes on in its turn, but no evidence is necessary, and the action is treated as if the statement of claim were true and uncontradicted; and such judgment is given, as, upon the statement of claim, the court may consider the plaintiff to be entitled to. In fact the action is treated as if the issues of fact had been tried before a jury and found in favour of the plaintiff, and the latter had then set down the action on motion for judgment.

(*a*) R. S. C., Ord. XXIX. rr. 2—8.   (*b*) Ib. rr. 10, 11.

However, any judgment by default may be set aside by a court or a judge on such terms as may seem just to him (c).

By Third Party. Where a third party is brought in, and makes default in pleading, the opposite party may apply for such judgment as he may appear to be entitled to. It is apprehended that this application should be made by an ordinary motion (or in very light cases by summons); and upon the application, such judgment may be given, and may be ordered to be entered, or such other order may be made as may be necessary to do complete justice (d).

By Plaintiff. Where a plaintiff fails to reply, or a defendant to deliver a subsequent pleading, within the proper time, the pleadings are closed at the expiration of that time, and the facts stated in the last pleading are taken to be admitted (e).

It would seem that a defendant cannot move for judgment on his counter-claim if the plaintiff discontinues the action; and, if this is good law, it would seem to follow that he cannot do so where the plaintiff simply makes default in pleading to it, the counter-claim not being an independent action, but merely a mode of cutting down the plaintiff's claim (f).

If a plaintiff, being bound to deliver a statement of claim, does not do so within the prescribed time, the defendant may move to have the action dismissed for want of prosecution; and on the hearing of such motion, such order may be made as may seem just (g).

(c) R. S. C., Ord. XXIX. r. 14.

(d) Ib. r. 13.

(e) Ib. r. 12.

(f) Vavasseur v. Krupp, L. R., 15 Ch. D. 474; Rolfe v. McLaren,

L. R., 3 Ch. Div. 106; but see contra, Beddall v. Maitland, L.R., 17 Ch. D. 183, and Aitkin v. Dunbar, 46 L. J., Ch. 489.

(g) R. S. C., Ord. XXIX. r. 1.

CHAPTER VII.

DISCONTINUANCE.

IT is convenient to notice at this place the subject of discontinuance of an action. The plaintiff may discontinue his action or any part or parts of his alleged cause of complaint by giving a notice of discontinuance to his adversary at any time before taking any further step after the delivery of the statement of defence (except on interlocutory application), and in that case he must pay the costs of the action or of so much of it as is discontinued (h).

Discontinuance may also be effected at any other stage of the action, even at or after trial, by leave of the court or a judge (i).

A defendant cannot withdraw or discontinue his defence or counter-claim without leave (i). Discontinuance does not prevent the institution of a new action (i).

The notice of discontinuance need not be formal—a mere letter will be sufficient (j).

Leave to discontinue will not be given where it would be unjust to the defendant, as where a verdict or award is substantially in his favour he is entitled to judgment so as to prevent the plaintiff bringing a subsequent action (k). And so also where a plaintiff has obtained an interlocutory injunction, subject to paying damages in case it is not confirmed at the hearing, he will not be

(h) R. S. C., Ord. XXIII. r. 1. 612.
(i) Ib.
(j) The Pomerania, 39 L. T. (k) Stahlschmidt v. Walford, L. R., 4 Q. B. D. 217.

allowed to discontinue without paying the damages (*l*). However, where a plaintiff discontinued a delivery of a defence, the defendant was not allowed to proceed with his counter-claim (*m*).

A defendant may sign judgment for the costs of a discontinuance (*n*).

(*l*) *Newcomen* v. *Coulson*, L. R., 7 Ch. D. 764.

(*m*) *Vavaseur* v. *Krupp*, L. R., 15 Ch. D. 474.

(*n*) R. S. C., Ord. XXIII. r. 2a.

Evidence.

———

CHAPTER I.

PRELIMINARY.

WHEN the pleadings are closed (*i. e.* when either party has joined issue, or when the plaintiff does not reply or demur within the proper period to the defendant's defence, or the defendant does not plead or demur to the plaintiff's reply within the proper time) the plaintiff has to consider whether any, and if so what, evidence it will be necessary for him to adduce at the hearing.

Evidence is the proof which a party produces of the truth of the material allegations of fact contained in his pleadings.

Now, where no statement of defence has been delivered, then as all the statements in the claim are to be taken as admitted as true (except as against infants and lunatics not so found), it is obvious that no evidence is required, and in such a case the action is heard without evidence upon motion for judgment. And so, where other pleadings are delivered besides the claim, all allegations not denied are taken to be admitted, and consequently no evidence is required with regard to them; and in administration actions, partition actions, foreclosure actions, and so on, it will very generally be found that enough is admitted by the defendant to enable the plaintiff to go to the hearing without evidence, because in such actions the judgment is but rarely the final settlement of the dispute, being generally a mere preliminary formality. Thus, in an administration action against trustees for misapplying trust funds the judgment would be that the trusts of the trust instrument be carried into execution by the court, and that the trustees do account for all sums received and paid by them.

It is obvious that such a judgment could only under the most exceptional circumstances be resisted, because every cestui que trust is entitled to have the trust estate administered by the court. The real fight would arise after the judgment, when the accounts are taken which were ordered by the judgment to be taken, and it is then that evidence would be material. In such cases, therefore, evidence is not very often necessary at the hearing. However, where an infant, or a lunatic not so found, is defendant, it is necessary to produce evidence unless the judgment asked for is purely formal.

Affidavits of Service. However, it must not be forgotten that in all actions, whether the facts are admitted or not, a party ought to be provided at the hearing of every application by the court (except of course mere *ex parte* ones), with an affidavit proving the service of the notice of the application on the other parties; for if the latter do not appear in court, either in person or by counsel, no order will be made, unless the party making the application produces such an affidavit to the registrar in court before the rising of the court on that day (*a*). Formerly, the party *served* had to be prepared with an affidavit of that fact, so that he may get his costs of attendance in case the party giving him the notice should fail to appear in support of his application; but this is no longer necessary (*b*).

Where, however, there are material issues of fact in dispute between the plaintiff and the defendant, as, for instance, where the action is for an injunction for infringement of a patent, or the creation of a nuisance, or the taking away of support from land, or the like, where the judgment is generally the final step in the action, then evidence of the disputed facts upon which each party relies must be produced at the hearing.

Such evidence may conveniently be divided into three groups, viz., 1st, the evidence of witnesses; 2ndly, the evidence of the opposite party elicited from him by means of interrogatories; and 3rdly, the evidence of documents.

It forms no part of the object of this Work to give a treatise on evidence. Such a treatise to be of any service would be as large as the book itself. In fact, the subject of evidence is one which has given rise to a great many works, among which Mr. Justice Stephen's scientific digest is by far the best for the purposes of the student, and Mr. Taylor's learned and complete treatise the most useful to the practitioner. In these works will be found all questions concerning the relevancy of evidence to the questions in issue, concerning

(*a*) But query, whether this is now necessary, *Chorlton* v. *Dickie*, L. R., 13 Ch. D. 160.

(*b*) *James* v. *Crow*, L. R., 7 Ch. D. 410.

primary and secondary evidence of documents, concerning judicial notice of facts, documents, decrees, judgments, and so on, and concerning presumptions, competency of witnesses, and the onus of proof.

To a work like this belongs only the task of stating *how* the evidence is placed before the court.

———

CHAPTER II.

THE EVIDENCE OF WITNESSES.

THE evidence of witnesses is given either *virâ voce* or by affidavit; and, if *virâ voce*, either in open court or before an examiner.

In the absence of any agreement between the parties, the witnesses *at the trial of any action* must be examined *virâ voce* in open court, but the court or a judge may at any time, for sufficient reason, order that any particular fact or facts may be proved by affidavit, or that the affidavit of any witness may be read at the hearing or trial on such conditions as the court or judge may think reasonable, or that any witness whose attendance in court ought for some sufficient cause to be dispensed with, be examined by interrogatories, or otherwise, before a commissioner or examiner. But where it appears that the other party *bonâ fide* desires the production of a witness for cross-examination, and that such witness can be produced, an order will not be made authorizing the evidence of such witness to be given by affidavit (*a*).

Usual Practice. The most usual practice in the Chancery Division is for the parties to agree to take the

(*a*) R. S. C., Ord. XXXVII. r. 1.

evidence of their witnesses by affidavit, but the witnesses attend in court at the hearing, or before an examiner, for the purpose of being cross-examined by the other party *vivâ voce*.

The agreement to take evidence by affidavit must be a formal written consent, signed by both solicitors, and not merely to be gathered from a correspondence (*b*).

There is, however, one difficulty about an agreement to take evidence by affidavit, viz., that, although a witness can be compelled to attend in court to give evidence *vivâ voce*, there is no means of forcing a witness to make an affidavit, and consequently it might happen, that if the agreement were irrevocable, a party might find himself left without the means of proving his case. In such an event, the proper course is to apply by summons in chambers for leave to be relieved from the agreement, and to have the witness examined *vivâ voce* at the trial (*c*), and this leave being granted, the witness can be compelled to attend by *subpœna*.

A *subpœna* is a species of writ, or letter missive, from the sovereign addressed to the witness, commanding him to attend before the court, or before one of the examiners of the court, or a special examiner, "to testify the truth according to your knowledge in a certain action depending in our High Court of Justice, Chancery Division, wherein A. B. is plaintiff, and C. D. defendant, on the part of the said A. B."

Where the witness only is required to attend, the writ is called a *subpœna ad testificandum*. Where he is

---

(*b*) *New Westminster Brewery Co.* v. *Hannah*, L. R., 1 Ch. D. 278.

(*c*) *Warner* v. *Moses*, L. R., 16 Ch. D. 100.

required to bring any document with him, it is designated a *subpœna duces tecum*.

The mode of issuing this writ is to procure a blank form at a law stationer's, fill it up, and take it, together with a document called a *præcipe* (which is a short memorandum or request to the proper officer to issue the writ), to the central office or district registry (as the case may be), where it will be sealed. The party then serves it on the witness, at the same time tendering his reasonable travelling expenses.

Neglect to attend to a *subpœna* is punishable by imprisonment for contempt of court, or the witness may be sued for the damages which the absence of his testimony may have caused.

Evidence by Affidavit. Where evidence is taken by affidavit, the affidavit must be intituled like a pleading, down to and including the names of the parties; must be made (on pain of costs being disallowed) (*d*) in the first person; contain a full and true address and description of the deponent (*e*) (*i. e.*, the person making it); and, if he be a party to the action, must state so. The body of the affidavit is divided into paragraphs, each paragraph as far as possible confined to a distinct portion of the subject (*f*), and should, if well drafted, be a clear and unambiguous account of the witness's story. In affidavits to be used *at the hearing*, the witness must (on pain of disallowance of costs) only speak to facts *known*, and not as to his belief, or information, or hearsay, nor must he be argumentative (*g*), or scandalous, or irrelevant. Affidavits used on interlocutory applications (motions, summons, &c.) may contain

(*d*) Cons. Ord. XVIII. rr. 1, 2.   (*f*) Ib. r. 3a.
(*e*) R. S. C., Ord. XXXVII.   (*g*) Ib. r. 3.
r. 3b.

allegations of mere belief. Every affidavit should state the deponent's means of knowledge. The affidavit is signed by the witness, or marked if he be illiterate.

Swearing. At the foot of the affidavit is the "jurat," which is a statement that the affidavit was sworn, where it was sworn, the date, and the commissioner before whom it was sworn, describing him as such commissioner. The affidavit may be sworn before any one of certain officers, but in practice affidavits are sworn either before (1) a master of the Supreme Court; (2) a District Registrar; or (3) a commissioner to administer oaths in the Supreme Court of Judicature; the commission being entrusted to a great number of solicitors of standing and position all over the country.

Where the affidavit is sworn out of England, but within the British empire, it may be sworn before any person entitled to administer oaths there (*h*). Outside the empire it may be sworn before the British ambassador, or minister, or the secretary of legation, or consular, or vice-consular, or acting consular officer (*i*), or before any person authorized to administer oaths in such country; but the latter alternative is practically never used, because the court would require evidence of the fact of such person being so authorized.

If the deponent cannot read, the affidavit must of course be read to him before it is sworn, which is usually done by the person before whom it is sworn, and in that case it must be certified in the jurat that the affidavit was so read by or in the presence of the swearing officer, and that the deponent seemed perfectly to understand it (*k*). If a person other than the swearing

(*h*) 15 & 16 Vict. c. 86, s. 22.   (*k*) R. S. C. Ord. XXXVII.
(*i*) Ib.   r. 3f.

officer reads the affidavit to the deponent, it must be so
stated, and such person must first be sworn to read
truly, and must attest the deponent's signature. Like
remarks apply to the case of a foreigner, to whom
the affidavit must be translated by a sworn interpreter.
Any such affidavit not having the required certificate
cannot be used, unless the judge or court is satisfied
that the affidavit was in fact read over and explained
and thoroughly understood.

Where an affidavit is made by more than one person,
and the whole of the deponents are not sworn at the
same time, there will be several jurats, and each must
state to whom it relates. If all are sworn together, the
jurat should state so (*l*).

Erasures, &c. No affidavit having in the jurat or
the body any interlineation, alteration or erasure can
be made use of without leave; unless the interlineation
or alteration (other than by erasure) is initialled in the
margin by the swearing officer, nor in the case of an
erasure, unless the words or figures appearing at the
time of swearing the affidavit to be rewritten, are also
written in the margin and signed or initialled by the
swearing officer (*m*).

Printing. Affidavits used at the hearing must, it
would appear, be printed (*n*), except where they have
been used on any proceedings without having been
printed (*o*); but they may *be sworn* either in print or
in manuscript, or partly in print and partly in manuscript (*p*).

<hr />

(*l*) R. S. C., Ord. XXXVII.
r. 3c.

(*m*) Ib. r. 3c.

(*n*) R. S. C., Ord. XXXVIII.
r. 6.

(*o*) Rules as to costs, Ord. II.

(*p*) R. S. C., Ord. LVI. r. 3.

How Written. Affidavits when written, must be written on foolscap paper done up bookwise, otherwise the filing officer may refuse to file them unless good cause is shown to the contrary. When printed they must (like all other printed proceedings) be printed on similar paper and in a similar way to that on which pleadings are printed.

At the foot of every affidavit it must be stated on whose behalf it is filed (*q*).

Exhibits. Sometimes documents or things are referred to in affidavits, and they are then called " exhibits." Thus, in patent cases, a model is, perhaps, exhibited to a witness, and he refers to it as " the exhibit now produced and shown to me and marked A." The exhibit is marked with the letter by which it is referred to, and a memorandum is put on it containing the short title of the action and a statement that it is the exhibit marked A. referred to in the affidavit, which memorandum must be signed by the swearing officer.

Filing Affidavits. When evidence is taken by affidavit, the affidavit must be taken, together with a printed or (where allowable) a written copy, to the central office or district registry, where the original is filed, and the copy is retained to be examined, and when examined is marked and returned as an office copy, except in certain urgent cases during the long vacation when the offices are not open, and in which the court will act on the original affidavit (*r*). It must be remembered, however, that affidavits used before the chief clerks or judge in chambers *must* be filed in London (*s*). Every affidavit must state, in a footnote, on whose behalf it is filed (*t*).

(*q*) Rules as to costs, Ord. V. r.11. (*s*) R. S. C., Ord. XIX. r. 29a.
(*r*) R. S. C. (Costs), Ord. V. r. 6. (*t*) R. S. C. (Costs), Ord. V. r. 11.

When a copy is wanted in a hurry the solicitor must get the copy marked as urgent at the divisional seat, in which case it will be examined before all others not so marked, and if filed before two p.m., will be ready on the next morning.

Time for filing Evidence. When evidence is taken by affidavit the plaintiff must cause his affidavits to be filed and deliver a list of them to the defendant or his solicitor within fourteen days after the consent to take the evidence by affidavit has been given (*u*).

The defendant on his part must file and deliver a list of his affidavits to the plaintiff or his solicitor within fourteen days after delivery of the plaintiff's list (*v*).

Within seven days after the expiration of the fourteen days given to the defendant the plaintiff must file and deliver a list of his affidavits in reply (if any), but these must be confined strictly to matters in reply (*w*), and if they are not, an objection may be taken to them at the hearing, but not before (*x*).

Where a party wishes to file further evidence after the time limited for filing his evidence has expired, he can only do so by leave of the court or a judge, which is applied for by motion before the hearing of the action (*y*).

Furnishing Copies. Where affidavits are printed, the party printing must furnish any number of copies (not exceeding ten) to any other party on demand, at the rate of one penny per folio for the first, and one halfpenny per folio for every other copy (*z*); and where they

(*u*) R. S. C., Ord. XXXVIII. r. 1.

(*v*) Ib. r. 2.

(*w*) Ib. r. 3; but see *Peacock* v. *Harper*, L. R., 7 Ch. D. 648.

(*x*) *Gilbert* v. *Com. Op. Co.*, L. R., 16 Ch. D. 594.

(*y*) 15 & 16 Vict. c. 86, s. 38; *Smith* v. *Pilgrim*, L. R., 2 Ch. D. 138; *Thaxton* v. *Edmonston*, L. R., 5 Eq. 373.

(*z*) Rules as to costs, Ord. V. r. 3.

are written, copies must be furnished on demand within twenty-four hours on payment of proper charges (*a*).

Cross-examination. Where one of the parties (as is almost invariably the case where the facts are disputed) desires to cross-examine a witness who has made an affidavit on behalf of the opposite party, he may serve on such party by whom such affidavit has been filed a notice requiring the production of the deponent for cross-examination before the Court at the trial. Such notice may be served at any time not later than fourteen days next after the end of the time limited for filing affidavits in reply (subject to the order of the judge).

If after such notice the maker of such affidavit is not produced, his affidavit will not be allowed to be used without special leave of the court (*b*); but the objection to their being used must be made at the hearing, and it is irregular to move to have the affidavits taken off the file (*c*).

The party whose witness is required to be cross-examined must bear the expense of his production in the first instance (*d*), and is entitled to compel his appearance by *subpœna* as if he were coming to be examined in his behalf (*e*).

In general the cross-examination or re-examination of a witness at the hearing takes place in open court, affidavits taking the place of the examination in chief, which, however, may also be taken *vivâ voce* if insisted on.

(*a*) Ib. r. 9.

(*b*) R. S. C., Ord. XXXVIII. r. 4.

(*c*) *Meyrick* v. *Jones*, 46 L. J.,

Ch. 579.

(*d*) R. S. C., Ord. XXXVIII. r. 4.

(*e*) Ib. r. 5.

Examination before an Examiner. However, the parties to an action may by writing signed by them or their respective solicitors, and filed at the central office, or the district registry as the case may be, agree, or a judge in chambers may order, that the *vivâ voce* examination, cross-examination and re-examination of any person, or cross-examination and re-examination of any person who has made an affidavit, shall be taken before one of the examiners of the court, or a special examiner, or before commissioners appointed for that purpose. And the court or a judge may *order* that this shall be done where it appears to him that, owing to age, infirmity or absence of such witness out of the jurisdiction of the court, or for any other cause which appears sufficient, or where it is expedient for the purposes of justice that such order should be made (*f*).

And where the witness resides in certain specified colonies, the court may award a writ to any court there, requiring the judges thereof to hold a sitting for the examination of witnesses within their jurisdiction (*g*).

Where the witness is abroad, it is not usual for the Chancery Division to appoint a commission, although it has power to do so. Generally, either a writ is issued to the Colonial Court (in colonies), or a special examiner is appointed in foreign countries (*h*).

Where the witness is in England, the evidence is either taken before the examiner of the court in Rolls

---

(*f*) Ord. as to Evid., Feb. 1861, r. 10, and Dan. Ch. Pr. 805, and R. S. C., Ord. XXXVII. r. 4.

(*g*) 13 Geo. 3, c. 63, s. 44 ; 1 Will. 4, c. 22, ss. 1, 2; Jud.

Act, 1873, s. 76.

(*h*) *Crofts* v. *Middleton*, 9 Ha. App. 18, 75; *Edwards* v. *Spaight*, 2 J. & H. 617 ; *Lond. Bank of Mexico* v. *Hart*, L. R., 6 Eq. 467.

Yard, or before a special examiner, who is usually a barrister.

An order for a special examiner will not usually be made (if opposed) unless strong reasons are shown by affidavit for adopting that course, as the expense to the parties is considerable, the special examiner being entitled to charge two guineas a day for his expenses for every day in which he is necessarily detained in the performance of his duties, and in addition three guineas for every day in which he is *bonâ fide* employed in examining witnesses, together with 1s. 6d. per mile travelling expenses (i).

The affidavit should also show the fitness for the office of the person proposed to be appointed.

In examinations before the examiner of the court 10s. per witness per hour is payable in stamps, and if the witness is (as is unusual) not examined at the examiner's office, 3l. per diem additional, besides reasonable travelling and other expenses (k).

The examination takes place in the presence of the parties, their counsel, and solicitors, and is conducted as an examination in court would be (l). The examiner administers the oath, and writes down, with his own hand (m), what the witness says, on foolscap paper, bookwise on both sides, or brief form on one side only (n). The general examination should be taken down in a narrative form, and not as question and answer; but where a question is objected to, it should be taken down,

(i) Sched. 1 to Regs. as to Fees, H. T. 1860.

(k) Ord. as to Court Fees, Oct. 1875, sched.

(l) 15 & 16 Vict. c. 86, s. 31.

(m) Ib. s. 32 ; *Stobart* v. *Todd*, 2 W. R. 617 ; but see *Bolton* v. *Bolton*, 2 Ch. D. 217.

(n) Ord. 6th March, 1860, r. 16.

together with the objection, and the examiner's opinion
as to its validity, which he is bound to state to the
parties; but he has no power to decide the point. He
may also state any special matter to the court (*o*).

When the examination is concluded, the examiner
reads over the deposition to the witness, who ought to
sign the same, and the examiner also signs it, and
transmits it to the central office or district registry (as
the case may be) to be filed (*p*).

When a deposition is intended to be used on the
trial, the rule as to printing affidavits applies to it
(sup. p. 116).

Evidence de bene esse. Where there is a pro-
bability of evidence being lost by the death or absence
of a witness, the court will allow his evidence to be
taken out of the regular course, or *de bene esse*, as it is
called (*q*). Evidence so taken can only be used con-
tingently upon the witness not being able to be produced
to be examined in the action in the usual way, and if,
when the time for the ordinary examination arrives, he
is alive and in the country, the evidence taken *de bene
esse* will be rejected.

The principal cases in which evidence is allowed to be
taken in this way are, where the witness is upwards of
seventy, or is dangerously ill, or about to leave the
country, or is the only person who can prove a fact of
great importance.

Where the application is made by reason of the age,
illness, or purposed emigration of the witness, it is
usually made by petition of course, although, in urgent
cases, it may be made by *ex parte* motion. Where it is

(*o*) 15 & 16 Vict. c. 86, s. 32.   (*q*) *Warner* v. *Moses*, L. R.,
(*p*) Ib. s. 34.   16 Ch. D. 100.

made by reason of the witness being the only person who can prove a fact of great importance, it must be made by motion on notice.

In every case the application must be supported by affidavit of the facts.

If the application is granted, the witness may be subpœnaed, and the examination, cross-examination, and re-examination is conducted before an examiner, or more usually a special examiner, and the depositions are filed by him in the usual way. They cannot, however, be used without an order of the court, which is absolutely discretionary (*r*).

CHAPTER III.

INTERROGATORIES.

ONE of the main distinctions which formerly existed between common law and Chancery procedure was, that the very object of the latter was to obtain from the defendant what was called "discovery," *i. e.*, an admission or denial *under oath* of the truth or falsehood of the matters upon which the plaintiff relied. This discovery was obtained by making the defendant answer by affidavit, certain written questions or "interrogatories." Under the early practice, these interrogatories formed part of the bill of complaint; afterwards (under the Chancery Procedure Act, 1852) they formed a

(*r*) See Hunter, 75, and *Forsyth* v. *Ellice*, 2 M. & G. 209.

separate and distinct document, being in fact the bill turned into the most searchingly interrogative form. Much useless questioning of course resulted from this procedure under which the whole of the bill was invariably interrogated upon. Indeed counsel used to teach their clerks how to turn bills into interrogatories in a mechanical kind of way, and it is still related of one of them that his master made a wager that if the first five lines of the Paradise Lost were interpolated in a bill, the clerk would quite unconsciously turn them into interrogatories, which in fact he did in the most approved fashion. " Was it of man's first or some other and what disobedience? and the fruit of that forbidden or some other and what tree? whose mortal or some other and what taste brought death into the world? or some and what part or parts thereof, or how otherwise?" &c.

However, that has all been changed, and instead of interrogatories being the invariable resort of the plaintiff, they are now used sparingly, and only where facts can be most readily ascertained by means of them. In fact, strictly speaking, they should be confined to material allegations of fact in the interrogator's pleading not admitted by the other party, or as to material allegations of fact pleaded by the opposite party, but not as to the evidence by which such facts are to be proved (a). However, such a principle is not strictly enforced, and a plaintiff is frequently permitted to interrogate before delivering his claim; in cases, for instance, where he cannot otherwise assess his damages.

Times for interrogating. The plaintiff may de-

(a) *Saunders* v. *Jones*, L. R., 7 Ch. D. 435; and see *Benbow* v. *Low*, 16 ib. 93.

liver interrogatories to the defendant (1) with his statement of claim, or at any subsequent time before the
close of the pleadings, or (2) by leave of the court or a
judge at any other time.

The defendant may deliver interrogatories to the
plaintiff (1) with his statement of defence, at any subsequent time before the close of the pleadings, or (2) by
leave of the court or a judge at any other time. There
is no objection in the Chancery Division to the plaintiff
delivering interrogatories before the delivery of the
statement of defence (b), but a defendant will not
usually be allowed to deliver interrogatories before
delivering his defence; and it is no ground for doing so
that he cannot otherwise tell what ground of defence to
take up (c). It is, however, submitted that a plaintiff
ought to be allowed leave to interrogate as to damages
suffered by him before he delivers his claim, and that a
defendant wishing to pay money into court ought to be
allowed to interrogate the plaintiff as to the amount to
be paid in before delivering his defence. No party can
deliver two sets of interrogatories to the same opponent,
without an order (d).

When an order is required for delivering interrogatories, it may be applied for by motion (c), or probably
by summons in chambers.

(b) *Harbord* v. *Monk*, L. R., 9
Ch. D. 616.

(c) *Disney* v. *Longbourne*, 2 ib.
704.

(d) R. S. C., Ord. XXXI. r. 1.
It requires the most exceptional
circumstances to obtain an order
for delivery *before* the statement
of defence. *Disney* v. *Longbourne*,
L. R., 2 Ch. D. 704.

(e) *Disney* v. *Longbourne* (*sup.*);
L. & P. Ins. Co. v. *Davies*, L. R.,
5 Ch. D. 775.

Form of Interrogatories. The form in which interrogatories are drawn up is as follows:—

1881. S. No. 1660.

In the High Court of Justice.
Chancery Division.
V.-C. Hall.

Between John Smith . . . . Plaintiff,
and
Thomas Jones . . . . Defendant.

Interrogatories on behalf of the above-named plaintiff for the examination of the above-named defendant.

1. Did not the defendant on the   day of   , 18   , or on some other and what date, receive, as trustee of the indenture of settlement in the pleadings mentioned, or how otherwise, a sum of 1,000*l.*, or some other and what sum, from A. B. or some other and what person, in discharge of a mortgage debt due from the said A. B. to the trustees of the said indenture or how otherwise?

2. Has the defendant invested the said sum of 1,000*l.*, or the sum so received by him as aforesaid, in some and which of the stocks, funds and securities authorized in that behalf by the said indenture, and if not, why not, or how otherwise?

3. Is it not a fact that the defendant invested the said sum of 1,000*l.* in his own name as part of his capital in the trade of a founder, carried on by him in co-partnership with divers other person at Birmingham, in the county of Warwick, and that the same sum still remains so invested : and if not, where is the said sum now invested, and in whose name, and when was the same invested upon its present security?

4. Is not the defendant's said trade of a highly speculative character?

The defendant is required to answer all the above interrogatories.

Time for answer. Interrogatories must be answered within ten days from the date of delivery, unless the court or a judge grant further time, usually applied for by summons (*e*).

Objections to answering. If the interrogatories

(*e*) R. S. C., Ord. XXXI, r. 6.

or any of them are objectionable, there are two ways of taking the objection to them, or to the one objected to, viz. :—

1. Where the ground of objection is that they are scandalous or irrelevant, or not asked *bonâ fide* for the purpose of the action, or that the matters inquired into are not sufficiently material at that stage of the action, or that an answer would tend to criminate the person interrogated, or on any other ground, the objection may be taken in the affidavit in answer (*f*).

2. Where the ground of objection is that the interrogatories are unreasonable, or vexatious, or scandalous, an application may be made in chambers to strike them out within four days after delivery of the interrogatories (*g*).

Interrogating Corporations. Where any party to an action is a corporation, or a joint stock company, or any body of persons empowered by law to sue or be sued in its own name, or in the name of an officer or other person, any opposite party may apply at chambers for an order allowing him to deliver interrogatories to any member or officer of such corporation, company or body (*h*). Before, however, a member can be interrogated, it must be shown that he has the required information, and that there is no *officer* capable of giving it (*i*).

Formerly it was usual to make an officer of a corporation a defendant, solely for the purpose of interrogating him, but the above rule now renders this unnecessary (*j*).

(*f*) Ib. r. 5 (1878).

(*g*) Ib.

(*h*) R. S. C., Ord. XXXI. r. 4.

(*i*) *Berkley* v. *Standard Co.*, L. R., 13 Ch. D. 97.

(*j*) *Wilson* v. *Church*, L. R., 9 Ch. D. 552.

However, it is still open to a plaintiff to join a person as defendant, solely for the purpose of discovery (*k*) where such a course is desirable.

Form of Answer. The form of the affidavit in answer to interrogatories is as follows :—

1881. S. No. 1660.
In the High Court of Justice.
Chancery Division.
  V.-C. Hall.
    Between John Smith . . . . Plaintiff,
                          and
        Thomas Jones . . . . Defendant.
The Answer of the above-named defendant to the interrogatories exhibited for his examination by the above-named plaintiff.

In answer to the said interrogatories I, the above-named   , make oath and say as follows :

1. I did on the   day of   , 18 , receive as trustee of the indenture of settlement in the pleadings mentioned a sum of 1,000*l.* from A. B.. in discharge of a mortgage debt due from him to the trustees of the said indenture.

2. I have invested 800*l.*, part of the said sum of 1,000*l.*, in mortgage of freehold hereditaments at   , in the county of   , by virtue of an indenture dated the   day of   , 188 , and made between Samuel Jones of the one part and me of the other part.

3. The sum of 200*l.*, residue of the said sum of 800*l.*, still remains in my hands uninvested, but is not used by me in my business, nor invested as part of my capital in the same.

4. I object to answer the 4th of the said interrogatories on the ground that the same is irrelevant and scandalous.

Sworn, &c.

This affidavit is sworn in the usual way, like any other affidavit, and should be *filed*, like an affidavit, at the central office or district registry. If it exceeds ten folios, it must (unless a judge orders otherwise) be printed under Order XXXI. r. 7.

Objections to Answer. Where a party objects to the sufficiency of the affidavit, the objection may be de-

(*k*) *Orr v. Diaper*, L. R., 4 Ch. D. 92.

termined on summons in chambers (*l*), as also, where he
omits to answer altogether; and the judge may order
the interrogated party to answer, or answer further, as
the case may be, either by affidavit or *vivâ voce* (*m*).

The summons should state specifically to what part or
parts of the interrogatories a further answer is required (*n*), and the order, when made, should be served
on the party or his solicitor.

If any party from whom discovery is sought objects
to the same or any part thereof, the judge may, if satisfied that the right to such discovery depends on the determination of any question in dispute in the action, or
that for any other reason it is desirable that any question
in dispute in the action should be determined before
deciding upon the right to such discovery, order that
such question in dispute be determined first, and reserve
the question as to the discovery (*o*). Thus, where a person disputed a horse-dealer's account, and the dispute
was, whether certain horses were sold on commission,
the court refused to order the horse-dealer to disclose
the prices until it had been decided whether the horses
had or had not been sold on commission (*p*).

Default in answering. If any party fails to
comply with any order to answer interrogatories, he is
liable to be attached (i. e., sent to prison for contempt),
and also, if plaintiff, to have his action dismissed for
want of prosecution, and, if defendant, to have his defence (if any) struck out, and to be placed in the same

(*l*) R. S. C., Ord. XXXI. r. 9 ;
Chesterfield Colliery Co. v. *Black*, 24
W. R. 783.

(*m*) R. S. C., Ord. XXXI.
r. 10.

(*n*) *Anstey* v. *Woolwich Co.*, L.
R., 11 Ch. D. 439.

(*o*) R. S. C., Ord. XXXI.
r. 19.

(*p*) *Re Leigh*, L. R., 6 Ch. D.
256.

U. K

position as if he had not defended (*q*), and the interrogating party may apply in chambers, or by motion, for an order to this effect (*r*).

Using Answer. With regard to using the affidavit in answer to interrogatories, at the hearing, any party may use all or *any* of the answers of *the opposite party ;* but the judge may look at *the whole* of the answers, and if he shall be of opinion that any others of them are so connected with those put in evidence, that the latter ought not to be used alone, he may direct them to be put in (*s*).

No party can use his own answers as evidence in his own favour.

The affidavit can only be cross-examined upon where any party gives notice that he means to use the affidavit as part of his evidence at the hearing, or upon any other proceeding against *any other party ;* in which cases, the party against whom it is used may cross-examine upon it (*t*).

Lastly, it must be remembered that if interrogatories have, in the opinion of the taxing officer, been unreasonably, or vexatiously, or lengthily administered, the party administering them will have to pay, not only the cost of them, but also of the answers (*u*).

(*q*) R. S. C., Ord. XXXI. r. 20.

(*r*) Ib. ; and *Freason* v. *Loe*, 26 W. R. 138 ; as to the evidence on such application, see R. S. C., Ord. XXXI. rr. 21, 22.

(*s*) R. S. C., Ord. XXXI. r. 23.

(*t*) *Manly* v. *Bewicke*, 8 D., M. & G. 470.

(*u*) R. S. C., Ord. XXXI. r. 2.

CHAPTER IV.

DOCUMENTARY EVIDENCE.

Notice to admit. A party who proposes to put in evidence documents which are in his own possession, should give notice to the other side to admit them. Such a notice is in the following form :—

In the High Court of Justice.
Chancery Division.
 V.-C. Hall.

Smith *v.* Jones.

Take notice, that the plaintiff (*or* defendant) in this action proposes to adduce in evidence the several documents hereunder specified, and that the same may be inspected by the defendant (*or* plaintiff) his solicitor or agent at   on the   of   instant, between the hours of   and   , and the defendant (*or* plaintiff) is hereby required within forty-eight hours from the last-mentioned hour to admit that such of the said documents as are specified to be originals were respectively written, signed or executed as they purport respectively to have been ; that such as are specified as copies are true copies ; and that such documents as are stated to have been served, sent or delivered were so served, sent or delivered respectively ; saving all just exceptions to the admissibility of all such documents as evidence in this action.

Dated, &c.
 To Mr.   .

       Solicitor (*or* agent) for the defendant (*or* plaintiff).
             (Signed)   JOHN BROWN.
       Solicitor (*or* agent) for the plaintiff (*or* defendant).

Description of Documents.	Dates.
Originals.	
Deed of Covenant between A. B. and C. D., first part, and E. F., second part	January 1st, 1848.
Letter, Defendant to Plaintiff	March 1st, 1879.
Copies.	
Letter, Plaintiff to Defendant	March 2nd, 1879.
Notice to produce Papers	December 2nd, 1879.

In case the party to whom this notice is given refuses or neglects to admit such documents, he will have to pay the costs of proving them ; unless, at the hearing, the court shall certify that the refusal or neglect was reasonable (*a*).

Omission to give Notice. In case a party omits to give such notice, he will not be entitled to his costs of proving the documents, unless the taxing master is of opinion that the omission was a saving of expense (*b*).

Proof of Admission. An affidavit of the solicitor or his clerk, of the due signature of any admission of the due execution of documents annexed to the notice, is sufficient evidence of the fact of such admission (*c*).

Where documents are not admitted, their execution must be proved in the ordinary way, for which see books on evidence.

Discovery of Documents. Where the opposite party has documents in his possession relating to the subject-matter of the action, the other party may, without any evidence, apply in chambers for an order directing such opposite party to make discovery on oath of the documents which are or have been in his possession or power relating to any matter in question in the action. A similar application may be made at any stage for the *production* of documents (*d*).

The affidavit to be made by a party against whom such order is made, must specify the documents, and also which (if any) of them he objects to produce (*e*).

(*a*) R. S. C., Ord. XXXII. r. 2.

(*b*) Ib.

(*c*) Ib. r. 4.

(*d*) R. S. C., Ord. XXXI. rr. 11, 12.

(*e*) Ib. r. 13.

This affidavit should be in the following form :—

1881. J. No. .

In the High Court of Justice.

Chancery Division.

V.-C. Hall.

Between John Smith . . . . Plaintiff,

and

Thomas Jones . . . . Defendant.

I, the above-named defendant Thomas Jones, make oath and say as follows :—

1. I have in my possession or power the documents relating to the matters in question in this action, set forth in the first and second parts of the schedule hereto.

2. I object to produce the documents set forth in the second part of the said schedule.

3. I object to produce such documents, on the ground that the same exclusively consist of letters which have passed between myself and my solicitor in relation to this action, and of a case submitted to counsel in relation thereto, and of his opinion thereon.

4. I have had, but have not now in my possession or power, the documents relating to the matters in question in this action, set forth in the third part of the said schedule hereto.

5. The last-mentioned documents were last in my power or possession on the   day of   last.

6. On that day I delivered them to   of   , in whose possession to the best of my belief the same now are.

7. According to the best of my knowledge, information and belief, I have not now and never had in my possession, custody or power, or in that of my solicitors or agents, or any of them, or of any other person or persons on my behalf, any document whatsoever, or any copy of or extract from any document whatsoever, relating to the matters in question in this action, or any of them, or wherein any entry has been made relative to such matters or any of them, other than and except the documents set forth in the said schedule hereto.

Sworn, &c.

It is one of the curiosities of our procedure, that the accuracy of this affidavit cannot be questioned by the other side, unless the deponent has in his pleadings or in the answer admitted the existence of some document not set forth in the schedule, or unless from the statements in the answer or pleadings it can be reasonably inferred that such document is in existence, in which cases only, a summons may be taken out for a further and better affidavit (*f*).

Inspection of Documents. The next step is to obtain *inspection* of the documents in the hands of the opposite party; and this is done by serving him with notice to produce them to the party or his solicitor, and to permit copies to be taken; and any party refusing to comply with such notice, forfeits the right to put such documents in evidence, unless he can satisfy the court that they relate solely to his own title (he being a defendant), or that he had some other sufficient cause for his refusal (*g*); and, in addition, the party requiring inspection may apply to the judge by summons for an order for compulsory inspection (*h*). Where, however, such order is applied for with respect to documents not disclosed by the pleadings of the opposite party on such an affidavit as above mentioned, the applicant must file an affidavit showing what documents he requires to inspect, that he is entitled to inspect them, and that they are in the possession or power of the opposite party (*i*).

Where a party means to comply with a notice to inspect, he must, within two days where the documents have been disclosed in his pleadings or affidavit, or within four days where they have not, deliver to the

---

(*f*) See *Saull* v. *Browne*, L. R., 17 Eq. 402; *Noel* v. *Noel*, 1 D., J. & S. 468; *Wright* v. *Pitt*, L. R., 3 Ch. Ap. 809; *Carver* v. *Pinto Leite*, 7 ib. 90.

(*g*) R. S. C., Ord. XXXI. r. 14.

(*h*) Ib. rr. 11, 17.

(*i*) Ib. r. 18.

party requiring inspection, a notice, stating a time within three days when the documents may be inspected at his solicitor's office, and stating which (if any) of them he objects to produce, and why (*j*).

Reserving Discovery and Inspection. The principles with regard to reserving interrogatories until after certain issues are tried, and the results of failure to comply with an order to answer interrogatories stated at p. 129, equally apply to the discovery and inspection of documents (*k*).

Putting Adversary's Documents in Evidence. A party having learnt the contents of documents in the possession or power of his adversary, may wish to put them in evidence at the trial. For this purpose he must give his solicitor notice to produce them at the hearing, and, if he refuses or neglects to comply with such notice, the party giving it may give secondary evidence of the document at the hearing.

Subpœna Duces Tecum. Where a document which a party proposes to put in evidence is in the possession of a third party, a writ of *subpœna duces tecum* must be taken out, and served in the same way as a *subpœna ad test.* (*ante*, p. 113). The writ must, however, specify the documents required to be produced.

Using Evidence taken in other Proceedings. Sometimes it is desired to use at the hearing evidence taken in another action. For this purpose an order (made on petition of course) is required: but at the hearing, the opposite party may of course object to any portion of the evidence, as if it were original evidence.

(*j*) Ib. r. 16.   (*k*) Ib. rr. 19, 20.

SUB-DIVISION V.

Trial of the Action, or of Issues of Fact in it.

CHAPTER I.

PRELIMINARY OBSERVATIONS.

By the trial of an action is meant the hearing in open court of the matters of fact in dispute.

Notice of Trial. The plaintiff may give notice of trial with, or at any time after, his reply; and if he does not do so within six weeks after the close of the pleadings, the defendant may do so, or may, in the alternative, apply to the judge in chambers to dismiss the action for want of prosecution (*a*).

The notice of trial must be given ten days at least before the date of the trial, unless the other party consents to take short notice, which is four days, and cannot be countermanded without leave (*b*): the notice must state whether the trial is to be the trial of the action, or only of issues therein (*c*), and must specify the mode of trial proposed by the notifying party. But either party may within four days apply by motion or

---

(*a*) R.S.C., Ord. XXXVI. r. 4a; *Evelyn* v. *Evelyn*, L. R., 13 Ch. D. 138; *Freason* v. *Loe*, 26 W. R. 138.

(*b*) R. S. C., Ord. XXXVI. rr. 9, 13.

(*c*) Ib. r. 8.

summons for a change of mode; or, by special leave, after four days (d).

Modes of trying Actions. There are three, viz. (1) before a judge and jury, (2) before a judge and assessors, and (3) before a judge alone, which is by far the most usual plan in the Chancery Division. Certain issues of fact in an action may also be tried before an official or special referee; but the action itself cannot (e).

If the party giving notice of trial chooses (as he usually does) any other mode than that of a judge and jury, the opposite party may within four days (or such extended time as a judge or the court shall allow) give notice of his desire to have the issues of fact tried by a judge and jury, and in that case, if the other party object, it lies upon him to convince the court, on motion or summons, that the matter is one which a jury is not competent to deal with, either from its great complexity as regards facts, or from fact and law being so intermingled together that it would be difficult (if not impossible) to direct a jury by separating the law from the fact; or because the questions, as regard the law, are of such a delicate nature, and require a knowledge of such refined law, that they could not be conveniently presented to a jury (.f). On the other hand, the judge may, either at or before the trial, *mero motu*, order the trial of any issue to be had before a jury, if he considers that it will be more convenient (g).

It is essentially a matter of discretion with the judge whether the case is proper for a jury or not, and the

---

(d) Ib. rr. 3, 5.

(e) Non obstante R. S. C., Ord. XXXVI. r. 2; see per Brett, L. J., *Layman* v. *East*, L. R., 3 C. P. D. 156.

(f) R. S. C., Ord. XXXVI. rr. 3, 4 and 26; and per Jessel, M. R., *Bordier* v. *Burrell*, L. R., 5 Ch. D. 514.

(g) R. S. C., Ord. XXXVI. r. 27.

Court of Appeal will rarely interfere with his decision, unless based on a misapprehension of law (*h*). But where personal character will be affected by the result of a trial, it is strong ground for insisting upon a jury (*i*).

The court, on motion, may order that different questions of fact in an action may be tried by different modes, and that one or more of such questions be tried before the other or others ; but such an order will only be made under the most exceptional circumstances (*k*).

Entry for Trial. An action cannot be entered for trial until after notice of trial, but *must* be entered within six days thereafter (except where it is to be tried at the assizes) (*l*). If the party giving notice does not enter it on the day of the notice, or the day afterwards, the other party may enter it within four days (*m*). Actions to be tried before a judge alone are entered at the registrar's office, or at the district registry, by leaving a præcipe (or request) there, together with two copies of the pleadings in print, where they are printed, one being for the use of the judge (*n*). Trials before a judge and jury, or at the assizes, are entered like common law actions with the district registrar (*o*).

(*h*) *Swindell* v. *Birm. Syndicate*, L. R., 3 Ch. D. 133; *Ruston* v. *Tobin*, L. R., 10 Ch. D. 565.

(*i*) *Leigh* v. *Brooks*, L. R., 5 Ch. D. 592 ; and see as to other cases, *Spratt* v. *Ward*, L. R., 11 Ch. D. 240 ; *Singer Co.* v. *Loog*; ib. 656; and *Wedderburn* v. *Pickering*, 13 ib. 769; *Garling* v. *Royds*, 25 W. R. 123; *West* v. *White*, L. R., 4 Ch. D. 631 ; *Mirehouse* v. *Barnet*, 26 W. R. 690.

(*k*) R. S. C., Ord. XXXVI.

r. 6; and see *Emma Mining Co.* v. *Grant*, L. R., 11 Ch. D. 918; and *Piercy* v. *Young*, 15 ib. 475.

(*l*) R. S. C., Ord. XXXVI. rr. 10, 10a.

(*m*) Ib. r. 14.

(*n*) Regs. Not. Feb. 1877; R. S. C., Ord. XXXVI. r. 17; ib. Ord. XXXV. rr. 1, 1a.

(*o*) Regs. Not. Feb. 1877; *Clark* v. *Cookson*, L. R., 2 Ch. D. 746 ; R. S. C., Ord. XXXVI. r. 15a.

CHAPTER II.

TRIAL BEFORE A JUDGE AND JURY.

WHERE a case is to be tried before a jury, it practically leaves the Chancery Division for that purpose, and goes either to the assizes or to the Middlesex or London sittings for trial in the same way as a common law action. If the *action* is being tried, judgment is generally given by a common law judge, or if only *issues* in the action are being tried, the action returns to the Chancery Division on motion for judgment.

Any application for a new trial in jury cases must be made in the Queen's Bench .Division (*a*). Where *an order* is obtained for a trial by jury, it is necessary that the order should state the reasons for which it was made (*b*) : but of course no reasons are necessary where the action is entered for a jury *without* order (*c*). Where an action has been entered for trial in the Chancery cause book before the judge, the officer of the Queen's Bench Division or the district registrar of the assize town will not enter it for trial before a jury, unless the solicitor brings either a judge's order, or a certificate of the Chancery registrar annexed to the statement of claim, that the action has been subsequently marked jury trial at defendant's [or plaintiff's] instance, in accordance with a notice given by the defendant [or plaintiff] (*d*).

(*a*) R. S. C., Ord. XXXIX. r. 1 ; *Hunt* v. *City of London Real Property Co.*, L. R., 3 Q. B. D. 19.

(*b*) R. S. C., Ord. XXXVI.

r. 29a.

(*c*) *Warner* v. *Murdoch*, L. R., 4 Ch. D. 750.

(*d*) W. N. 1877, Pt. II. page 162.

———◆———

CHAPTER III.

TRIAL BEFORE A JUDGE AND ASSESSORS.

WHEN a trial takes place before a judge and assessors it is heard in such manner and upon such terms as the court or a judge shall direct (*a*); and it is therefore apprehended that in such cases the proper course is to move the court for the appointment of an assessor or assessors, and for directions as to the manner and time of trial. Such modes of trial are, however, very rare in the Chancery Division, although the judge not unfrequently orders a particular skilled person to view property, and to report to him upon its condition.

CHAPTER IV.

TRIAL BEFORE A JUDGE ALONE.

As I have said before, by far the most usual course in the Chancery Division, is to have an action tried before a judge alone. In that case he invariably decides both facts and law at the same time, and delivers his judgment at the conclusion of the trial, so that there is no occasion to move for judgment subsequently.

The action having been set down, will appear in the paper and be called on for hearing in its turn. It generally happens that where a judgment is likely to be resisted, some weeks (or even in busy times, months) elapse before an action is reached.

Short Actions. But besides these really litigated actions (such as actions for injunctions to prevent the

(*a*) R. S. C., Ord. XXXVI. r. 28.

commission or continuance of wrongs, whether *ex con-
tractu* or *ex delicto*), in which the judgment concludes the
action, there is a class of actions peculiar to the Chancery
Division, in which the judgment is rarely resisted, and
merely forms the prelude to further proceedings in the
judges' chambers, and in court on further consideration.

To this class belong actions for the administration of
the estate of an intestate, or of the trusts of a will or
settlement, the partition of estates held by tenants in
common, foreclosure actions, and other administrative
business. In actions of this class, the judgment asked
for is generally such as cannot be decently resisted.
For instance, in an action for foreclosure, the plaintiff
generally asks that an account may be taken of what is
due to him on the mortgage, and that the defendant
may be ordered to pay the amount by a day certain
(generally six months), or in default, that he may be
declared to be foreclosed of his equity of redemption.
It is obvious, that, supposing the mortgage to exist,
there can be no valid resistance offered to such a claim,
although when the account comes to be taken in chambers, a fierce fight may be made over the items. So,
where a *cestui que trust* asks, that the trust may be
administered by the court, he has a right to the relief
prayed, and the trustee cannot prevent him getting it,
although in chambers afterwards many nice points may
arise in reference to how the trust should be carried out.

In such cases as these, therefore, where the trial is
not likely to last more than ten minutes, the action may
be set down as "a short action" on the certificate of
counsel that it is fit to be heard as short, and it will
then be placed in the paper for the first succeeding
short action day (one day a week being devoted to this
class of work). The certificate of counsel is a *primâ*

facie ground for setting an action down as short. If the other party considers that the action ought not to be heard as short, he should appear when the action is called on, and if he can show the court any fair reason why it should not be heard as a short action, it will be ordered to be put into the general list; but the mere desire of the defendant that the action should not be heard as a short action, is not sufficient (*a*). Of course an action with witnesses ought not to be marked short.

Notice of an action, being marked short, must be at once given to the other party in the usual way.

Briefs. Some days before an action (whether marked short or otherwise) is likely to be in the paper, the solicitors for the party or parties wishing to be heard, should deliver their briefs to counsel. In contested actions, two counsel are usually employed for each party (although in very important cases three or even four may be justified), one generally being a Q. C., and the other the junior, who has drawn the pleadings and advised on the case; and even in short actions, where the property involved is large, the employment of two counsel may be justified. The briefs should consist of a copy of the pleadings and affidavits (if any), counsel's opinion on the case (if any), observations of the solicitor, copies of documentary evidence, and (where evidence is to be taken *vivâ voce*) proofs, *i. e.*, statements of what each witness is prepared to prove. If it is intended to cross-examine the opponent's witnesses, and they are known, the solicitor should find out their several characters, and should notify the same in the briefs of his counsel, together with any hints or information relative to their intended cross-examination which may strike him. Such observations are frequently

(*a*) *Filstead* v. *Grey*, L. R., 18 Eq. 92.

of the greatest service. Where real property is in question, a plan should be furnished to counsel.

It is an excellent and usual plan to bind up the pleadings and affidavits bookwise, together with a table of contents.

Party appearing in two Capacities. Where a person appears in two capacities in an action, for instance as an executor or trustee and in an individual capacity, he should instruct two sets of counsel.

Order of the Proceedings. The plaintiff's counsel opens the case by reading the pleadings and commenting on them; and, where evidence is taken by affidavit, and the cross-examination is not to be taken in court, he reads his evidence, and so much of the evidence of his opponent's as he wishes to comment upon. When he has finished, if the court thinks that he has not made out a *primâ facie* case, the action is at once dismissed without calling on the defendants; but if he has made out a *primâ facie* case, the defendants' counsel are called upon in the order in which the defendants appear on the record, unless any of them happen to be in the same interest with the plaintiff, in which case they immediately follow him.

If the defendants' counsel do not show a *primâ facie* answer to the plaintiff's case, the court does not call upon the plaintiff's counsel to reply; but if they do raise a reasonable case against the plaintiff, the leading counsel for the plaintiff in court is called upon to reply. After the reply, the court either reserves judgment or pronounces judgment at once, the heads of which are taken down by the registrar in court, and by the several counsel, and are subsequently put into formal shape by the registrar.

Where evidence is heard *virâ voce* in court, the plaintiff's witnesses are examined, cross-examined and re-examined, immediately after his counsel has opened his case, and the defendants' witnesses are examined, cross-examined and re-examined, immediately after the defendants' counsel has opened his defence; but the defendants' counsel in that case has the right of making a second speech, summing up his evidence.

Non-appearance at Trial. Sometimes on the trial of an action a party does not appear: in that case, if the defendant does not appear, the plaintiff may, on producing an affidavit of service of notice of trial, prove his claim so far as the proof lies on him; if the plaintiff does not appear, the defendant will be entitled to judgment, unless he has a counter-claim, in which case he must prove it so far as the proof lies on him (*b*).

However, any judgment obtained in default of a party appearing, may be set aside upon motion or notice made within six days after the trial (*c*).

Affidavit of Service. Whether an action is marked "short" or not, it must never be forgotten that in case (as is not unusual) the defendant does not appear on the case being called on, the fact of notice of trial having been duly given (and where the action is marked short, of notice of the action being so set down) must be proved to the satisfaction of the registrar *before the rising of the court on the day of the hearing*, by affidavit in case of actual service, or (where the defendant has not appeared to the writ) by certificate of the proper

---

(*b*) R. S. C., Ord. XXXVI. rr. 18, 19.

(*c*) Ib. r. 20; and see *Burgoine* v. *Taylor*, L. R., 9 Ch. D.

1; *Wright* v. *Clifford*, 26 W. R. 369; *Michell* v. *Wilson*, 25 W. R. 380.

officer that such notice has been duly filed (*d*). (Seo *ante*, p. 110.)

Hearing in Camerâ. It is occasionally desirable that the facts of a case involving family honour, or the like, should not be mado public, and in such cases the court will consent that tho action be heard in tho judge's private room, and judgment is either delivered thero or in court.

Compromise. It sometimes happens that after an action is entered for trial the parties como to terms. In such a case it may be withdrawn by either party upon producing to the registrar the written consent of both parties; but otherwise it cannot be withdrawn without leave of a judge (*e*). It may be here mentioned, however, that if one of the parties withdraw from a compromise, the terms cannot be enforced in that action, but must form the subject of a new action for specific performance (*f*).

———◆———

CHAPTER V.

TRIAL OF ISSUES BEFORE REFEREE.

Consent. Where. the parties consent, the court may send *any* or *all* questions or issues of fact in an action (but not the action itself) for trial before one of the official referees or a special referee. But even by

---

(*d*) *Cockshott* v. *Lond. Gen. Cab Co.*, 26 W. R. 31; but see a query contra, per Fry, J., *Chorlton* v. *Dickie*, L. R., 13 Ch. D. 160. Until the point is decided finally the above rule should be observed.

(*e*) R. S. C., Ord. XXIII. rr. 1, 2.

(*f*) *Pryer* v. *Gribble*, L. R., 10 Ch. Ap. 534.

L.

consent, questions of law cannot be so referred (a) (unless of course the action is regularly referred to arbitration).

Compulsory Reference. Where the parties do *not* consent, and there are any issues requiring a prolonged examination of documents or accounts, or requiring any scientific or local investigation which cannot in the opinion of the court or a judge conveniently be made before a jury or conducted by the court through its ordinary officers, all the issues of fact may be compulsorily referred to an official or special referee (b).

Limited to Trial of Issues. The powers of trial before official or special referees are limited to the above. In spite of the R. S. C. (many of which contemplate the trial of *actions* before official or special referees), no such trial can be had before them. They are merely to act as the eyes of the court, to investigate facts, and to report those facts to the court, and upon that report the court gives judgment on the action being set down on motion for judgment. " If by consent, all the questions of fact in a cause are sent to an official referee, and if there are no issues of law to be afterwards decided by the court, then I incline to think that the parties may relieve the official referee from reporting or finding expressly as to each question of fact, and that they may consent to his reporting to the court the general effect of his finding of all the facts in the form ' that, having tried all the issues of fact, he found the result to be in favour of the plaintiff or the defendant.' But I think that the referee has no juris-

---

(a) Jud. Act, 1873, s. 56; and per Brett, L. J., *Longman* v. *East*, L. R., 3 C. P. D. 151.

(b) Jud. Act, 1873, s. 57; and

Longman v. *East, supra;* and *Ward* v. *Pilley*, L. R., 5 Q. B. D. 427; *Re Leigh*, L. R., 3 Ch. D. 292.

diction to order judgment to be entered, that must be the act of the court " (c).

The report of any referee upon any question of fact is equivalent to the verdict of a jury (d). In the case of a report by an official referee under a reference of issues to him by consent under sect. 56, the court or a judge may differ from him as to any finding *which is an inference from the facts which he has reported*, but with regard to the facts themselves, and with regard to his findings where issues have been referred to him under sect. 57, the court must accept his finding unless they can set it aside according to the ordinary rules which would be applicable to the finding of a jury. It is open to appeal, therefore, whether improper evidence has been received, or whether the referee in considering the facts has, so to speak, misdirected himself. The court can set aside the finding of the referee if they consider that the finding is a finding against the evidence, and in that case, if the issue were a material one, the court would have to send back that issue to the referee or to some other referee to be tried (e).

But although *quà* referee, a referee, official or special, can only report to the court, and only takes the place of a jury, yet if the parties agree that he shall act as *arbitrator*, it is within his option to accept or refuse such a reference. If he accepts it, he is no longer acting as referee under the statute; he is merely an arbitrator between the parties (f).

Method of getting Issues referred. Issues may be referred to an official or special referee at or at

(c) Per Brett, L. J., *Longman* v. *East*, supra.

(d) Jud. Act, 1873, s. 58.

(e) Per Brett, L. J., *Longman* v. *East*, supra.

(f) Ib.

any time before trial; even when the action has been specially transferred to the junior judge for trial (g). When the application is made before trial a summons should be taken out for that purpose, and an order obtained in chambers. When the order is made, the order, or a duplicate of it, must be produced to such one of the registrar's clerks whose duty it is to distribute the business among the official referees, who thereupon indorses on each order the name of the official referee to whom it is assigned (h). But the court may nevertheless, where expedient, refer an action to a particular official referee (i).

When the official referee to whom the action is referred is settled, the solicitor should take the order to the chambers of the referee in question, and ask for an appointment for the hearing of the questions referred to him. The referee's clerk will thereupon draw up an appointment, notice of which must be forthwith served on all the other parties. The official referee may (subject to the order of the court or a judge) hold the trial at, or adjourn it to, wherever he deems it convenient, and have any inspection or view, and evidence is taken before him, and the attendance of witnesses enforced by subpœna, and generally the trial is conducted as a trial before the court would be, except that it is not public, and that he must (unless otherwise ordered by the court or a judge) proceed *de die in diem* (j).

The official referee has the same authority in the conduct of a *trial* as a judge (k). But he cannot

(g) R. S. C., Ord. LI. r. 1a.   (i) Ib. r. 29c.
(h) R. S. C., Ord. XXXVI. r.   (j) Ib. rr. 30, 31.
29b.   (k) Ib. r. 32.

commit any person to prison, or enforce any order by attachment or otherwise (*l*); nor make an order for production of documents or other interlocutory order (*m*). He may either during the trial, or by his report to the court, submit any question for the decision of the court, or state any facts specially, with power to the court to draw inferences therefrom, and in any such case the order to be made on such submission or statement is to be entered as the court directs (*n*). The court also has power to require any reasons or explanations from a referee, and to remit the cause or matter, or any part thereof for re-trial, or further consideration, to the same or any other referee; or the court may decide the question referred to any referee on the evidence taken before him, either with or without additional evidence, as the court may direct (*o*).

References for Inquiry. Besides referring issues for trial, the court or judge may refer any question arising in an action or matter to an official or special referee for inquiry and report (*p*). In such cases the referee does not act as a jury, but rather as an assessor; and the court is not bound by his report, and a summons to adopt the report should be taken out, on the report being made (*q*).

(*l*) R. S. C., Ord. XXXVI. r. 33.

(*m*) *Dauvilliers* v. *Myers*, L. R., 17 Ch. D. 346.

(*n*) Ib. r. 31.

(*o*) Ib.

(*p*) Jud. Act, 1873, s. 56.

(*q*) *Wood* v. *Barnicot*, W. N. 1878, pp. 25, 36.

Sub-division VI.

Motion for Judgment.

With regard to the facts in respect of which relief is claimed, they are either :—

    (1) Disputed and tried—
        (a) before a judge ;
        (b) before a judge and assessors or a jury ;
        (c) before a referee ; or

    (2) Undisputed and—
        (a) specifically admitted ;
        (b) impliedly admitted by default of pleading.

When facts are disputed and tried before a judge, judgment is invariably pronounced by him either forthwith, or after he has taken time to consider his decision; and so where the whole action is tried before a judge and jury, very frequently the judge will deliver judgment forthwith where the matter is simple (*e. g.*, where an injunction, or specific performance, or the like, is claimed). But it is obvious that in all the other cases mentioned above something further has to be done after the facts are determined or admitted before judgment can be had. With regard to the case of facts specifically admitted, we have already fully considered it (page 100), and, therefore, we have now only to consider (1) cases in which facts have been referred to a referee, and (2) cases in which default has been made in pleading, and in both these cases judgment is obtained on motion for judgment.

Judgment on Referee's Report. If only some of the issues in an action have been referred for trial to a referee, then unless the result of such reference makes it unnecessary to determine the rest, judgment cannot be had until the other issues are decided, and therefore those issues will be tried in the ordinary way, and then the judge will either at the trial, or on motion for judgment afterwards, give judgment on the whole case. But where all the issues in an action have been referred to a referee, then as there is nothing more to be determined, the proper course is for the plaintiff to set down the action on motion for judgment. He may do this immediately, and if he does not do so, and give notice of motion to the other parties within ten days after his right accrues, then at the expiration of such ten days, any defendant may do so and give such notice (a). And so where some only of the issues have been decided, but the decision of them has rendered the decision of the rest unnecessary, or has rendered it desirable to postpone the decision of them, any party may apply to the court or a judge for leave to set down the action on motion for judgment without waiting for the determination of such other issues, which leave may be granted on such terms as may appear just, and the judge may give any directions as to postponing the undetermined issues (b).

As we have seen in Chapter VI. of Sub-division III., the proper course in default of pleading is to set down the action on motion for judgment.

(a) R. S. C., Ord. XL. r. 7. It would seem, however, that in that case the defendant cannot claim judgment on his counterclaim. See *Vavaseur* v. *Krupp*, L. R., 15 Ch. D. 474 ; but see contra, *Beddall* v. *Maitland*, 17 ib. 183.

(b) Ib. r. 8.

Procedure on Motion for Judgment. No action can, except by leave of the court or a judge, be set down on motion for judgment after one year from the date when the party might first have set it down (c). Motions for judgment are not brought on as ordinary motions on a motion day, but are set down in the cause book, and come in ordinary course among the actions for trial.

Notice of Motion for Judgment. The party setting down should first give to the other parties two clear days' notice of his motion, and produce a copy of such notice to the registrar on setting the motion down. The day named in the notice (although generally not the day on which the motion is likely to be heard) must be a day on which the court sits (d).

The notice should be served in the same manner as the pleadings; that is to say, at the address for service where an appearance has been entered, or by filing in any other case. And it must be particularly remembered that unless the parties appear personally or by counsel on the hearing of the motion, it will be necessary to produce to the registrar *before the rising* of the court, an affidavit of the service or a certificate of the filing (e).

Where a motion for judgment cannot from the nature of it last long, it may be marked "short" on production of counsel's certificate, and will then be heard on the next succeeding short cause day, but in that case the notice of motion should state that it is intended to set it down as short.

(c) R. S. C., Ord. XL. r. 9.　　(e) But query, now see *Chorlton*
(d) *Daubney* v. *Shuttleworth*, L.　v. *Dickie*, L. R., 13 Ch. D. 160.
R., 1 Ex. D. 53.

Final or interlocutory. Upon a motion for judgment, the court may either give final judgment, or direct the motion to stand over for further consideration, and direct such issues or questions to be determined, and such accounts and enquiries to be made and taken, as it may think fit (*f*).

Liberty to apply. A judgment unless absolutely final almost invariably reserves "liberty to apply as the parties may be advised," but it would seem that, even where this is omitted, liberty to apply is implied in every judgment and order of the court (*g*).

(*f*) R. S. C., Ord. XL. r. 10.   (*g*) *Fritz* v. *Hobson*, L. R., 14 Ch. D. 542.

The Judgment.

THE judgment in actions *properly* commenced in the Chancery Division is always delivered by the court. In actions appropriate to the Queen's Bench Division, the plaintiff may, in many of them, *sign* judgment himself in default of appearance, and then of course the judgment is not delivered by the court. Such actions are actions for liquidated demands, and for recovery of land; or where the claim is for damages for detention of goods, and for return of the goods or either of them, he may enter interlocutory judgment, and a writ of enquiry to the sheriff to assess damages will be issued, or some other mode of ascertaining the damages will be directed (*a*). Such actions are, however, inappropriately brought in the Chancery Division, and judgment in all actions properly brought in that division must be delivered in court, either on the hearing of the action, or on motion for judgment.

Minutes. On short actions, where the parties are agreed or practically agreed on the form of the judgment, minutes are usually prepared by the plaintiff's counsel, which are submitted to the counsel for the defendants for their approval. These minutes are in effect a draft of the operative part of the judgment, omitting the recitals of evidence, &c., which are afterwards added by the registrar.

(*a*) R. S. C., Ord. XIII. rr. 5, 7 and 6.

Bespeaking Judgment. In contested actions, the registrar in attendance on the court, and also the counsel engaged, take a note of the judgment as delivered by the judge. Within seven days after the judgment is pronounced (*b*), one of the ·parties must "bespeak" or request judgment to be drawn up, and leave with the clerk of the registrar, his senior counsel's brief, and any documents or evidence required to be produced at the court (*c*) ; office copies of affidavits and exhibits used (*d*) ; orders authorizing the proof of documents at the trial by *vivâ voce* evidence or by affidavit, and the documents themselves (*e*) ; the certificate of the paymaster-general's chief clerk with regard to funds in court dealt with by the judgment, and any restraining order with regard to any such funds (*f*) ; probates or letters of administration (*g*) ; and generally all such other documents as may be necessary to enable the registrar to draw up the judgment.

The practitioner must never forget that where any ' party does not appear at the hearing or motion, an affidavit of service of the notice of trial or notice of motion, as the case may be, or (where such party has not entered an appearance) a certificate of the filing of such notice, must be produced to the registrar before the rising of the court on the day of the hearing (*h*).

At the time named by the clerk to the registrar, the solicitor to the party bespeaking the judgment applies at the registrar's office for a draft of the judgment,

---

(*b*) Cons. Ord. I. rr. 20, 21, 22.

(*c*) Regs. Rules, March, 1860, r. 15.

(*d*) Ib. r. 27.

(*e*) Ib. r. 28.

(*f*) Ib. r. 16.

(*g*) Ib. r. 17.

(*h*) Ib. r. 21; but query, now see *Charlton* v. *Dickie*, L. R., 13 Ch. D. 160.

and with this draft the registrar delivers a written appointment of the time fixed by him for settling the same (*i*); copies of this appointment must be served on the other parties at the place for service, either by hand or by post, one clear day at least before such day (*j*).

On the day appointed, all parties who please, attend before the registrar at his office, with their briefs and other documents, and the judgment is then settled. If any party fails to attend, the party bespeaking the judgment must produce the original appointment, with a memorandum of service on it, signed by the person who served it; but the registrar may, if he thinks fit, require this memorandum to be verified by affidavit (*k*).

Varying Judgment. If any question arise as to the proper form of the judgment, the action is replaced in the paper to be "spoken to on the minutes," and thereupon the judge states what was the exact decree pronounced; but unless by consent, he will not vary the judgment as pronounced.

When a mistake is obvious on the minutes, and the registrar refuses to make the necessary alterations, the court must be moved, on notice of motion, to vary the minutes; but the registrar may by consent make such alterations himself as the court would sanction (*l*).

Passing the Judgment. The minutes having been thus settled, the registrar names a time for passing the judgment, or delivers out a written appointment for that purpose (and in the latter case copies of such appointment must be duly served). On the day named,

(*i*) Cons. Ord. I. r. 23.
(*j*) Ib. rr. 24 and 25.
(*k*) Ib. r. 26.

(*l*) *Davenport* v. *Stafford*, 8 B. 503.

the judgment having been drawn up from the minutes, by one of the registrar's clerks, is perused by the registrar in the presence of such of the parties as please to attend; and, if found correct, he passes the decree, by inserting his initials in the margin at the end, as an authority to the entering clerk to enter it in the registrar's book.

Entering Judgment. The registrar's assistant clerk leaves the judgment for this purpose with the entering clerk at his seat in the registrar's office, together with a copy of the pleadings (*m*), and the latter enters it: the judgment may generally be obtained on the second day after it is left for entry, on application to the assistant clerk.

The registrar's books contain copies of all judgments made by the court, and two of these books are provided every Michaelmas term, one being reserved for actions where the first letter of the first plaintiff's name is found in the earlier half of the alphabet, and the other for actions where such first letter is found in the latter half. The books themselves are designated A. and B., and are referred to by the year and folio or page, thus: Reg. Lib. 1880, f. 250."

Form of the Judgment. The judgment consists of the title and date on which the judgment is delivered, a statement of the proceeding on which the judgment was given, of the presence or absence of the parties or any of them, and of the evidence; then comes what may be called the operative part, which consists (where necessary) of a declaration of right (which is equivalent to the verdict of a jury on a matter of fact), and then comes the ordering part, where necessary.

(*m*) R. S. C., Ord. XLI. r. 1.

With regard to the statement of the evidence it is important to remember, that even where a plaintiff is nonsuited without the defendant being heard, yet it is sometimes desirable to have the defendant's evidence stated in the judgment; for if an appeal be brought, and the respondent use evidence which was not used on the hearing in the court below, he will often be left to bear his own costs, and the Court of Appeal cannot look to anything but the judgment to ascertain what was used on the former occasion.

Sometimes a judgment ends with a declaration of right, without ordering anything to be done; such cases most frequently occur in actions instituted for the purpose of ascertaining the true construction of written instruments.

On the other hand, judgments sometimes contain no declaration of right, the operative part being merely composed of the ordering part. Sometimes (as in cases of injunction, specific performance and the like) the order is final and immediate, but more often it is merely for accounts and enquiries to be taken in the judges' chambers; and where damages are claimed, they are never assessed by the judge in court, but the right to *some* damages having been declared, an enquiry is directed to assess them, either before the judge's chief clerk, or an official or special referee.

When a judgment orders a party to *do* some act other than the payment of money, it should name a time within which the act is to be done (*n*), otherwise it will be defective; and before execution by attachment can be issued, it will be necessary to get a supplemental order naming such time. This order will be

(*n*) Cons. Ord. XXIII. r. 10.

made on motion, of which the ordinary notice must be given (o).

Office Copies. When a judgment has been passed and entered, office copies of it can be obtained in the usual way.

Mistake in Judgment passed and entered. A consent to a judgment, if given by mistake, may be withdrawn before the judgment is passed and entered, and application may be made to the court to vary it accordingly ; but after it has been passed and entered, a judgment cannot be varied or added to, except where , there has been a mistake, such as would suffice to set aside an agreement to the like effect (p), or unless by consent (q), or unless there is a trivial error, slip or omission (r) ; by which I mean, not a mere clerical error, but any obvious slip, such, for instance, as where the direction to mortgagor in a redemption suit to pay principal, interest and costs within six months (s), or a direction to have a deed settled in chambers, has been omitted (t). In all such cases the application to vary should be by motion (u), although in case of very trivial errors the registrar will sometimes make the alteration himself.

Further enquiries, &c. Where, however, it appears that further enquiries or accounts should be taken or made, the judge may order the same on summons in chambers (v) ; and where a person, not a party, has been served with notice of the judgment,

(o) Daniell's Ch. Pr. 904.

(p) Holt v. Jesse, L. R., 3 Ch. D. 177 ; Att.-Gen. v. Tomline, L. R., 7 Ch. D. 388.

(q) King v. Savory, 2 Jur. 431.

(r) Cons. Ord. XXIII. r. 21.

(s) Bird v. Heath, 6 Ha. 236.

(t) Trevelyan v. Charter, 9 B. 140.

(u) R. S. C., Ord. XLI.r.

(v) Cons. Ord. XXXV. r. 19.

he may, within one month after service, apply to add
to it.

In all other cases, the judgment can only be varied
or added to, either by getting an order on petition to
have the case reheard, or on appeal, unless the parties
consent (*u*).

Amending Irregularities. It is convenient to
state at this place, that non-compliance with the rules
of procedure does not render the proceedings void unless the court or a judge so direct, but such proceedings may be set aside or varied on terms or otherwise (*v*),
and the court or judge may at any time upon terms or
otherwise amend any defect or error in any proceedings (*w*).

(*u*) *King* v. *Savery*, 2 Jur., N. S.
431 ; *Hughes* v. *Jones*, 26 B. 24.

(*v*) R. S. C., Ord. LIX. r. 1.
(*w*) Ib. r. 2 (1880).

Proceedings in Chambers under the Judgment.

CHAPTER I.

THE SUMMONS TO PROCEED.

IN many actions, for instance, where an injunction or a declaration of a right or the construction of a document or similar simple relief is sought, the action ends with the judgment, save so far as the taxation of costs and enforcing of the judgment are concerned, of which hereafter. But in many other actions, such as those for administration of trusts or the estates of deceased persons, for foreclosure or sale of mortgaged estates, specific performance of contracts for the sale of real estate, and the like, the judgment is (as has been remarked above) preliminary to the real fight, and merely consists of an order to take certain accounts and inquiries (a). As was stated in the introduction, each of the four senior judges has a staff of three chief clerks, each of whom has his junior clerks,

---

(a) R. S. C., Ord. XL. r. 10.

and it is to these chief clerks that the duty of taking accounts and making inquiries is delegated.

These officials attend at chambers daily (with certain modifications during vacation), and the business of each judge is divided among his chief clerks by the first letter of the plaintiff's name, one taking from A to F; another from G to N, and the third from O to Z. A list of the causes to be disposed of by each is daily hung up outside the door of the chambers.

Summons to proceed. When a judgment is pronounced which orders accounts or inquiries to be taken or made, the party having the carriage of the judgment (who is usually the plaintiff), takes a copy of the judgment, indorsed by the solicitor with a certificate of its correctness, to the judge's chambers, and presents it to the clerk sitting in the outer room. This official then consults the appointment book of the chief clerk to whom the case falls, and informs the solicitor of the earliest day and hour at which the chief clerk will be disengaged, so as to be able to proceed with the business ordered by the judgment. The time so fixed is then entered by this clerk in the "summons and appointment book," and he seals a summons in the following form:—

1880. B. No. 150.

In the High Court of Justice. ·

Chancery Division.

V.-C. Hall.

Between John Brown . . . . . . Plaintiff,

and

Joseph Smith . . . . . . Defendant.

Let all parties concerned attend at my chambers, Royal Courts of Justice, Middlesex, on the 29th day of November, 1880, at 11 o'clock in the forenoon, on the hearing of an application on the part of the plaintiff to proceed with the accounts and inquiries directed to be taken and made by the judgment in this action dated the 1st day of August, 1880.

Dated this 20th day of November, 1880.

This summons is taken out by George Robinson, of No. 700, Cheapside, in the City of London, solicitor for the above-named plaintiff.

To Mr. William Jones, solicitor for the above-named defendant.

Issue and Service of Summons to proceed.

This summons is prepared by the plaintiff's solicitor, who takes two copies to the judge's chambers, one of which is filed and the other sealed by the clerk there. Further copies are then made for service, which is effected by delivering a copy, and at the same time showing the sealed original; or where default has been made in appearance, service is effected by filing with the proper officer. The summons must be served seven clear days before it is returnable (*i. e.* the day fixed for the hearing of it); and if this cannot be effected, the latter day will be altered, and a new one endorsed, the endorsement being sealed.

Hearing of the Summons. At the time appointed, the parties attend personally or by their solicitors (but not by counsel), and the chief clerk then gives directions as to how the accounts and inquiries are to be taken and made, and fixes times for the accounts to be brought in, and for the inquiries to be made, and for the further attendance of the parties.

Summoning Witnesses. By the 30th section of the Chancery Procedure Act the chief clerks have power to summon witnesses to attend and give evidence. Such summonses are served like, and have the effect of, subpœnas.

M 2

CHAPTER II.

ACCOUNTS.

Bringing in the Account. At the time fixed by the chief clerk on the hearing of the summons to proceed, the accounting party makes an affidavit verifying the statements of an account which is annexed to the affidavit by way of exhibit; and this affidavit and the exhibit are brought into chambers and left with the junior clerk in the outer room.

The form of such an affidavit and exhibit will be found in Daniell's Forms, by Upjohn.

The account is written on foolscap paper, bookwise (*b*), and the items on each side of the account are numbered consecutively. No costs paid to the solicitor of the accounting party should appear, as they are costs in the action, and are disposed of subsequently. If necessary, further accounts must be brought in from time to time, to bring the account down to the date of the chief clerk's certificate.

The accounting party, on the same day that he leaves the account at chambers, should give notice of the fact to the other parties, and also state that he has (as he must have done) filed an affidavit in support, and they may then obtain copies on application (*c*).

Vouchers. Besides the affidavit, the account must be supported by the production of receipts for every payment over 2*l.*, which are accepted as *primâ facie* evidence of the payments in respect of which they are expressed to have been given; but if any reasonable ground is shown for doubting their genuineness, the affidavit of

(*b*) Regs. 8th Aug. 1857, r. 17.   (*c*) Cons. Ord. XXXVI.

the party giving the receipt is required, or evidence of his handwriting must be produced.

This is the usual mode of verifying accounts, but the court may give special directions, either when directing the account to be taken or subsequently; and in particular may order that in taking the account, any book of account in which the accounts required to be taken have been kept, shall be *primâ facie* evidence of the truth of the matters contained in it (*d*).

Objections, how taken. When the account has been brought in, any party interested may give notice to the accounting party of any objections which he may entertain to particular items, specifying them by their numbers, and specifying the grounds of his objection.

Taking the Account. On the day appointed for going into the accounts, the chief clerk goes through them, sees that they are properly verified, and also disposes of the objections, or marks such of them as queried which cannot be then and there satisfactorily explained, and the accounting party must then obtain further time for explaining and verifying them, or they will be disallowed.

Finally, if the alterations in the account are considerable, a transcript is made of the whole as altered, and the result of the account is finally summed up in the form of a certificate of the chief clerk, which he subsequently submits and explains to the judge, who usually adopts and signs it.

(*d*) 15 & 16 Vict. c. 86, s. 54.

CHAPTER III.

INQUIRIES.

THESE generally relate to incumbrances affecting property, or to title to property; to the persons beneficially entitled to property; to heirs, next of kin, creditors, legatees, devisees and annuitants; or as to damages or other facts necessary to be known before a proper and final judgment can be pronounced.

Advertisements. With respect to inquiries concerning incumbrances, title to property, damages or the like, such matters are generally proved by affidavit, and by production of the documents in the usual way; but in the case of inquiries as to persons beneficially entitled, whether as heirs, next of kin, or creditors, or as devisees, legatees or annuitants *not specifically named in the will*, it is generally necessary to advertise for them in the London Gazette and the Times. These advertisements are prepared by the party having the carriage of the judgment, and are submitted by him to the chief clerk for approval, and when approved are signed by the latter, which is sufficient authority to the printer of the Gazette to insert them (c).

Where, however, the usual statutory advertisements for creditors have been already made by the executor or administrator, it is not usual for the chief clerk to direct any further advertisements.

One advertisement only is usually ordered, but under special circumstances any number may be directed (f). As evidence of the advertisements, the party having the carriage of the judgment should produce to the chief

(c) Cons. Ord. XXXV. r. 36.　　　　(f) Ib. r. 35.

clerk copies of all papers wherein the advertisements have been inserted (*g*).

Party claiming an Interest. Any person (other than a creditor) wishing to make any claim in consequence of an advertisement, may do so by entering his name at the judge's chambers in the claim book, and filing an affidavit in support, and giving notice thereof to the solicitors in the action within the time fixed by the advertisement (*h*) : on the day appointed for going into the inquiry, the parties attend, and the chief clerk adjudicates on the matter, or adjourns it, either simply or for further evidence, and either with or without special directions as to the nature of such evidence (*i*).

In case of an adjournment, any new claimant may enter his claim within four clear days before the hearing is resumed; provided that the chief clerk has not in the meantime made any certificate of debts or claims (*j*).

Creditors' Claims. With respect to the claims of creditors, the procedure is different, as such claims have not to be entered, but must be sent to the executor or administrator of the deceased, or to their solicitor, or to such other person as the chief clerk may direct, and must specify (1) the name and address of the claimant; (2) full particulars of his claim, and statement of his account; and (3) the nature of his security, if any (*k*).

In any action for the administration of the estate of a deceased person, no party other than the executor or administrator, or such other party appointed as aforesaid, is entitled to appear on the claim of a person not a party (*l*).

(*g*) Daniell's Prac. 1092.
(*h*) Cons. Ord. XXXV. r. 38.
(*i*) Ib. r. 40.
(*j*) Ib. r. 41.
(*k*) Ord. XXVII., Mar. 1865, r. 1.
(*l*) R. S. C., Ord. XVI. r. 12b.

Date for sending in Claims by Creditors.
Claims are usually directed to be sent in within one
month, and the date of the adjudication upon them is
fixed for three or sometimes four weeks subsequently.

No claim is received after the date fixed, unless by
special leave, granted on summons (*m*), or unless the
day of adjudication is adjourned, when claims may be
sent in up to four days before the day to which it is
adjourned (*n*).

The person to whom the claims are to be sent examines
them, and must, at least seven clear days before the
date of the adjudication, file an affidavit, either alone
or jointly, with the solicitor or other skilled party,
or otherwise as the chief clerk directs, verifying a list
of the claims, the particulars of which have been sent
in, and stating to which of such claims, or parts thereof
respectively, the estate of the deceased is, in the opinion
of the deponent, justly liable; and his belief that such
claims, or parts thereof respectively, are justly due and
proper to be allowed, and the reasons for his belief (*o*) ;
but the chief clerk may direct the making of this affidavit to be postponed until after the day of the adjudication, and it is then to be subject to such directions as
he may give (*p*).

Adjudication on Claims of Creditors.   On the
day fixed for the adjudication the chief clerk goes through
the list, and allows such of them as he thinks fit without
evidence, and directs such investigations to be made of
all or any of the claims not allowed, and requires such
further particulars, information, or evidence in respect
of them, as he thinks fit; and he may also require any

(*m*) Ord. XXVII. r. 10.   (*o*) Ib. r. 5.
(*n*) Ib. r. 9.   (*p*) Ib. r. 6.

creditor to attend and prove his claim, and the adjudication is then adjourned to a date then named (q).

Notice is then given to each creditor, by the party to whom claims are to be sent, informing those whose claims are admitted of that fact, and requiring those whose claims are not admitted to attend on the day to which the adjudication has been adjourned, and prove their claims; and unless they attend their claims will be disallowed (r).

These notices must be sent out, not less than seven days before the date fixed for the adjourned adjudication (s), by prepaid letter addressed to the claimant or his solicitor at the address mentioned in the claim (unless otherwise directed) (t): and unless this notice be given, the creditor need not attend or prove his claim, either on the original day of the adjudication, or on the day of the adjourned adjudication, unless, indeed, he holds a security, when he must produce it on the day of the original adjudication (u).

When a claim is allowed, the chief clerk marks it as allowed, and he may require an alphabetical list to be left at the chambers of all claims which are eventually allowed (v).

Evidence. With regard to the proof of claims for which proof is required, simple contract debts are proved by affidavit (filed in the central office and not in the district registry (w)), verifying the particulars of the account, which latter must be referred to by way of exhibit. Specialty debts are similarly proved, the spe-

---

(q) Ib. r. 7.
(r) Ib. r. 8.
(s) Ib.
(t) Ib. r. 13.

(u) Ib. r. 2.
(v) Cons. Ord. XXXV. r. 11.
(w) R. S. C., Ord. XIX. r. 29a.

cialty being exhibited; and a claimant may be cross-examined on his affidavit before an examiner, or before the chief clerk himself (x).

Where a creditor cannot prove his claim without the aid of documents in the possession of the executors or administrators of the deceased, he may compel them to produce them on oath (y).

Creditors' Costs. A creditor who has established his claim, is entitled to his costs, to be fixed by the chief clerk, unless he thinks fit to direct that they be taxed; and the amount of such costs is added to the debt (z). On the other hand, where a claim is successfully resisted, the court may order the costs of resisting it to be paid by the claimant (a).

CHAPTER IV.

SALES.

It is frequently ordered by the judgment, that real estate " be sold with the approbation of the judge." In such cases, whenever the action is for the administration of a trust, and the trust instrument contains a trust for, or power of, sale in, the trustees, they are the proper parties to conduct the sale unless the court directs otherwise (b). In other cases, the plaintiff is the proper party, and is considered the agent for all parties concerned (c).

(x) *Cast* v. *Payser*, 26 L. J. (N. S.) Ch. 353; *Lenton* v. *Brudenell*, 12 W. R. 1127.

(y) *McVeagh* v. *Croall*, 1 De G., J. & S. 399; and R. S. C., Ord. XXXI. r. 11.

(z) Cons. Ord. XL. r. 24; and Gen. Ord. May 27, 1865, r. 14.

(a) *Hatch* v. *Searles*, 2 Sm. & G. 146; *Colyer* v. *Colyer*, 10 W. R. 748; *Bentley* v. *Bentley*, 7 L. T., N. S. 819.

(b) R. S. C., Ord. LII. r. 6a.

(c) *Dally* v. *Pullen*, 1 R. & M. 296; *Dale* v. *Hamilton*, 10 Ha. App. 7.

Incumbrances. Where the property is incumbered, it cannot be sold free from incumbrances, without the incumbrancer's consent; and the judgment directing the sale, runs "free from the incumbrances of such of the incumbrancers as consent thereto, and subject to the incumbrances of such of them as do not," and an inquiry is invariably directed as to what incumbrances there are, and what are their priorities, proof of which is usually furnished by the affidavit of the party conducting the sale.

Mode of Sale. The chief clerk, on the hearing of summons to proceed, gives directions as to the mode of sale (usually by auction), and as to the place and auctioneer. Sometimes a sale by private contract is sanctioned upon evidence of beneficial character of the offer. The chief clerk also directs an advertisement to be prepared and published in the Gazette, and also in some of the local papers. This advertisement is prepared by the solicitor of the party having the conduct of the sale, and is then submitted by him to the chief clerk for approval, and, being signed by him, is duly published.

Abstract and Conditions of Sale. The solicitor of the party having the conduct of the sale, also prepares an abstract of the title and particulars and conditions of sale (in the form provided by Sched. 7 of the Reg. 8th August, 1857), which must (unless otherwise ordered (*d*)) be submitted to one of the conveyancing counsel to the court, who advises on the title and on the necessary conditions. For this purpose, the solicitor obtains from the chief clerk a short memorandum or minute signed by him, directing a reference to the conveyancing counsel. This minute is taken to such one

(*d*) See *Gibson* v. *Woolland*, 24 L. J. (N. S.) Ch. 56.

of the registrars' clerks whose duty it is to distribute the business among the six conveyancing counsel, and he indorses upon it the name of the counsel to whom it is assigned, unless the matter is referred to a particular counsel. This minute so indorsed, together with a copy of the particulars and conditions marked by the chief clerk, and the abstract, are then taken to the chambers of the conveyancing counsel, by whom the particulars and conditions are settled in the usual way.

The conditions when settled are fair-copied, carried in to the judges' chambers, marked as approved by the chief clerk, and then printed in the usual way, and two printed copies (certified as correct by the solicitor) must then be left at chambers (*e*).

Reserve Price. Very frequently the chief clerk fixes a reserve bidding for each lot, and in that case a valuation must be made, by a competent surveyor, of the property as a whole, and of each lot; and he must make an affidavit referring to the valuation by way of exhibit (*f*). This affidavit must be filed, and the chief clerk attended with an office copy of it. He then fixes the reserve biddings in writing, and encloses them in a sealed envelope, and delivers them to the person appointed to sell. They must, however, not be opened until the sale, and must not then, or afterwards, be communicated to any person. If no bidding reaches the reserved price, the property is declared not sold.

Where there is a reserved bidding, it should be made the subject of a condition (*g*).

The Sale. The auctioneer having been appointed, a copy of the particulars and conditions (signed by the

(*e*) Regs. 8th Aug. 1857, r. 11.   (*g*) Ib. r. 14.
(*f*) Ib. r. 13.

chief clerk), and a form of bidding paper and affidavit
of the result of the sale, are obtained by the solicitor
(for the use of the auctioneer) at the judges' chambers ;
and where there are reserved biddings, these papers are
enclosed with them in a sealed envelope.

The sale is conducted in much the usual way, the
result, however, being marked in the bidding paper as
thereby directed. No party to the action can bid except by leave, which is occasionally given in the judgment, but is more usually obtained in chambers on
summons. As a general rule, the leave will not be
given to the party conducting the sale (h), nor to persons
in fiduciary positions (i). After the sale the auctioneer
makes his affidavit of the result of the sale, which must
be filed, and an office copy left at the judges' chambers
one clear day at least before the day appointed for
settling the chief clerk's certificate of the result. On
the latter day, the certificate is signed by the chief
clerk, like any other certificate. (for which see *infra*),
and this certificate must be adopted and signed by the
judge before the sale is considered to be approved.

Delivery of the Abstract. Within the period
appointed by the conditions (generally eight days after
the approval of the certificate), an abstract of title is
sent to the purchaser, and he sends in his requisitions ;
and the solicitor having the conduct of the sale replies
to them in the usual way; but the nature of the objections and answers are matters of substantive law,
which will be found noticed in works on the Law of
Vendors and Purchasers.

(h) *Sidney* v. *Ranger*, 12 Sim. 118.

(i) *Geldard* v. *Ramble*, 9 Jur. 1085 ; *Pooley* v. *Quilter*, 2 De G. & J. 327.

If the solicitor neglects to deliver the abstract within the time fixed by the conditions, the purchaser may take out a summons to compel delivery of it.

Purchaser's Requisitions and Objections. If the solicitor of the party conducting the sale and the purchaser cannot agree on the requisitions, the disputed point may be raised on summons, either by the purchaser for an inquiry into the title, or by the party conducting the sale for an order on the purchaser to pay the purchase-money into court. The point in dispute is then adjourned into court for argument, or sometimes referred to the conveyancing counsel; and if the title is certified to be bad, the purchaser applies by summons (which must be served on *all* parties to the action) to be discharged, and to have a return of his deposit with interest at 4 per cent. per annum and his costs (*k*).

Payment of Purchase-money. If, however, the title is approved, the next step is the payment of the purchase-money into court, for which purpose an order will be made on the application of the purchaser by summons, or (on his default) on the application of the party conducting the sale; and where the estate is encumbered, and is sold free from incumbrances, the summons should be for leave to pay off the incumbrancer, and to pay the residue only into court.

The summons should also ask that the purchase-money be not paid out without notice to the purchaser, so that he may have a lien thereon until the conveyance is duly executed, in which case it will be necessary to serve him with any summons, petition or notice of any

---

(*k*) See Seton on Decrees, 4th ed. 1411 et seq.

other proceeding asking for payment out, and to file an affidavit of such service in case of his non-appearance.

The order having been obtained, it is taken to the office of the paymaster-general, and the money paid in as described in Sub-division IX. If the order directs that the purchase-money and interest are to be paid, an affidavit of the amount of the interest must be made and taken with the order.

Conveyance. The purchaser should not take possession until he has accepted the title, as his doing so is considered a waiver of all objections disclosed by the abstract (*l*); unless, indeed, the judge or the conditions of sale authorize his doing so, subject to objections (*m*); but this is rarely conceded (*n*).

The conveyance is prepared by the purchaser, and forwarded for perusal to the solicitor of the party conducting the sale, and executed in the ordinary way, unless the parties cannot agree, in which case it must be left at chambers to be settled there, and from thence it is sent to the conveyancing counsel.

If any party having the legal estate refuses to execute it, he may be ordered to do so on summons, or (as is more usual) a vesting order may be obtained on summons, vesting the lands in the purchaser (*o*).

Any delay in the preparation, or perusal, or execution of the conveyance may be remedied by summons (*p*).

Opening Biddings. It was formerly the very inequitable practice of the court, even after the result of

(*l*) *Wilding* v. *Andrews*, 1 C. P. Coop. 380; *Bown* v. *Stenson*, 24 B. 631.

(*m*) *Simpson* v. *Sadd*, 4 De G., M. & G. 665.

(*n*) *Hutton* v. *Mansell*, 2 B. 260; *Morris* v. *Bull*, 12 Jur. 4.

(*o*) 15 & 16 Vict. c. 55, s. 1; and Cons. Ord. XXXV. r. 1.

(*p*) Dan. 1172, 1173.

the sale had been certified, to order the estate to be again offered for sale in case any person offered a large increase of price. This was called " opening the biddings," and has now been put an end to except in cases of fraud or gross misconduct bordering on fraud in the management of the sale (*q*), both in regard to sales by auction and by private contract (*r*).

Resale. Where the property or any part of it is not sold at the sale, or for any reason the contract is rescinded, it may (if thought advisable) be again offered for sale. For that purpose, a summons to proceed is taken out, and served on all parties entitled to attend; and on the hearing of it a new time of sale is fixed, and any necessary alterations made in the particulars or conditions; but generally it will not be necessary to have the conditions again submitted to the conveyancing counsel, nor is it necessary to get fresh orders for the sale (*s*).

CHAPTER V.

THE CHIEF CLERK'S CERTIFICATE.

WHEN everything has been done in chambers which is directed by the decree, the result is embodied in the form of a certificate by the chief clerk, to which is annexed, by way of schedule, the account (if any) on which it is founded (*t*). This certificate is prepared by the chief

----

(*q*) 30 & 31 Vict. c. 48, s. 7 ; *Griffiths* v. *Jones*, L. R., 15 Eq. 279 ; *Brown* v. *Oakshot*, 38 L. J., Ch. 717 ; *Delves* v. *Delves*, L. R., 20 Eq. 77.

(*r*) *Newman* v. *Hook*, L. R., 16 Ch. D. 561.

(*s*) Dan. 1163.

(*t*) Hunter's Suit, 116.

clerk, and the solicitor having the conduct of the proceedings obtains the draft, and furnishes copies of it to the other solicitors in the action, upon being paid for them after the usual rate, which is 4*d.* per folio of seventy-two words.

Settling Certificate. An appointment is made by the chief clerk (upon the adjourned summons) to settle the certificate, and notice of this must be given to all parties : at the time appointed the respective solicitors attend, and suggest any alterations which they may desire, and the chief clerk settles the draft. The law stationer of the judges' chambers then transcribes the certificate, the solicitor who has the conduct of the action paying his charges ; and when so transcribed, it is signed by the chief clerk at an adjournment made for that purpose. But where from the nature of the case (*i. e.*, where it is very brief) the certificate can be drawn and copied in chambers while the parties are present before the chief clerk, it must be then completed and signed without adjournment (*u*).

Judge's Signature. Except where otherwise directed by a judgment or order in relation to the computation of interest or the apportionment of a fund (*x*), the certificate must be signed by the judge before it can be acted on. This will be done without investigation after four clear days have elapsed, unless any party in the meantime takes out a summons to take the opinion of the judge as to any point (*y*). The parties have the same opportunity of taking the judge's opinion upon any point directly the point is decided by the chief clerk, and before the certificate is made, but they may postpone doing so until the certificate is made, and within the four days above mentioned ; but the rule at

(*u*) Cons. Ord. XXXV. r. 48.   (*x*) Ib. r. 45.   (*y*) Ib. rr. 49, 50.

U.   N

the Rolls has hitherto been that the objection must be left in writing at chambers *before the* signing of the certificate by the chief clerk (*z*). Upon hearing the summons the judge will either at once sign the certificate, or will remit it to the chief clerk with a direction to vary it as the case may require ; and in some cases a direction will be given to review or reconsider it (*a*).

Filing. After the certificate is signed by the judge it is forthwith filed by the chief clerk (*b*), and any party may obtain office copies at the usual rate of 4*d.* per folio. It may be here remarked, that all proceedings, affidavits, &c. in chambers are filed in the central office, and not in the district registry (*c*).

Varying Certificate. After the certificate has been signed, if any party wishes to vary or discharge it, he must apply by summons or motion within eight clear days after the filing (*d*) ; and unless he does so, the certificate will not afterwards be varied, except upon very special grounds, such as fraud, accident, mistake, or the like (*e*).

Where the application to the judge requires to be argued, and the further consideration of the action is about to be heard, the summons is frequently adjourned into court to come on at the same time as the further consideration of the action. In that case the registrar will set down the summons with the action, upon production to him of a note by the chief clerk to that effect.

(*z*) Rolls' Notice, 4th Mar. 1871.

(*a*) *Daubeny* v. *Coglan*, 12 Sim. 507.

(*b*) R. S. C., Ord. XIX. r. 29a ; Cons. Ord. XXXV. r. 55.

(*c*) R. S. C., Ord. XIX. r. 29a.

(*d*) Cons. Ord. XXXV. r. 52.

(*e*) 15 & 16 Vict. c. 80, s. 31 ;

and see *Howell* v. *Kightley*, 8 De G., M. & G. 325; *Ashton* v. *Wood*, ib. 698 ; *Re Jones*, 1 Giff. 284 ; *Lambe* v. *Orton*, 29 L. J., Ch. 286 ; *Turner* v. *Turner*, 1 J. & W. 39 ; *Prowse* v. *Spurgin*, L. R., 5 Eq. 99 ; *Briant* v. *Tibbutt*, 17 W. R. 271.

Proceedings in the Chancery Pay Office.

ONE of the commonest proceedings in an action involving the administration of property, is the payment of money, or the transfer of stock into or out of court.

Whenever a defendant admits that he holds a definite sum of money or stock upon trust, the plaintiff is entitled to have it brought into court, and can compel this by interlocutory motion. The court may also order a plaintiff to pay money or transfer stock into court. The object of the court in all such cases, is to secure the safety of the fund or stock in question as far as possible, and of course the payment or transfer does not affect the ultimate rights of the parties who may be eventually adjudged to be beneficially entitled to it. The procedure as to paying and transferring money or stock into or out of court, is now regulated by the statute 35 & 36 Vict. c. 44, and by the Chancery Funds Rules, 1874. The act is hereafter called the Chancery Funds (or C. F.) Act, and the rules the Chancery Funds (or C. F.) Rules.

The C. F. Act then abolished the old practice and the office of accountant-general of the court, and transferred his duties to the paymaster-general for the time being, vesting in him all funds and money then standing in the name of the accountant-general, and making the consolidated fund liable to make good to the suitors of the court all money and securities which by that act became vested in the paymaster-general. The new office thus created is called the Chancery Pay Office, and its procedure is regulated by the very elaborate provisions of the C. F. Rules, with which practitioners are continually coming in collision, owing to the somewhat technical and uncompromising manner in which they are enforced.

Judgments and Orders to be acted on by Paymaster-General. Every order which is to be acted on by the paymaster-general must be drawn up by and entered with the registrars of the court, and, unless very urgent, must be printed, except in cases where a form can be used, in which cases they may be partly printed and partly written. The printing must be on judicature paper, and in a particular kind of type, and the order itself must be intituled in the action or matter, and must *also* (in the body of it) state not only the title of the action or matter, but also the separate account (if any) to which the money or securities are to be placed, and the title of which account must not exceed in length thirty-six words exclusive of the title of the action or matter, unless good cause be shown for extending the title (*a*). The order must also state the exact amount of the money or securities to be dealt with, and also the amount at the date of the order already in court to the credit of the same action or matter, and if the money or securities or dividends of securities to be dealt with under the order are not in court, the order must specify the source from which they will be derived (*b*) ; and the names of persons directed to pay in or transfer money or securities must be stated in full, and not by reference (*c*) ; and in every case the exact amount of

(*a*) C. F. rr. 7, 94.   (*b*) Ib. r. 8.   (*c*) Ib. r. 12.

money or stock to be dealt with must be expressed in the order when it can be ascertained (*d*), and all sums in the body of the order are to be expressed in words; but dates and sums in the schedule (if any) are to be in figures (*e*). However, we need not dwell upon these regulations, because the duty of drawing up such orders, and the control of the printing of them, is assigned to the registrars, and they may be assumed to know their own business, although it is well for the practitioner to see in passing the order that no error has been made.

Every order to be acted on by the Chancery paymaster is passed and entered in the usual way, but the registrar at the same time must cause a duplicate to be made. This duplicate and the original order is transmitted by the registrar to the clerks of entries, who examine them and file the duplicate, and after marking and stamping the original order return it to the registrar for delivery to the parties (*f*).

The registrar may also, according to the requirements of the parties, cause additional copies of such orders to be printed, and he then sends them to the central office, whence they are duly certified and issued as office copies (*g*).

Clerical errors in an order may be amended in writing, the order being sealed by the clerk of entries or a master of the Supreme Court, as evidence that the duplicate kept by them has been amended. No amendment is allowed, however, to provide for a new state of circumstances which may have arisen since the order, nor to

(*d*) Ib. r. 8. (*f*) Ib. r. 18.
(*e*) Ib. r. 15. (*g*) Ib. r. 19.

extend the time named for paying in money or transferring securities (*h*).

Procedure. Money or securities may be paid or
transferred into, or deposited in court in an action or
matter with or without an order ; but in the latter case
it can only be paid in to the credit of the action generally, and not to the credit of a separate account in the
action, except a security for costs account (*i*).

When it is desired to pay money into court under an
order, the order is taken to the Chancery Pay Office,
and a direction bespoken from the paymaster-general
to the Bank of England to receive the money, and
place it to the credit of the Chancery Pay Office account.
If there is no order, then a request is left at the Chancery Pay Office, asking for the issue of a similar
direction.

This direction will in due course be issued, and must
be taken to the bank when the payment is made, and
the cashier will give a receipt for the money. The
bank returns the direction to the Chancery Pay Office,
together with a certificate of payment. The paymaster
then files in the central office a certificate of the payment having been made, an office copy of which certificate is good evidence of the facts therein stated (*k*).

When securities are to be transferred into court, a
similar application must be made for a direction addressed
to the bank or company in whose books such securities
are standing, to make such transfer, which direction will
be a sufficient authority to them to effect the transfer.

After the transfer, the bank or company will return
the direction to the Chancery Pay Office, together with

(*h*) C. F. r. 16.   (*i*) Ib. r. 25.   (*k*) Ib. rr. 28—30.

a certificate of the transfer, and the paymaster will then make his certificate as in the case of money paid into court (*l*).

Where securities are desired to be *deposited* in court, the procedure is the same as upon payment in of money, the securities being handed over to the Bank of England for safe custody (*l*).

Where no Order. The following is the form of request where there is no order for payment, transfer or deposit :—

Chancery.

To the Paymaster-General.

A direction is requested to enable John Smith to pay into court [*or* transfer into court, *or* deposit in court] the sum of one thousand pounds [*or* the sum of one thousand pounds Three per Cent. Consolidated Annuities, or the following securities, that is to say,—*stating them*] to the credit of an action of *Jones* v. *Smith*, 1881. J. No. 500, pursuant to Rule 25 of the Chancery Funds Consolidation Rules, 1874, such money [*or* annuities *or* securities] not having been directed to be paid into [*or* transferred into *or* deposited in] court by an order, and not being money or securities to be paid into [*or* transferred into *or* deposited in] court in pursuance of any act of parliament, or general order by which some particular authority is required to enable the payment to be made.

Dated this 5th day of May, 1881.

JAMES ROBINSON,

28, New Inn,

Strand, W.C.,

Solicitor for the said John Smith.

This request must be sealed by a master of the Supreme Court, to show that the reference to the action and record is correct (*m*), and notice must be forthwith given to the solicitors of the other parties (*n*).

(*l*) Ib.

(*m*) Ib. r. 26.

(*n*) Ch. F., Amended Orders, r. 4.

Urgent Cases. Where it is desirable to pay money before a direction can be obtained, it may be lodged at the bank to the Chancery suspense account upon a request to the bank to receive the same, very similar in form (with necessary variations) to the above form of request to the paymaster-general (*p*); but a direction from the latter in the usual way should be at once sought, and the money carried over to the Chancery Pay Office account.

Tardy Payment. A person ordered to pay money into court by a day certain is not precluded from paying it in afterwards; and he may pay in any interest which may have become due by reason of his default, upon a request to the paymaster-general, as money paid in without an order; but any payment in after the date specified, does not relieve the party from paying any liability which he may have incurred through disobeying the order (*q*).

Ascertaining Dividends. Where dividends or interest are ordered to be paid into court, and the amount cannot be ascertained at the date of the order, it may be ascertained by affidavit or statutory declaration, income tax being deducted unless ordered to the contrary (*r*).

Securities. It must be remembered that the only securities which can be transferred into court are securities of the United Kingdom, or of any colony, or of any foreign state, or of any corporation or company in the United Kingdom, or stock standing in books kept by any corporation, company or person, in the United Kingdom (*s*); all others must be deposited in a box.

(*p*) Ch. F. r. 31.
(*q*) Ib. r. 27.

(*r*) Ib. rr. 8, 10, 86.
(*s*) C. F. Act, ss. 3, 6.

Investment of Money paid into Court since the 7th January, 1873.

Money exceeding 10*l.* paid into court, is forthwith placed on deposit, and bears interest at 2 per cent. per annum (*t*), computed half-monthly on every complete pound (*u*), except in the case of money arising from the realization of securities in court, or from dividends of securities in court, or money brought over from the credit of some other action or matter, with regard to all of which a request signed by the party or his solicitor desiring the money to be placed on deposit is necessary (*v*).

Where, however, money is directed to be otherwise dealt with, it will not be placed on deposit (*w*); nor will money paid in to the appeal deposit account (*x*); nor where the party claiming to be entitled to or interested in the money leaves a request at the Chancery Pay Office signed by his solicitor that the money be not placed on deposit; but this request may be at any time withdrawn, and a request to the contrary substituted (*y*). Money in court may also be invested, by *order*, in Consols, Reduced 3 per Cents., New 3 per Cents., Bank Stock, East India Stock, Exchequer Bills, $2\frac{1}{2}$ per Cent. Annuities, or freehold or copyhold mortgages in England or Wales (*z*).

Where investment of a fund is desired, and is not directed by the original order, a summons served on all parties interested should be taken out, asking for the necessary order.

(*t*) C. F. Act, s. 14, and C. F. r. 73.

(*u*) C. F. rr. 76, 77. See this latter rule as to commencement of interest in sums exceeding 500*l.*

(*v*) C. F. r. 68.

(*w*) Ib. r.

(*x*) Ib. r. 72.

(*y*) Ib. rr. 67, 69.

(*z*) Gen. Ord., 1st Feb. 1861, r. 1; C. F. rr. 36, 65, 66.

The method of procuring the investment, is by taking the order, together with a request, to the Chancery Pay Office for a direction, which will be in due course issued, ordering the bank to pay the money out to the Chancery broker (*b*), conditionally upon his causing the securities to be transferred or deposited to the account of the paymaster-general (*c*). The bank, corporation, or company, in whose books, or with whom the transfer or deposit of the securities is made or deposited, then issue their certificate of transfer, or deposit, as in the ordinary case of transfers into or deposits in court of securities (*d*). Money invested on deposit must, however, be withdrawn from deposit before applying for a direction for its investment (*e*).

Dividends. The order for investment should state what is to be done with the dividends, and if (as is proper where they amount to 40*l.* half-yearly) they are to be invested and accumulated; the order is left at the pay office, with a direction to carry it into effect (*f*). Where, however, the dividends do not amount to 40*l.* half-yearly, they will not be invested, even although the order directs their investment (*g*).

Payment or Transfer or Delivery out of Court. Payment of money, or transfer or delivery of securities out of court, can only be made in pursuance of an order (*h*), which, if interlocutory, can only be obtained on petition, or (where the fund in court is under 300*l.* on summons), intituled in the *action* to the credit of which the money is standing, but not in any *separate*

(*b*) *Re Undertaking of West Riding Railways Bill*, W. N. 1876, pp. 48, 80.

(*c*) C. F. r. 60.

(*d*) Ib.

(*e*) Ib. r. 94.

(*f*) Ib. r. 61.

(*g*) Ib. r. 64.

(*h*) C. F. Act, s. 10; and C. F. r. 36.

account in the action, and of course marked with the reference to the record (*i*).

The order for payment out is taken to the Chancery Pay Office, and in due course a cheque for the money will be issued; but before money on deposit will be paid out, it is necessary for the party entitled to leave a request, asking that it may be withdrawn from deposit (*j*). The paymaster-general may also demand a request for payment of the money out, in addition to the order (*k*); but this right is never enforced.

Where securities are to be sold or transferred, or delivered out of court, it is necessary to get the certificate from a registrar of the exact amount of money to be raised by the sale, or the exact amount and description of the securities to be sold, transferred or delivered out. On applying for this certificate the original order must be produced to the registrar, or, if it cannot be produced, a satisfactory reason for its non-production must be given, and an office copy must be produced (*l*); and where securities are to be transferred, the solicitor must append a memorandum to the certificate, stating the name, address and description of the transferee.

In case of the death of a payee after the order, and before payment, transfer or delivery, the payment, transfer or delivery will be made to the person entitled, on proper proof of his title (*m*). And in the case of a woman marrying after the order, but before payment, transfer or delivery, it will be made to her and her hus-

---

(*i*) C. F. r. 7; C. F., Amended Order 17.

(*j*) C. F. r. 75.

(*k*) Ib. r. 37.

(*l*) C. F. Act, s. 10; C. F. r. 42.

(*m*) C. F. rr. 53, 54; but see r. 56 as to money unpaid for six years after the order.

band, where the amount or value does not exceed 200l.,
on proof of the marriage and production of an affidavit
of the woman and her husband stating that no settlement or agreement for one has been made, or, if one
has been made, identifying it, and, also, in the latter
case, on production of an affidavit of their solicitor,
stating that such settlement or agreement does not affect
the fund or securities (n). In other cases, it would
seem necessary to have the married woman examined.
Where, however, a fund is standing to the credit of a
married woman, and does not exceed 500l., it will as a
general rule be ordered to be paid to her on her separate
receipt without examination (o).

Payment to Third Party. Generally, no one
can receive the money except the party entitled; but
where there are several parties, each of whom is entitled
to less than 10l., it will be ordered to be paid to the
solicitor having the conduct of the action, or to one of
the parties, on his undertaking to distribute it. Even
in that case, however, it is very usual, except in the case
of creditors, to require a written authority of such
persons.

Payment out of Dividends. The practice is
similar to that relating to the payment out of money,
and where dividends have accrued on securities after the
order for their transfer or delivery out of court, such
dividends will be paid to the person to whom the securities are to be transferred or delivered (p).

Certificates of Paymaster-General. The paymaster-general may, *in his discretion*, upon the written
request made by or on behalf of a person claiming to

(n) C. F. r. 52.
(o) Daniell's Forms, 1085.

(p) C. F. rr. 46, 47, 48, 49.

be interested in money or securities standing in the books of the Chancery Pay Office, to the credit of an action or matter, issue (1) a certificate for the information of a judge or other officer of the court of the amount and description of such money or securities, and notifying the dates of any restraining and charging orders affecting the same, and the names of the persons in whose favour such orders have been made (q); (2) a certificate of all purchases, sales, transfers, deliveries or carryings over of, or other dealings with, such moneys or securities (r); (3) a transcript of the account in his books in reference to the cause or matter, and, if so required by the party to whom it is issued, such transcript must be authenticated at the Chancery Audit Office.

The paymaster may also, in his discretion, on a similar request, supply such information with respect to any transactions in the office as may be required in any particular case (s).

Such, then, is an account of the practice in the vast mass of cases in the Chancery Pay Office. It would be impossible in a small work like this to go into exceptional cases, and the reader is referred for information upon any such cases to Morgan and Chute's Chancery Acts and Orders, and the notes to Daniell's Chancery Forms.

Dormant Causes. The London Gazette of June 28th, 1881, gives a list, extending over forty pages, "of the titles of causes, matters and accounts in the books at the Chancery Pay Office, to the credit of which funds were standing on the 1st of September, 1880, which had not been dealt with during the fifteen years immediately preceding that date, prepared pursuant to Rule 91 of

(q) Ib. r. 87.   (r) Ib. r. 89.   (s) Ib. r. 90.

the Chancery Funds Consolidated Rules, 1874." The following notice applies to all inquiries respecting the causes in question :—"No information is to be given by the Chancery paymaster respecting the money or securities to the credit of any cause, matter or account in this list until he has been furnished with a statement, in writing, by a solicitor requiring such information, of the name of the person on whose behalf he applies, and that in such solicitor's opinion the applicant is beneficially interested in such money or securities. Every petition or summons affecting any money or securities to the credit of a cause, matter or account inserted in this list is to contain a statement that it has been so inserted. In cases in which the money or securities affected by such petition may amount to or exceed in value 500*l.*, a copy of such petition, and notice of all proceedings in court or at chambers, unless the court otherwise directs, are to be served on the official solicitor of the court."

Further Consideration.

As has been said before, many actions are not finally
disposed of by the judgment pronounced on the hearing,
that judgment being often a mere general declaration
that justice ought to be done between the parties, and a
direction that certain inquiries be made and accounts
taken in chambers, the making and taking of which are
necessary before the judge can form a conclusion as to
what his final judgment on the matters in dispute between the parties ought to be. For instance, suppose a
testator charges his residuary real and personal estate
with debts, and, subject to their payment, leaves the
real estate to A., and the personal estate to B., and then
directs that a certain mortgage debt charged on a specific
property, specifically devised to C., shall be paid out of
his *personal* estate, and C. claims to have (if necessary)
the realty and personalty marshalled, it would be necessary before deciding the point of law whether or no he
was entitled to have them marshalled, to ascertain the
amount of the testator's debts, legacies and personal and
testamentary expenses, and the value of his personal
estate, so as to see whether the latter was not capable of
bearing all the testator's debts including the mortgage
debt. The judgment, therefore, on the hearing would
direct these matters to be ascertained in chambers, and
the result being certified by the chief clerk's certificate,
the action is again set down on " further consideration,"

in order that the points of law arising on the facts, as found by the certificate, may be argued and decided.

It must not, however, be supposed that further consideration always follows whenever there is a reference to chambers, for sometimes the object of an action will be completely attained by what is done in chambers, as, for instance, in the case of a redemption suit by a mortgagor. In such a case the decree directs an account of what is due on the security for principal, interest and costs, and of what the mortgagee has received (in case he has been in possession), and that on payment of the balance by the mortgagor the mortgagee shall reconvey to him. If these accounts be taken in chambers, and the deed of reconveyance be there settled and executed by the parties without further compulsion, there is no need to again apply to the court. In such a case, from the nature of the suit the costs would be disposed of under the original judgment ; but in most cases of reference to chambers the judgment says nothing about the costs, and that question, therefore, at least, will usually remain to be dealt with on further consideration, even when the result of the inquiries and accounts leaves no other point for argument.

Further Consideration in Chambers. Sometimes, where damages are directed to be ascertained in chambers, and in other cases where the points which are likely to arise on the certificate are simple (as in creditors' administration actions, and the like), further consideration is "adjourned into chambers," so that the action does not again come into court, and the further consideration is brought on by summons.

Setting down. An action may be set down on further consideration, by the *plaintiff*, or other *party* *having the conduct of the proceedings,* after eight, and within fourteen, days after the filing of the chief clerk's certificate. After that period, *any party* may set it down (*a*). By consent, an action may be set down immediately after the filing of the certificate.

The way of setting down an action on further consideration is to take a written request of the solicitor of the party setting it down, together with the judgment, and an office copy of the chief clerk's certificate, to the registrar's clerk at the order of course seat, and he will set the action down accordingly.

The action must not appear in the cause list until ten days have elapsed since it was set down; and notice of the fact that it has been set down must be given to all parties at least six days before the first day on which it can possibly appear in the list (*a*). Where persons who are not parties have been served with notice of the judgment, but have not applied for leave to attend the proceedings, they must be served with notice of the further consideration if it is sought to make them personally liable (*b*).

Where the further consideration is to be had in chambers, the times for taking out and serving and hearing the summons are the same as those above specified in relation to setting down, giving notice, and hearing in court; and the summons may be adjourned into court for hearing, where important, in the usual way.

Setting down as a Short Action. An action may be marked "short" on further consideration in the usual certificate of counsel where the minutes are agreed on, or the points involved are easy and not susceptible

---

(*a*) Cons. Ord. XXI. r. 10.   (*b*) *Re Rees*, L. R., 15 Ch. D. 490.

of being argued at great length; and in that case it will be set down on the short action day next after the expiration of the ten days from the date when it is set down (c). Of course, notice of the action having been so marked must be given.

Leaving Papers. At least one *clear* day before the hearing on further consideration, the solicitor for the party setting down the action must leave with the usher of the court, for the use of the judge, "the papers," *i.e.* copies of (1) the original judgment, (2) the certificate of the chief clerk, (3) any intermediate orders or certificates, and (4) where minutes have been prepared, two copies thereof.

Briefs and Evidence. The briefs will consist of the old briefs used at the original hearing, together with copies of the original judgment, the chief clerk's certificate, and the minutes (if any), together with any other matter which the solicitor may consider it desirable for counsel to know; and, where any new affidavits have been filed, copies of them. With regard to these however, it is a rule that the court will not allow facts to be brought before it on further consideration for the purpose of obtaining a judgment not warranted by the original judgment; although any facts which have occurred since the original judgment altering the situations of the parties, or affecting their rights, and which are not directly in issue, may be proved by fresh evidence (d).

Hearing. The case will be called on in due time in its turn, and will be argued, and the judgment on further consideration pronounced, drawn up, and passed

(c) Regs. R. 15th Mar. 1860, r. 10.

(d) Daniell's Ch. Pr. 1229; and 13 & 14 Vict. c. 35, s. 28.

and entered, like an original judgment. Like it, too, it may be either final, or may direct a further reference to chambers, and on this reference further proceedings are taken and a further certificate made and filed; and the action may, if necessary, be again set down on further consideration. Most usually, however, the judgment on further consideration finally disposes of the action, including the question of costs.

Affidavit of Service. It must not be forgotten that where parties entitled to attend on further consideration fail to do so, the solicitor setting down the action must, as in every other like case, produce to the registrar an affidavit of service of the notice on such parties before the rising of the court on the day of the hearing; and where a purchaser has been served, the affidavit must state that the conveyance has been delivered to him.

Payment of Costs by Solicitors. Solicitors should also bear in mind that if the hearing cannot be conveniently proceeded with owing to the absence of the solicitor for any party, or by reason of his having neglected to deliver "the papers" to the usher, he may be ordered *personally* to pay to any of the parties, such costs as the court may award (*e*).

(*e*) Cons. Ord. XXI. rr. 11, 12.

Interlocutory Applications.

CHAPTER I.

PRELIMINARY.

IN the foregoing pages, frequent reference has been
made to motions, petitions and summonses for the purpose of obtaining incidental orders in the course of an
action ; for instance, to obtain temporary protection for
property until the hearing of the action, to amend
pleadings, to strike out irrelevant or impertinent matter
in pleadings, to set aside the writ of summons, to get

guardians *ad litem* appointed, to strike out interrogatories, to get a further and better answer to interrogatories, to refer issues of fact to an official or special
referee, and the like. Such applications are called
interlocutory applications, and are made either (1) by
way of motion, when no lengthened statement is required in addition to the pleadings to indicate the point
to be decided; (2) by way of petition, when it is necessary to have a written statement of the grounds of the
application in addition to the pleadings; and (3) by
way of summons, when the point is simple and capable
of being disposed of in the judge's chambers. Let us
first examine the different modes of making such applications, and then we shall be in a position to consider
certain of the more important interlocutory applications
which have not hitherto been noticed.

CHAPTER II.

THE DIFFERENT MODES OF MAKING INTERLOCUTORY
APPLICATIONS.

SECTION 1.

By Motion.

ALTHOUGH it is generally said that an application should
be made by motion when no written grounds of the
application are needed beyond the pleadings, such a rule
is not a safe guide, and as Mr. Hunter observes in his
" Concise View of a Suit in Equity," " in fact no general

rule exists on the point, and the practitioner must trust to his experience alone." In this work, therefore, in speaking of any particular interlocutory application, I have always specified whether it should be made by motion, petition or summons.

Special, or of Course. Motions are either "special," or "of course." The former are, *par excellence*, called motions; and in this Work, wherever a motion is spoken of, it means a special motion unless otherwise stated. Motions of course are now of rare occurrence, petitions of course having almost entirely supplanted them.

Motions of Course. It may be as well, however, at once to say that there are certain cases in which a party is entitled of right to a particular order, which he therefore obtains "of course," that is, without any judicial action or discretion being called into play, but merely on satisfying the proper officer that the circumstances are such as to entitle him to it. A motion of course then is made by giving counsel a brief, which is endorsed with a statement of the order required.

This brief the counsel takes to the registrar in court, who marks it with his initials, whereupon the order is drawn up, passed and entered in the usual way, but without notice being given to the other side to attend, and copies are then served on the solicitors of the opposite parties.

If the registrar refuses to mark the brief, the judge should be moved, *ex parte*, to order him to do so, and if an order of course has been improperly obtained, a special motion on notice should be made in court to have it discharged. Owing to the fact that counsel have to be briefed in order to obtain an order on motion of course, it is now rarely used, petitions of course being a less expensive method of arriving at the same result.

Special Motions. Special motions are oral applications made to a judge in open court, and not founded on any written application. They are either (1) *ex parte*, *i. e.* without notice to the other side and without giving the other parties any opportunity of opposing them, or (2) upon two clear days' written notice (*a*) served on the other parties, or (except in cases involving imprisonment) their solicitors at the address for service, or where they have not appeared, by filing the notice in the same way as pleadings are served under like circumstances (*b*).

A shorter notice may, however, be given by special leave, which leave is obtained upon *ex parte* motion made by counsel, and in general made immediately on the judge returning into court after the mid-day adjournment. Such an application is colloquially, and in professional slang, called "a shot."

A notice of motion cannot be given without leave, until the defendant has appeared, or the time limited for appearance has expired (*c*); but leave may be obtained, *ex parte*, to serve notice of motion along with the writ of summons, or at any time after (*d*), and such leave is granted in all cases which are *primâ facie* urgent without the necessity of producing any evidence of their urgency.

Ex parte Motions. No precise rule can be laid down as to when a motion can be made *ex parte*, and when only upon notice; but except where it is specifically said to

---

(*a*) R. S. C., Ord. LIII. s. 4. Ch. D. 694.

(*b*) R. S. C., Ord. XIX. r. 6; and (*c*) R. S. C., Ord. LIII. r. 7.
Morton v. *Miller*, L. R., 3 Ch. D. (*d*) Ib. r. 8.
516; *Parsons* v. *Harris*, L. R., 6

be *ex parte*, or is merely to obtain leave to give short notice of motion, or is made to obtain an order calling on the other side to show cause only, or to obtain an order where delay caused by proceeding in the ordinary way would or might cause irreparable or serious mischief, the motion can only be made upon notice (*e*). *Ex parte* motions may be made on any day on which the court sits; and in vacation may be made to the vacation judge, either in court or chambers or at his private residence; they are generally only granted (when the order injuriously affects another's rights) for a few days until proper notice can be given and the motion duly heard, and upon such terms as the court may consider just; and any party affected may forthwith move to set such an order aside (*f*). For instance, a person claiming to be a bill of sale holder, takes possession of property claimed by the plaintiff, and intends to sell it by auction within two days. Here if the ordinary notice of motion to restrain the sale were given, it would be useless, because the sale would be over before the motion could be heard. In such a case counsel would go into court and directly he could catch the judge disengaged, he would move for an injunction restraining the bill of sale holder and the auctioneer, their servants, agents and others from proceeding with the sale *until the next ordinary motion day*, and for leave to serve notice of motion along with the writ of summons for a similar order to be made on that day, and to remain in force up to the trial of the action. Such an *ex parte* application as this, affecting another's alleged right, would have to be supported by an affidavit duly filed.

(*e*) R. S. C., Ord. LIII. r. 3.   (*f*) Ib.

Motion upon Notice. When notice of motion has to be given, it must be by a formal document, served two clear days, at least, before the day named for moving (*g*), unless leave to serve a shorter notice has been obtained *ex parte*. The following is an example of a notice of motion :—

1881. No. .

In the High Court of Justice.
   Chancery Division.
      V.-C. Hall.
         Between John Smith . . . Plaintiff,
                   and
          Thomas Jones . . Defendant.

Take notice, that this Honorable Court will be moved before his lordship the Vice-Chancellor Sir Charles Hall, on the 2nd day of July next, and so soon thereafter as counsel can be heard, by Mr. ——— of counsel for the plaintiff, that the defendant, his servants, agents and workmen, and John Jones of ——— auctioneer, may be restrained by injunction from selling or attempting to sell the property, or any part of the property comprised in the bill of sale in the statement of claim mentioned, until the court shall make other order to the contrary.

Dated 29th June, 1881.

WILLIAM SMITH,
Plaintiff's solicitor.

No. 118, Darlington Street,
To Mr. Elliot,   Wolverhampton.
   Defendant's solicitor, and to the said John Jones.

In drafting a notice of motion care should be taken to state the object of the motion clearly, as the court cannot make any order, except that stated in the notice, or differing from it only in being less to the advantage of the party moving (*h*).

It is not generally necessary to give notice to all the parties to an action, but only such whose interests are

---

(*g*) Ib. r. 4.   (*h*) Hunter's Suit, 135.

affected by the particular application (*i*); but of course if the court considers any party to be interested who has not been served, the motion may be dismissed with costs, or adjourned in order that such party may be served (*j*).

If a party is unnecessarily served, he should not appear on the hearing of the motion, or he will not be allowed his costs; but if he has incurred expense in ascertaining whether or not his interest requires that he should appear, then even though it turns out that his appearance is unnecessary, yet it has been held that he may appear for the purpose of receiving the repayment of the expenses which he has so incurred (*k*).

One day in each week called "seal day," or now more commonly "motion day," is set apart for the hearing of motions by each judge, and motions on notice are only heard on such days (except by leave); but in vacation when the court is not sitting, the motion may be made to the vacation judge at his residence (if urgent), or in court on the day when he sits in court.

Evidence. The evidence adduced on the hearing of a motion is not usually *vivâ voce*, but by affidavit (*l*); and in this respect is unlike the evidence adduced at the trial, which must be *vivâ voce* except by consent to the contrary (*m*). The court or a judge may, however, on the application of either party, order the attendance for cross-examination, of the person making any such affidavit (*n*), or order his cross-examination before an examiner, or special examiner, or other officer of the court.

(*i*) Hunter's Suit, 134.

(*j*) R. S. C., Ord. LIII. r. 5.

(*k*) *Heneage* v. *Aikin*, 1 Jac. & W. 377; sed quære Morg. & Dav. Costs, 43.

(*l*) R. S. C., Ord. XXXVII. r. 2.

(*m*) Ante, p. 112.

(*n*) R. S. C., Ord. XXXVII. r. 2.

If time allows of it, this order may be obtained on summons or *ex parte* motion, but it is a very usual practice to ask at the hearing of the motion that it may be adjourned until the next motion day, and that the witness may then be in attendance to be cross-examined.

Affidavits to be used on interlocutory applications also differ from those used at the trial in this respect, that a deponent is allowed to speak, not only to his *knowledge*, but also to his *belief*, giving, however, the grounds for it (*o*).

Briefs. The briefs to be delivered to counsel consist of the writ of summons and pleadings (if any), a copy of the evidence, and of the notice of motion, together with any remarks which the solicitor may think desirable.

Hearing. On motion day, there is no list of the business to be transacted, like there is on the days when actions are being tried, but on the judge coming into court, he says to the senior counsel present, "Do you move Mr. —— ?" If Mr. —— is instructed to move in any case he proceeds to do so, reading his notice of motion, stating the facts, and reading his evidence, and arguing on the law applicable to his contention. If there be two counsel engaged, the junior follows his leader if he thinks proper to do so.

The counsel for the other party then oppose the motion, and finally the leading counsel for the party moving, replies, and the judge delivers his decision, and either makes the order asked for, with or without variations, or dismisses the motion, and either orders costs to be paid by one party, or orders that the costs shall be

(*o*) Ib. r. 3.

costs in the action, which leaves them to be dealt with along with the general costs of the action at the trial, or makes no order as to costs, in which case the unsuccessful parties bear their own costs, and all others, whether successful or passive, are entitled to their costs as " costs in the action."

When the first motion is finished, the senior counsel is again and again called on, until he has made two opposed, and any number of unopposed motions, after which the next senior has similar opportunities afforded to him. When all the Q.C.'s have been called on thus, the junior bar are called on in a similar manner, but a junior barrister can only make one motion at a time, and not two or more consecutively like a senior can.

When all the bar have been called on, the judge recommences with the senior, and so on until there are no more motions to be made, or until it is time for the court to rise for the day. If all the motions are not disposed of, they stand over until the next motion day ; but if a motion *can* be brought on, and is *not* brought on, the party giving the notice will have to pay the costs, and his motion will be taken to have been abandoned (*p*). To prevent this, the counsel of the party giving the notice should " save his motion," by asking that it may stand over until the next seal.

The Order. An order made on motion is drawn up, passed and entered, and enforced in the same way as a judgment.

(*p*) *Re Smith*, 23 Bea. 284; *Aitken* v. *Dunbar*, 25 W. R. 336; *Yelles* v. *Biles*, ib. 452.

SECTION 2.

Petitions.

Where an interlocutory order is desired for the payment of money out of court, or where any other application is to be made of such a nature that it cannot be explained without a narrative in addition to the pleadings, a petition is the proper form of application.

Petitions of Course. Petitions, like motions, are either special or of course; and it is more convenient that we should at once dispose of petitions of course, and then we can devote ourselves to the consideration of special petitions. Petitions of course then, like motions of course, are used for the purpose of obtaining orders to which a party is entitled of right, and without any judicial action or discretion being brought into play. Such petitions have been hitherto usually presented to the M. R., although the action may not be attached to his branch of the court; but as a bill is now pending before parliament providing for his transfer to the Court of Appeal, such petitions will, in future, be assigned to any judge. Such a petition is in the following form :—

188 . No.

In the High Court of Justice.

    Chancery Division.

        Vice-Chancellor Hall.

            Between John Smith . . . . . . Plaintiff,

and

                Thomas Jones . . . . . Defendant.

    To Her Majesty's High Court of Justice.

    The humble petition of the above-named plaintiff

Sheweth as follows:

1. In this action the writ was issued on the   day of   last, and the statement of claim delivered on the   day of   last. The defendant has not yet delivered his statement of defence.

2. Thomas Thomas, of 58, New Street, Haverfordwest, in the county of Pembroke, is a material witness in this action for your

petitioner; without whose testimony your petitioner cannot safely proceed to a trial of this action.

3. The said Thomas Thomas is about to proceed on the   day of   next, to the colony of Natal, and your petitioner is desirous to examine him *de bene esse*.

> Your petitioner therefore humbly prays that he may be at liberty to examine the said Thomas Thomas as a witness on his behalf in this action *de bene esse*, saving all just exceptions; and that William Johnson, of Lincoln's Inn, barrister-at-law, may be appointed an examiner to take such examination. And your petitioner will ever pray, &c.

The petition, when drawn and engrossed on paper, is lodged with the Lord Chancellor's secretary of causes, and need not be served on any one. Such a petition is not heard, but the secretary merely draws up and initials such an order as the party is entitled to, and this order is entered in a book kept for that purpose at the secretary's office, open during office hours to the inspection of suitors and their solicitors. Every order so entered and initialed, has the same force as an order of the court, passed and entered by the registrar (*q*). If an order of course has been irregularly obtained on petition, any party wishing to set it aside, should apply to the judge to whose court the action is attached (*r*).

Special Petitions. Special petitions are usually prepared by counsel. As will be seen in the second division of this work, petitions are presented in " matters" as well as in " actions." A special petition in an action is in the same form as a petition of course, setting out the facts on which the petitioner relies, and praying for the order to which he considers himself entitled, " or that such other order may be made in the premises as to this honorable court shall seem meet." In a special petition it is also necessary to state in a foot-note whether, and upon whom, it is intended to be

(*q*) Cons. Ord. XXIII. r. 17.   (*r*) Hunter, 156.

served; thus, "It is intended to serve this petition on the above-named defendant," or "It is not intended to serve this petition on any person." Petitions, like pleadings, should be clear and unambiguous, and generally the principles above specified in relation to pleadings may be observed as guides in the preparation of petitions.

The petition having been prepared, is engrossed on brief paper, in words at length (except figures), and folded like a brief, and endorsed with the record reference, court, division and judge, and with the name of the action, and marked "petition," "opposed" or "unopposed," as the case may be. It is then left with the clerk of the secretary of the Lord Chancellor, who will "answer" it, by writing a memorandum in the margin, to the effect that "his Lordship doth order that all parties concerned do attend him thereon on" the next petition day, and that notice is to be given forthwith. Petitions assigned to the Rolls Court have hitherto been left with the secretary of the Master of the Rolls, but if the latter is transferred to the Appeal Court, no petitions will in future be assigned to him. The petition, when answered, is returned to the petitioner's solicitor, and will be set down for hearing by the secretary. At the time of presenting the petition a fair copy on brief paper is left for the use of the judge on the hearing.

Service. At the foot of every petition, the petitioner must state the parties (if any) intended to be served, and he must choose these parties at his own risk, in the same way as parties are chosen on whom to serve a notice of motion. Service is effected in the same way as service of a pleadings, and consists in delivering a copy of the petition with the memorandum of the secretary copied on it, and showing the original petition and memorandum, and must be effected two clear days at least before the date fixed for the hearing (*s*), unless special leave is given to the contrary.

Where it is doubtful whether a petition should be served on a party or not, the petitioner may serve him, and at the same time offer him 40*s*. to enable him to get legal advice, and if he afterwards appears on the hearing, the court will consider whether his appearance is justified, and will not give him his costs of appearing unless he was justified in appearing (*t*).

Evidence. The evidence on a petition is the same as on a motion, and where no opposition as to facts is anticipated, the affidavit is generally an echo of the statements in the petition.

Briefs. The briefs consist of a copy of the petition and evidence, and any observations of the solicitor which he may consider desirable.

Hearing. One day in each week of the sittings is set apart by each judge for the hearing of petitions. A list of petitions to be heard by each judge is made out by the secretary to whom they are presented, and on the day named the petitions are called on in the order in which they appear in this list, the unopposed ones, however, being heard first.

Sometimes a petition presented as unopposed will turn out to be opposed; and in that case it stands over until the unopposed ones have all been heard.

If when a petition is called on, the petitioner's counsel are not in court, the registrar passes on to the next, but when all the list is exhausted he goes through it a second time, and if no one answers on this occasion the petition is struck out.

(*s*) Cons. Ord. XXXIV. r. 2.   Eq. 697; *Wood* v. *Boucher*, L. R.,
(*t*) *Duggan's Trusts*, L. R., 8   6 Ch. App. 77.

Standing over. Where for any reason the petitioner is not ready to have his petition heard, he should (when it is called on) ask for it to stand over until a future fixed day, or "generally:" in the latter case it will, if unopposed, be set down again by the registrar in attendance, for the next petition day, on the request in writing of the petitioner's solicitor. In other cases it will be set down again upon the like request, accompanied by evidence that the object for which it was ordered to stand over, has been accomplished; and notice of its restoration to the list must then be given to the respondents.

Leave to amend. It frequently becomes necessary to amend petitions: it is usual to make the application for such amendments at the hearing, but amendments will be made even after the hearing.

Adjournment to Chambers. Sometimes in cases where money has to be paid out of court, and the titles of the different parties have to be investigated, and also in cases of infant wards of court asking for leave to marry, the petition is adjourned into chambers, and a summons to proceed is issued and worked out in the usual way; but a formal certificate may be dispensed with, and the order made in chambers, and a memorandum is then sent to the registrar to enable him to draw it up. It may, however, be ordered to be again brought on in court, and in that case the chief clerk annexes to the judge's copy petition, a minute of the result of the chief clerk's investigation, and a note of the evidence for the use of the registrar in drawing up the order (*u*).

Filing. Petitions on which any order is founded

<hr>

(*u*) Seton, 4th ed. 54 ; Haynes, 480.

must be filed at the central office, and an office copy transmitted to the District Registry; and until this is done the order cannot be passed (*v*).

———

SECTION 3.

Summonses.

We have already considered the manner in which the chief clerks make the enquiries and take the accounts directed by an order, and the result of which are incorporated in a certificate. But besides this ministerial business under judgments and orders, the chief clerks have certain judicial duties to perform, of the same nature as those performed by the judge in court; and like the judge's duties, these judicial duties of the chief clerks may arise either in actions or matters, and in the latter case (as will be seen in the second division of this work) such matters are sometimes *originated* in chambers and never come into court at all.

In this place, however, we are only concerned with such interlocutory applications in *actions* as are capable of being made in the judge's chambers, a method of proceeding which, from its superior economy, ought always to be pursued when possible, unless the object of the application is of such importance as to be hotly contested; in which case, as the summons in chambers would probably be adjourned into court for formal argument, it would be cheaper to commence the application by motion in the first instance.

Every application in chambers is made by a proceeding called a summons (*x*), which is in form a requisition by the judge, requiring all parties concerned to attend

———

(*v*) Cons. Ords. I. r. 44, and   Ord. XXXV. r. 2.
XXXIII. r. 23; and R. S. C.,   (*x*) R. S. C., Ord. LIV. r. 1.

at his chambers at a certain day and hour, when the application will be heard. With the exception of the matter to be heard, every such summons is similar in form to the summons to proceed under a judgment, an example of which has been given on page 162, and it is taken out and served (where service is necessary) in the same way. A summons, like a motion, may be either *ex parte* or on notice, and in the next chapter some of the more usual applications by summons (both *ex parte* and on notice) will be specified.

Counsel are not usually heard by the chief clerks (although V.-C. Bacon's and V.-C. Hall's chief clerks will hear counsel). Solicitors and suitors in person usually appear before them ; but if a case is of importance, either party can of right have it adjourned before the judge himself, and in that case counsel will be heard in his chambers (except in V.-C. Bacon's) ; and if there is any difficult point involved, it will be adjourned, either by the chief clerk or by the judge himself, into court for argument, and will then be placed in the list on the next adjourned summons day.

Service. A summons on notice must be served on all necessary parties two clear days at least before the day fixed for its return (*y*) ; and where this is found to be impracticable, an application should be made at the judge's chambers to extend the time for the return of the summons, and to make a new appointment. If the summons has not been served on anyone, this will be done, simply by altering the date named in the summons and re-sealing it. But if any party has been served, a memorandum will be made on the summons adjourning it (as to the parties not served) until a future date. At the original date the hearing will be

(*y*) Cons. Ord. XXXV. r. 7.

adjourned as to the parties already served for that date, until the date named in the memorandum (z).

Affidavit of Service. It must be remembered that where a party served does not appear, the usual affidavit of service must be produced to the chief clerk on the day of the hearing.

The Order. Orders in chambers, when of a simple nature, are drawn up by the chief clerks; but the judge may direct any order to be drawn up by the registrar, like an order made in court; and in that case a minute of the order is endorsed by the chief clerk on the summons, and signed and transmitted by him to the registrar attending in court on that day, by whom the order is drawn up, passed and entered, in the same way as an order made in court (a). Orders drawn up by the chief clerks must also be entered in the same manner, and in the same office, as orders made in open court (b).

Orders made in chambers have the same force and effect as orders made in court, and may be enforced in the same way (c).

Setting aside and varying Orders made in Chambers. Any order made by a judge in chambers may be set aside or varied by him on motion in court (of which notice must be given to the other side), made within twenty-one days of the order, unless the judge enlarges the time (d); and no appeal to the Court of Appeal will be heard unless such re-hearing has been had or refused, or unless the judge gives a certificate that he has heard the case in chambers and does not wish to have it further argued before him in court (e).

(z) Daniell's Ch. Pr. 1025.
(a) Ib. 1066.
(b) Cons. Ord. XXXV. r. 32.
(c) 15 & 16 Vict. c. 80, s. 15; R. S. C., Ord. XLII. r. 20.

(d) Jud. Act, 1873, s. 50; and *Dickson* v. *Harrison*, 26 W. R. 730.

(e) Ib.; and *Thomas* v. *Elsom*, L. R., 6 Ch. D. 346.

District Registrars. Where an action proceeds in a district registry, the registrar has power to exercise all the authority and jurisdiction of a judge in chambers on summons, and may refer any matter to the judge for his decision or direction. There is, however, this distinction, that an appeal from a registrar is not effected by adjournment of the summons to the judge himself, but by a new summons taken out in the judge's chambers within four days after the decision complained of (*f*); such an appeal is no stay of proceedings unless so ordered by the registrar or judge (*g*).

CHAPTER III.

SOME OF THE PRINCIPAL INTERLOCUTORY APPLICATIONS.

In a small work like this, it would be impossible to describe every kind of interlocutory application. In cases of doubt or difficulty the reader is referred to Daniell's Chancery Practice, in the second volume of which lists are given of all kinds of interlocutory applications, specifying whether they should be by motion, petition or summons. No attempt is here made to do more than mention a few of the ordinary and most important kinds of interlocutory applications.

SECTION 1.

Interlocutory Injunctions.

An injunction was formerly described to be a writ issuing out of Chancery, in the nature of a prohibition ;

(*f*) R. S. C., Ord. XXXV. rr. 4, 7.   (*g*) Ib. r. 8.

that is to say, a writ which had the same operation as a prohibition issued out of a court of common law. *Writs* of injunction are now, however, abolished, and an injunction is merely an order or judgment; and such order or judgment of itself has exactly the same effect as a writ of injunction formerly had, without the necessity of going to the trouble and expense of suing the writ out (*h*).

As has more than once been pointed out, this work only relates to procedure, and, therefore, the practitioner is referred to works treating of the substantive law and rules of equity for information as to when, and under what circumstances, an injunction will be granted.

Injunction should be claimed by the Writ of Summons. It is a general rule that no injunction will be granted unless it be asked for in the writ and claim; and, consequently, wherever there is a fear that a defendant *may* do an act which it is desirable that he should be prevented from doing, it is usual to claim an injunction *ex abundanti cautelâ*, although it may not be necessary to move for one.

Mode of Application. Assuming that an interlocutory injunction is considered desirable in any case, the proper mode of applying for it is by motion on notice. If, however, the need is urgent, an interim injunction will be granted on *ex parte* motion, founded on an affidavit. Such an injunction is usually only granted until the next motion day after due notice of motion can be given.

Undertaking in Damages. It may here be at once mentioned that an interlocutory injunction when

(*h*) R. S. C., Ord. LII. r. 8.

granted, is almost always granted only upon the terms of the plaintiff undertaking to pay all damages which the defendant may suffer in consequence of the injunction, if it shall turn out, on the hearing of the action, that the interlocutory injunction has been improperly granted. Occasionally this rule is not enforced where the right to the injunction is clear and undoubted; but in the vast majority of cases it is otherwise.

Notice of Injunction. As soon as an interlocutory injunction has been granted, notice should be served on all parties affected by it that the order has been made; and if any person disobeys the order after notice of it, he will be liable to be committed or attached for contempt (*i*). The order is finally drawn up and passed and entered in the usual way, and disobedience to it is enforced in the same way as disobedience to any other order or judgment.

Dissolving an Injunction. An interlocutory injunction may be always dissolved on motion made for that purpose, of which notice should, of course, be given. If the need for dissolving the injunction is urgent, an *ex parte* motion (or "shot") should be made, for leave to serve short notice of motion. Of course such cases are fought tooth and nail, and strong evidence is required to dissolve an injunction granted on a contested motion.

It must not be forgotten that an interlocutory order remains in force only until the hearing; and, therefore, if an injunction is to be perpetual, it should be expressly " continued " by the judgment.

(*i*) See *Ex parte Langley*, L. R.,   that a telegram was a sufficient
13 Ch. D. 110, where it was held   notice.

SECTION 2.

Receivers.

As in the case of an injunction, it is no part of this work to enter into the consideration of the circumstances which will authorize the appointment of a receiver. It is assumed in speaking of the procedure, that circumstances exist which render the appointment desirable.

Mode of applying. The mode of applying for a receiver is, in all important cases, by motion; but where the subject-matter is small, it would seem that a receiver will now be appointed on summons in chambers (*k*).

As in the case of an injunction, if the appointment of a receiver is a substantial part of the action, a receiver should be asked for in the writ and statement of claim (*l*).

Inquiry as to Fitness. The appointment of a *specified* person as receiver is not usually made by the court on the hearing of the motion, although it sometimes is; and when one of the parties will undertake to be responsible for the person proposed, he will sometimes be appointed interim receiver, *i. e.* until a receiver is appointed in the ordinary way. The ordinary order is, that a "proper person be appointed receiver," in which case the chief clerk inquires at chambers (on a summons to proceed in the ordinary way) as to the fitness of any person proposed to him, and of persons or societies who must be proposed as sureties for such receiver (*m*); and, if he is satisfied, a recognizance of the

(*k*) *Macauley* v. *Pocock*, L. T., 8th Dec. 1877, p. 100; R. S. C., Ord. LII. r. 4.

(*l*) R. S. C., Ord. II. r. 1; Ord. III. rr. 1, 3; *Colebourne* v. *Colebourne*, L. R., 1 Ch. D. 690.

(*m*) Cons. Ord. XXIV. r. 1.

receiver and two sureties to the two senior Chancery judges is taken by way of security. It is only under most exceptional circumstances that sureties will be dispensed with (n), and each surety must make an affidavit that he is worth the amount for which he binds himself, after payment of all his debts. The recognizance and affidavit having been left at the judge's chambers and approved, a further summons to appoint the party approved as receiver is necessary.

Even where a specified party is appointed receiver in the order made on the motion in court, his appointment is almost invariably made conditional upon his "bringing in his security;" and in such a case he will not be a receiver in fact, until his security is given (o): but of course in such a case the appointment is complete on the security being given, and no final summons to appoint him is necessary.

Appointment of a Party to the Action. Where a party to the action wishes to propose himself as receiver, he must obtain leave to do so, which is usually applied for on the hearing of the application for the appointment of a receiver. In such cases he is usually appointed *without* salary; and sometimes, if largely interested, without giving security. A stranger appointed receiver is usually paid 5 per cent. of the gross receipts; but this is reduced where the estate is large, or may be augmented under exceptional circumstances (p).

Refusal to pay or hand over Property to a Receiver. Where persons in possession of property, ordered to be paid or delivered to a receiver, refuse to

(n) See Daniell's Ch. Pr. 1584.

(o) *Edwards* v. *Edwards*, L. R., 2 Ch. D. 291.

(p) See *Potts* v. *Leighton*, 15 Ves. 276; *Re Ormsby*, 1 Ba. & B. 189.

pay or deliver over the same, the order should be personally served upon them; and if they still refuse, an *ex parte* motion should be made to the court (founded on an affidavit of service of the order and non-compliance), for an appropriate writ of execution. Any attempt to disturb a receiver is a contempt of court, and will be punished accordingly.

Powers. The consideration of the powers of a receiver belongs rather to a work on Equity jurisprudence than to one treating only of procedure, but it may generally be stated that they are very limited, and that he should, when in any doubt as to what course he ought to take, request the party who has the conduct of the action to apply by summons for directions, and if such party neglects to apply, he may do so himself (*q*).

A receiver may, however, without leave, let lands from year to year, or for a term not exceeding three years, or may put an end to such tenancies, but may not eject on his own responsibility (*r*); nor should he pledge the estate to any expense, nor entrust money belonging to the estate to improper persons.

Accounts. The order appointing the receiver, appoints the days on which he must pass his accounts (*s*), and such accounts must be made out in a form which can be obtained at the law stationers.

On the day named, the receiver leaves the account at the chambers, and (on the first occasion only) also a copy of the order appointing him receiver, certified to be a true copy by his solicitor. At the same time he takes out a summons to proceed on his accounts, which

(*q*) *Ireland* v. *Eade*, 7 Bea. 55; *Parker* v. *Dunn*, 8 Bea. 497.

(*r*) Daniell's Ch. Pr. 1597.
(*s*) Cons. Ord. XXIV. r. 2.

is served in the usual way (t). The account is then gone through in the same manner as other accounts.

If a receiver does not leave his account at the appointed dates, any party concerned may take out a summons calling upon him to do so, and if he disobeys the order made on such summons, he may be committed for contempt in the usual way. If a receiver does not pay in balances found to be due from him on his account, a similar course should be pursued; but in that case a certificate of the paymaster-general will be necessary that the payment has not been made (u). The receiver will in such cases also be charged with 5 per cent. interest, and he may be required to attend at chambers, to show cause why he has not passed his accounts or paid his balances, and directions may be given proper to ensure the prosecution thereof by some interested party for the discharge of the receiver and the appointment of another, and payment of costs by the receiver. Or a certificate by the chief clerk of the receiver's default or neglect, or of any abandonment of the proceedings, may be filed; and after such certificate, unless discharged, none of the parties are to be at liberty to further prosecute proceedings in chambers without order; but on the certificate becoming binding, any party may apply to the court, and the court may make such order as may seem proper. And for that purpose the official solicitor may be directed to summon the person whose attendance is required, and to conduct any proceedings, and carry out any directions, his costs being paid, as the judge may direct (x).

Discharge. When all the receiver's duties are

(t) Ib. r. 3.　　　　et seq.
(u) See Daniell's Ch. Pr. 1602　(x) Cons. Ord. XXXV. r. 23.

effected, he will be discharged, and his recognizances vacated, on an affidavit of the balance having been paid to the proper parties, or a certificate of the paymaster-general, as the case may be. Such discharge is granted on further consideration, or by motion, petition, or summons. A receiver (like a trustee) will not without good cause be discharged before all his duties are effected, without paying all the costs occasioned by the change (*y*).

SECTION 3.

Ne exeat Regno.

A *ne exeat regno* is a writ addressed to the sheriff of the county in which a defendant is resident, commanding him to take bail from the defendant not to quit England without leave of the court (*z*).

It used to be a rule that this writ would only issue where the plaintiff had a claim enforceable in a court of equity, and since the passing of the Judicature Acts the rule is only so far modified that the writ will also be issued where the case can be brought within sect. 6 of the Debtors Act, 1869 (*a*). However, it is outside the province of this work to discuss the substantive law relating to the issue of the writ.

How applied for. The writ is applied for by *ex parte* motion, which may be made (if advisable) before the writ of summons is issued. The motion must be supported by a positive and strong affidavit, stating that the defendant is about to leave England for the purpose of avoiding the demand of the plaintiff. Mere

(*y*) Daniell's Ch. Pr. 1613.
(*z*) Hunter's Suit, 147.

(*a*) *Drover* v. *Beyer*, L. R., 13 Ch. D. 242.

belief will not be sufficient (b).   Like an *ex parte* injunction, the writ is rarely issued except upon the
plaintiff undertaking to pay damages if adjudged to
do so.

An order being obtained, the writ is engrossed on
parchment, and indorsed with the name and address of
the party or solicitor issuing it, in the same way as a
writ of summons, and also with the amount of security
to be taken by the sheriff.   The writ is then taken to
the central office, together with a *præcipe* or request to
seal it, which is done.   The writ is then forwarded to
the under-sheriff of the county into which it issues, by
whom it is executed and returned (c).

Discharging the Writ.   As in the case of an injunction, so in that of a *ne exeat*, the party against whom
it is issued may move on notice to discharge it, on the
ground, either that the plaintiff has no case, or that the
defendant is not intending to go abroad, or upon his
paying the money into court (d).

Where a defendant wishes to obtain damages for the
unnecessary issue of the writ, he should lose no time in
applying for its discharge, as otherwise he may be taken
to have waived his claim (e).

———

SECTION 4.

Accounts.

In all cases of ordinary accounts, as for instance in
the case of a partnership or executorship, or ordinary

(b) Daniell's Ch. Pr. 1554.   L. J., N. S. 374 ; Daniell's Ch.
(c) Ayckbourne, 8th ed. 285.   Pr. 1559.
(d) *Sichel* v. *Raphael*, 4 L. T.,   (e) *Lees* v. *Patterson*, L. R., 7
N. S. 114 ; *James* v. *North*, 28   Ch. D. 866.

trust account, where the plaintiff in the first instance desires to have an account taken, the writ of summons should be endorsed with a claim that such account be taken (*f*) ; and in that case in default of appearance, and also after appearance, unless the defendant by affidavit or otherwise satisfy the court or a judge that there is some preliminary question to be tried, an order for the account claimed with all usual directions will be forthwith made (*g*) on an application by summons or notice, supported by an affidavit stating concisely the grounds of the plaintiff's claim for an account (*h*).

It would seem that where the account claimed is an executorship or administration account, or where there is, in fact, no issue to be tried, the usual administration judgment will be made on the hearing of the summons without the necessity of afterwards going into court (*i*), and in that case the further consideration will be adjourned with liberty to apply (*j*).

A district registrar can only make an order for an account where default has been made in appearance (*k*).

In addition to the accounts above referred to, the court or a judge may at any stage of the proceedings direct any necessary inquiries or accounts to be made or taken, notwithstanding that it may appear that there is some special or further relief sought for, or some special issue to be tried, as to which it may be proper that the action should proceed in the ordinary manner (*l*).

(*f*) R. S. C., Ord. III. r. 8.

(*g*) R. S. C., Ord. XV. r. 1.

(*h*) Ib. r. 2.

(*i*) Haynes, 61 ; and Seton, 4th ed. p. 8 ; *Re Hackwell, David* v. *Dalton*, W. N. 1879, p. 86.

(*j*) See *Gatti* v. *Webster*, L. R., 12 Ch. D. 771.

(*k*) *Irlam* v. *Irlam*, L. R., 2 Ch. D. 608.

(*l*) R. S. C., Ord. XXXIII. ; *Turquand* v. *Wilson*, L. R., 1 Ch. D. 85.

Of course accounts ordered under these provisions are taken in the ordinary way.

SECTION 5.

Allowance pending Litigation.

Wherever any property forms the subject of any proceedings, and the judge is satisfied that it is more than sufficient to answer all claims on it which ought to be provided for in the action, he may on summons on notice, at any time make an allowance to any of the parties, of the whole or part of the annual income; or (where it is personalty) of part of the corpus, up to such time as the court shall think fit (*m*). Strong circumstances are, however, necessary to induce the exercise of this power, and there must be no doubt as to the title of the parties claiming it (*n*).

SECTION 6.

Consolidation of Actions.

Where two or more actions are brought by one plaintiff against the same defendant, they may be ordered to be consolidated. And so also where divers actions are brought by one plaintiff for the same cause of action against several defendants, the court or a judge will, on motion, or on summons on notice, stay proceedings in all but one, making that one a test action (*o*). And it would seem that where a series of

(*m*) 15 & 16 Vict. c. 86, s. 57.   652.
(*n*) *Rowley* v. *Burgess*, 2 W. R.   (*o*) R. S. C., Ord. LI. r. 4.

actions are brought by several plaintiffs against one defendant, a test action will be ordered, and the others will be stayed in the meanwhile (*p*); and in the case of administration actions they will be consolidated or all stayed but one, so far as they ask for the same relief (*q*).

Where the actions are in different divisions of the court or (all being in the Chancery Division) they are assigned to different judges, they must (before being consolidated) be transferred to one division and judge, and then he must be asked to consolidate or stay them (*r*).

Section 7.

Transfer of Actions.

Any action may be transferred from one *division* of the court to another, either by an order of that division or of a judge thereof, on motion or summons (*s*), or by an order of the Lord Chancellor (*t*), but only with the permission of the president of the division to which it is to be assigned; and any action may be transferred from one *judge* of the Chancery Division to another by an order of the Lord Chancellor (*u*).

The Lord Chancellor will direct the transfer of any action on a written application to his secretary, accom-

---

(*p*) *Smith* v. *Chadwick*, L. R., 4 Ch. D. 867 ; 9 Ch. D. 457.

(*q*) See *Re Aird, Maton* v. *Quick*, 26 W. R. 441.

(*r*) *Evans* v. *Debenham*, 24 W. R. 900 ; *Holmes* v. *Harvey*, 25 W. R. 80.

(*s*) R. S. C., Ord. LI. r. 2 ; *Hillman* v. *Mayhew*, L. R., 1 Ex. D. 132.

(*t*) R. S. C., Ord. LI. r. 1.

(*u*) Ib. ; and *Chapman* v. *Real Property Co.*, L. R., 7 Ch. D. 732.

panied by the written consent of all parties; but where all parties do not consent, the application should be made to his lordship in court (*x*). An order transferring an action to the Chancery Division should name the judge to whom it is transferred (*y*).

An action will be transferred to a division in which it can be more appropriately and conveniently disposed of (*z*) ; and in one case (*a*), V.-C. Hall stated that an opinion existed among the judges, that where issues of fact were to be tried by a jury, it would be better to transfer the action to the Queen's Bench Division. But this principle has not been very freely put into practice.

Transfer of Administration Actions. There is a very important exception to the general rule as to the transfer of actions, viz., in the case of administration actions, in which the judge to whom they are assigned may after judgment, or order for administration, and without any further consent, order the transfer to himself of any action pending in any *other division* (but not in the court of any other judge of his own division (*b*)), brought or continued by or against the executors or administrators of the deceased person whose assets are being administered (*c*).

Such an order may be obtained on *ex parte* motion, leaving it to the other side to move to discharge it (*d*).

(*x*) Memorandum, Nov. 10th, 1875, L. R., 1 Ch. D. 41.

(*y*) R. S. C., Ord. LI. r. 3.

(*z*) See *Hillman* v. *Mayhew*, L. R., 1 Ex. D. 132 ; *Holloway* v. *York*, L. R., 2 Ex. D. 333 ; *Humphreys* v. *Edwards*, 45 L. J., Ch. 112.

(*a*) *Clements* v. *Norris*, W. N. 1878, p. 4.

(*b*) See *Re Madras, &c. Co.,* L. R., 16 Ch. D. 702.

(*c*) R. S. C., Ord. LI. r. 2a.

(*d*) *Field* v. *Field*, W. N. 1877, p. 98 ; *Whitaker* v. *Robinson*, ib. 201 ; *Re Landore Steel Co.*, L. R., 10 Ch. D. 487.

The same rule applies to cases of the winding-up of joint stock companies; but these are " matters" and not " actions."

<hr>

SECTION 8.
Removal of Proceedings from District Registry.

As we have already seen a *defendant* can remove an action from a district registry, to the central office without leave ; but *any party* may apply to the court or a judge, or to the district registrar, for an order for the removal on reasonable grounds ; and, on the other hand, an action may be similarly removed from the central office to a district registry (*a*).   The application should be made by summons served in the usual way, and if granted the district registrar transmits to the proper master of the Supreme Court at the record and writ office all original documents filed with him, and a copy of all entries in his books of proceedings in the action (*b*).

Where an application in an action is made to the court the proceedings are *ipso facto* removed thenceforward to the central office (*c*).

<hr>

SECTION 9.
Special Cases.

By Agreement or Compulsorily. Sometimes the question in dispute is merely a question of law, and in that case the parties may, after the issue of the writ, concur in stating it in the form of a special case for the opinion of the court (*d*) ; and where no such

(*a*) Jud. Act, 1873, s. 65; R. S. C., Ord. XXXV. r. 13.
(*b*) Ib. r. 14.
(*c*) *Dyson* v. *Pickles*, 27 W. R. 376.
(*d*) R. S. C., Ord. XXXIV. r. 1.

agreement is come to, the court, or more usually the judge on summons on notice, may in its or his discretion make an order ordering a special case, wherever there is a question of law which it would be convenient to have decided before any evidence is given or any question of fact tried (e). Where the fact that a question of law has to be determined appears on the pleadings, no further evidence is required in support of such application; but where it is made before the pleadings are delivered, an affidavit of the facts should be made, showing that the determination of the question of law may render it unnecessary to go into the facts (f).

Printing. Special cases must be printed by the plaintiff, and signed by the parties or their solicitors, and filed by the plaintiff, who must also deliver printed copies for the use of the judge (g).

No special case, where a party is under disability, can be set down for argument without leave of a judge, obtained on summons, supported by affidavit that the statements of fact in such case, so far as they affect the party under disability, are true (h).

The parties may, if they think fit, enter into a written agreement (which is not subject to stamp duty), that according as the judgment of the court is in favour of one or the other, a fixed sum or sums to be ascertained shall be paid by one party to the other, either with or without costs; and the judgment of the court may be entered for the sum so agreed or ascertained with or without costs, as the case may be, and execution may issue on such judgment forthwith (i).

(e) Ib. r. 2.
(f) *Metropolitan Board* v. *New River Co.*, L. R., 1 Q. P. D. 727
(g) R. S. C., Ord. XXXIV. r. 3.
(h) Ib. r. 4.
(i) Ib. r. 6.

A special case may be set down for argument by either party, by delivery to the registrar of a memorandum of entry, and production of the order, where an order is necessary, giving leave to set it down (*k*).

A special case is argued like a demurrer; and as the decision of the points of law is only a decision or finding of the specific issues or questions in dispute between the parties, it is necessary to formally move for judgment. On setting down the case therefore, it should be set down not merely for argument, but *also on motion for judgment*, and notice of motion should be duly given to the other parties, otherwise motion for judgment will have to be made subsequently (*l*).

It may be mentioned, that the old method of stating special cases under 13 & 14 Vict. c. 35, has been abolished (*m*).

———

Section 10.

Miscellaneous Interlocutory Applications.

In addition to those above referred to, there are numerous interlocutory applications which may be made in actions, the most usual of which have been incidentally referred to under other heads.

Applications by Summons. For instance, the following applications may be made by summons:—

1. As to the guardianship of infants (except the appointment of guardian *ad litem*), and as to maintenance or advancement of infants; and as to allowing a ward of court to go out of the jurisdiction, and generally as to the administration of the estates of infant wards of court.

(*k*) R. S. C., Ord. XXXIV. r. 5.   (*m*) R. S. C., Ord. XXXIV.
(*l*) Seton, 4th ed. 14.   r. 7.

2. For payment of money out of court, where the fund does not exceed 300l. cash or stock. In all other cases the application must bo by petition.

3. All applications for enlarging time.

4. All questions relating to the conduct of actions or matters.

5. All applications for payment into court of purchase-moneys under sales by the court, and for investment of the same.

6. In all cases of arbitration to appoint an umpire under the Common Law Procedure Act, 1854.

7. Applications for payment to any person of the dividends or interest of any stock, bonds, or securities, standing to the credit of any cause or matter depending to the separate account of such person.

8. Applications for special orders for taxation, or reviewal of taxation of costs.

9. Applications for transferring an action from or to a county court.

10. Applications for divers orders as to the conduct of an action in chambers, and the procedure in chambers under judgments.

11. Applications as to the management of property—as to receivers when appointed—inspection of mines, in the course of an action—for change of investments—for leases and management of estates in litigation by trustees who are parties to the action.

Applications by Motion of course. With regard to interlocutory orders obtainable by motion of course, and *not by petition of course*, there are now only four, viz.—(1) A final order of foreclosure or redemption; (2) Orders *nisi* and absolute to confirm the commissioners' certificate in partition actions; (3) Orders making an order of the House of Lords an order of the court; and (4) Orders for *subpœna duces tecum* to prove exhibits at the hearing.

Orders obtainable on Petition of course. These are very numerous, and include orders by consent, to enable a defendant to enter an appearance after judgment; to enter a conditional appearance (without consent); to withdraw appearance entered for defendant by mistake (by consent); for sheriff to return writ of attachment; for leave to attend proceedings where served with decree; to discharge process of contempt (by consent); to examine a witness *de bene esse* where he is dangerously ill, or very old, or about to leave the kingdom; to discharge a *distringas* on the application of the party who lodged it: for the appointment of a guardian *ad litem* to an infant, or married woman, or lunatic, on their own application; to dissolve injunction (by consent); to appoint a new next friend or relator in place of a deceased one; for security for costs where plaintiff's residence abroad appears by the writ; to change the solicitor; to stay proceedings (by consent); and some others not of a sufficiently usual character to need notice here.

DIVISION II.

———◆———

OF MATTERS.

PRELIMINARY.

HAVING now finished the consideration of actions, it is desirable that some notice should be taken of "matters," or summary proceedings not commenced by writ of summons. Matters are commenced in several ways, the method of instituting them being generally prescribed by the statutes by which they are authorized. The most usual method of commencing a matter is by petition. Some are, however, commenced by summons, and some by affidavit, and some by motion. With regard to those commenced by petition, motion or summons, the remarks upon these proceedings, as used in actions, contained in Sub-division XI., Chapter II. of the first Division of this Work, are equally applicable to petitions, motions and summonses in "matters;" save only that, with regard to summonses by which matters are commenced (and which are called "originating summonses"), the form is slightly different to the form of summonses used upon interlocutory applications.

It may also be remarked, that in all documents relating to matters, the parties are not stated as in actions, but the document is intituled "In the matter of," &c., stating the matter to which it refers.

Matters relating to Trustees.

———◆———

CHAPTER I.

PETITIONS FOR THE OPINION OF THE COURT (*a*).

ANY trustee, executor or administrator, or any beneficiary (*b*), is at liberty, without the institution of an action, to apply by petition (*c*) to the High Court (assigning the petition to any judge of the Chancery Division except the junior judge), for the opinion or direction of such judge on any question of minor importance arising in the administration of the trust (*d*); for instance, as to investments, payment of debts, maintenance of infants and lunatics not so found, repairs, leasing, consenting to a sale, and the like (*e*).

But the court will not give an opinion or direction on points involving questions of complicated detail (*f*),

(*a*) 22 & 23 Vict. c. 35, s. 30.

(*b*) *Re Ward*, 13 L.T., N.S. 495.

(*c*) The act also says by summons, but in practice the application should be by petition. *Re Dennis*, 5 Jur., N. S. 1388.

(*d*) *Re Muggeridge*, Johns. 15; *Re Mockett* (loc. cit.); *Re Spiller*, 8 W. R. 333; *Re Leslie*, W. N. 1876, p. 93; *Re Jacob*, 9 W. R. 474.

(*e*) *Re Knowles*, 18 L. T., N. S. 809; *Re Box*, 1 H. & M. 552; *Re Lord Hotham*, L. R., 12 Eq. 76; *Re Breed*, L. R., 1 Ch. D. 226; *Re Kershaw*, L. R., 6 Eq. 322; *Re T——*, L. R., 15 Ch. D. 78; *Cuthbertson* v. *Wood*, 19 W. R. 265; *Re Shaw*, ib. 129; *Earl Powlett* v. *Hood*, L. R., 5 Eq. 115.

(*f*) *Re Barrington*, 1 J. & H. 89.

nor on questions of difficulty (g), nor on questions of construction (h), nor on hypothetical cases (i).

Effect of Judicial Opinion. The advice of the court, if acted on, operates as an indemnity to the trustee who has not been found guilty of any fraud, or wilful concealment, or misrepresentation in obtaining it (j); but it binds no one, and does not prevent an action being brought to administer the trust; and in any such action the opinion of the judge is subject to be overruled (k).

Title of Petition. A petition under this act must be headed like a pleading and intituled in the matter of the act, and in the matter of the particular will, trust, or administration; and must be addressed to Her Majesty's High Court of Justice, and marked with the name and division of the court, and of the judge to whom it is assigned (l).

Service. The act says that it must be served seven clear days before the hearing upon all persons interested, or such of them as the judge shall think expedient (m); and it would seem that the trustees should serve all such persons as they think necessary, and state in the note at the end of the petition whom they have served. It is not permissible to bring on the petition merely to find out who should be served (n), but of course, if all

(g) *Marsh* v. *Att.-Gen.*, 2 J. & H. 61.

(h) *Re Evans*, 30 Bea. 232; *Re Lorenz*, 1 Dr. & Sm. 401; *Re Hooper*, 29 Bea. 657; but see *Re Michel*, 28 Bea. 39; *Re Green*, 8 W. R. 403; *Re Davies*, 9 W. R. 134; *Re Elmore*, 6 Jur., N. S. 1325; *Re Pett*, 27 Bea. 576; *Re Peyton*, 10 W. R. 515.

(i) *Re Box*, 1 H. & M. 552.

(j) 22 & 23 Vict. c. 35, s. 30.

(k) *Re Mockett*, Johns. 628.

(l) Gen. Ord. 20th Mar. 1860.

(m) 22 & 23 Vict. c. 35, s. 30; and Gen. Ord. March, 1860, r. 3.

(n) *Re Green*, 8 W. R. 403, overruling *Re Muggeridge*, sup.; *Re Tuck*, W. N. 1869, p. 15. In *Re Larken*, W. N. 1872, p. 85, it was said that it was generally unnecessary to serve anyone.

. necessary parties are not served, the petition will be ordered to stand over in order that they may be; and, on the other hand, service may be dispensed with (o).

Presentation and Hearing. The petition is presented and answered and set down by the secretary, and heard in the ordinary way, but no evidence is admitted, and no inquiries will be directed (p). The opinion when given is passed and entered like an order, and is called "a judicial opinion," or "advice," or "direction," as the case may be (q).

Formerly the petition had to be signed by counsel (r), but whether this is now necessary would appear doubtful (s). However, there can be no harm in signing it, and until the point is decided, it will be well to do so.

CHAPTER II.

THE TRUSTEE RELIEF ACTS AND THE LEGACY DUTY ACT.

IF a person have in his hands trust moneys, or any government or parliamentary securities, and a difficulty arises in determining the ownership of them, the trustee need not incur the risk of paying it over to the person whom he considers to be entitled, although *he may* do so if he likes to run the risk of having to refund it, in the event of it appearing that he has paid the wrong party. A trustee, placed in a situation of difficulty of this nature, may either commence an action for the administration of the trust, or he may pay the money, or

(o) *Re Larken,* W. N. 1872, p. 85.

(p) *Re Mockett,* sup.

(q) Gen. Ord. 20th Mar. 1860, r. 4.

(r) 23 & 24 Vict. c. 38, s. 9.

(s) R. S. C., Ord. XIX. r. 4.

transfer the securities, into court under the above acts (*t*), which is a much cheaper and easier method; the only difference being, that in the action the trustee could pass his accounts, and get his discharge, whereas, by paying the money into court under the Trustee Relief Acts, he still remains a trustee, and is liable at any time to be called on to account for his trusteeship (*u*).

Affidavit. A trustee who wishes to take advantage of these acts must file an affidavit, which requires very careful preparation, and is, therefore, almost invariably drafted by an equity counsel. This affidavit is headed, " In the High Court of Justice, Chancery Division," but no particular judge is mentioned. It is intituled in the matter of the trust, shortly describing it, as, for instance, thus: "In the matter of the trusts of the will of A. B., the sum of 1,000*l*. bequeathed in favour of C. D." The affidavit is further intituled, "In the matter of the Act 10 & 11 Vict. c. 96, intituled, ' An Act for better securing trust funds, and for the relief of trustees.' "

The affidavit then proceeds to state the facts under which the money is paid in, and the draftsman must take particular care to set forth :—

1. The deponent's name and address.
2. The place where the deponent is to be served with any petition, summons or order, or with notice of any proceeding relating to such money or securities.
3. The amount of money (in words, not figures (*x*)), and description, and amount, of securities in question, and the credit to which he wishes such

(*t*) 10 & 11 Vict. c. 96 ; 12 & 13 Vict. c. 74.

(*u*) See Underhill on Trusts, 167.

(*x*) *Re Watts*, 21 W. R. 701.

money or securities to be placed, remembering that a separate account must not exceed thirty-six words : and if such money or securities are chargeable with legacy or succession duty, a statement whether such duty, or any part of it, has or has not been paid.

4. A short description of the trust, and of the instrument creating it.

5. The names of the persons interested in the money or securities, and their places of residence to the best of the deponent's knowledge and belief.

6. The deponent's submission to answer all such enquiries relating to the application of the money or securities, as the court or judge may make, or direct.

7. A statement whether the money in question, or the dividends on the securities in question, and all accumulations of dividends thereon, are desired to be invested in consols, or reduced annuities, or New Three per Cents.; or whether it is deemed unnecessary so to invest them, or to place them on deposit (y).

Printing Affidavit. This affidavit *must* be printed and filed in the usual way; and on production of a printed office copy to the paymaster-general he will give the necessary directions (z).

Notice. The money, stock or securities having been paid or transferred into, or deposited in, court, the trustee should give notice of the fact to all parties interested (a); but where this cannot be done, at least without great trouble and expense, the trustee must use his discretion as to advertising and otherwise taking steps for bringing the

(y) C. F. r. 34. (z) Ib. (a) C. F. Am. Ord. V.

matter to the knowledge of the party interested. No directions will be given to the trustee with regard to dispensing with notice on application by him for that purpose; but when a party interested applies to the court by petition for payment out of the money, the court will then consider whether all requisite notices have been given, and, if not, the petition will be ordered to stand over until they are given (b).

Supplemental Affidavit. Not infrequently errors occur in the original affidavit, and in that case a supplemental one may be filed, intituled like the original, and commencing, " I, A. B. &c. of, &c. by way of supplement to and in correction of any affidavit filed in this matter on the   day of   18 , make oath and say as follows." A trustee has even been permitted to pay into court a further sum, on such an affidavit, when he has omitted to pay in such sum on, and mention it in, the original one.

Petition. The money, stock or securities will be dealt with on the petition of (or where they are under 300l. in amount or value on summons taken out by) the parties, or some or one of the parties named in the affidavit as being interested (c). Any person claiming an interest, who is not named in the affidavit, must proceed by action (d). The petition must be intituled like the affidavit (e), and must be marked with the name of the judge to whose court it is desired to be assigned.

(b) *Re Hardley*, L. R., 10 Ch. D. 664; and see *Re Hansford*, 7 W. R. 199, 254; *Re Goodman*, W. N. 1870, p. 152; *Re Palmer*, W. N. 1873, p. 101.

(c) 10 & 11 Vict. c. 96, s. 2; and C. F. Am. Ord. VI.

(d) *Re Jephson*, 1 L. T., N. S. 5; *Crause* v. *Cooper*, 1 J. & H. 207.

(e) C. F. Am. Ord. X.

The petition should first state the trust instrument, then the affidavit under which the payment or transfer into or deposit in court was made, and then such other facts as are necessary to support the petitioner's contention; and where the fund is chargeable with legacy or succession duty, it must be stated whether such duty has or has not been paid (*f*). The petition or summons must also name a place where the petitioner or applicant may be served with any petition or summons, or notice of any proceeding or order relating to the trust fund (*g*).

The petition is presented, answered and set down in the ordinary way, and must be served on the trustees, and on all parties claiming any interest in the property, unless of course they join as co-petitioners (*h*); and, on the hearing, the court will (if necessary) decide the question which occasioned the difficulty to the trustee (*i*), and may even order payment to a person not petitioning (*j*). If not satisfied as to the facts by affidavit, at the request of the parties the court may order an inquiry in chambers (*k*). But, on the other hand, the court may direct an action to be instituted, where it appears that the fund cannot be safely distributed without (*l*).

(*f*) C. F. Am. Ord. XI.

(*g*) Ib. Ord. IX.

(*h*) Ib. Ords. VII. VIII.

(*i*) *Re Bloye*, 1 M. & G. 488; *Lewis* v. *Hillman*, 3 H. L. 607; *Re Allen*, Kay, Append. 51; *Re Dalton*, 1 D., M. & G. 265; and see cases collected in Morgan's Ch. Acts, p. 71, 5th ed.

(*j*) *Re Woolland*, 18 Jur. 1012.

(*k*) *Re Wood*, 15 Sim. 469; *Re Trower*, 1 L. T., N. S. 54; R. S. C., Ord. XXXIII.

(*l*) 10 & 11 Vict. c. 96, s. 2. For instance, a breach of trust cannot be remedied on petition. *Re Lloyd*, 2 W. R. 271; and see for other cases, *Re Foyard*, 24 L. J., Ch. 441; *Thorp* v. *Thorp*, 1 K. & J. 438; *Re Sharpe*, 15 Sim. 470.

Several Petitions. It sometimes happens that two or more petitions, praying for payment or transfer out of court are presented and heard at the same time by the different parties claiming; and where a claim is disputed, this is the proper course to adopt, unless by arrangement the necessity of a cross petition is dispensed with (*m*). In such cases one or more of the petitions will generally be dismissed, and the order made on one only.

Costs. The trustees are, as a general rule, entitled to their costs of appearing on the petition; but by paying, transferring into, or depositing in court, the trustees submit themselves to the jurisdiction, and may even be ordered to *pay* costs, where they have availed themselves of the act vexatiously or improperly; as where they require an unreasonable amount of evidence of identity or otherwise (*n*).

Where Accounts disputed. The Trustee Relief Acts do not afford any means of taking accounts, and therefore if a *cestui que trust* disputes the amount of the money paid in, he must bring an action against the trustees in the ordinary way.

Dissentient Trustees. Where all the trustees do not consent to pay or transfer into or deposit in court under the act, the majority may petition the court to be allowed to do so, and the court may order any person in whose hands the monies or securities may be, to pay or deliver them up to the majority of the trustees, for the purpose of being paid or transferred into or depo-

---

(*m*) *Lewis* v. *Hillman*, 3 H. L. Ca. 607.

(*n*) See *Re Elliott*, L. R., 15 Eq. 194; *Cater's Trusts*, 25 Bea.

366; *Knight's Trusts*, 27 Bea. 45; *Wyllys' Trusts*, 8 W. R. 645; Underhill Tr. 167 et seq.

sited in court (*o*). The petition should be intituled in the matter of the trust, and in the matter of the Trustee Relief Act, and of the act 12 & 13 Vict. c. 74, and should be served on the trustees who do not concur (*p*).

Legacy Duty Act. Under the Legacy Duty Act (36 Geo. 3, c. 52, s. 32), a cheaper method exists of paying money or transferring stock into court where, by reason of the infancy or absence beyond the seas, of any person entitled to a legacy, or to the residue of any personal estate, or any part thereof, chargeable with legacy duty, such money or stock cannot be paid to the party entitled. Under this act money may be paid in on a simple request to the paymaster-general; but stock cannot be transferred without an order obtained on *ex parte* motion, petition or summons. The money or stock will be dealt with on petition or (where under 300*l.*) on summons, or even on motion.

CHAPTER III.

THE TRUSTEE ACTS.

Principal Enactments of the Acts. Although it is not intended in this work to treat in any way of substantive law, it seems absolutely necessary that a very short account should be given of the alterations in the *law* made by the above acts, in order to render the *practice* under them intelligible: but the reader must remember that such an account is merely by way of

(*o*) 12 & 13 Vict. c. 74.　　(*p*) *Re Bryant*, W. N. 1868, p. 123.

" inducement," as the old special pleaders would have put it, and is not intended as in any way a treatise on the Trustee Acts, for which the reader is referred to Mr. Lewin's work and to Morgan's Chancery Acts and Orders.

The acts in question were passed to remedy the difficulty which formerly existed, when it became necessary to appoint new trustees and the legal estate in the property was outstanding in a lunatic, or infant, or a person who refused to obey an order of the court commanding him to execute a proper conveyance. Formerly the court could only appoint new trustees in a suit commenced for that purpose, which was of course an expensive and dilatory mode of procedure; and when the new trustees were appointed, it had no means of vesting the legal trust estate in them, except by ordering the person in whom it was vested to convey it on pain of imprisonment or sequestration, a method which was of course inapplicable to the case of persons *non compos mentis*, or infants, and was of no avail even against a contumacious sane adult who had sufficient fortitude to defy the court.

But by these acts, it was provided that where a lunatic, or person of unsound mind, or an infant, or person out of the jurisdiction, or a person who cannot be found, or about whom it is uncertain whether he be living or dead, is seised or possessed, as trustee or mortgagee, of lands, or of a contingent right therein, or solely or jointly of stock, or a chose in action, or where it is not known which of several trustees of land was the survivor, or where a trustee of lands has died intestate and without leaving an heir, or where such heir or devisee is not known, or where stock is standing in the name of a

R 2

deceased person whose personal representative is a lunatic or person of unsound mind, or where a chose in action is vested in such a personal representative, or where lands are subject to a contingent right in any unborn person or class of persons who upon coming into existence would, in respect thereof, become seised or possessed of such lands upon any trust, or where trustees of lands in stock refuse to convey such lands, or transfer such stock for twenty-eight days after demand by a person entitled to require such conveyance or transfer, then in any of such cases, the Lord Chancellor or Lords Justices (as to such persons as are lunatics so found) or the Chancery Division of the High Court as to such other persons, may make orders vesting such lands in such person or persons, in such manner, and for such estates as may be thought fit, and releasing lands from such contingent rights, or disposing of the same, and vesting the rights to transfer such stock or to receive the dividends or income thereof, or to sue for and recover such chose in action or any interest in respect thereof in any person or persons (*r*). And when any person or persons is or are entitled *jointly* with any such person as before mentioned, to any stock or chose in action as trustee or mortgagee, the Lord Chancellor or Lords Justices as to lunatics, and the Chancery Division in other cases, may make an order vesting the right to transfer such stock or to receive the dividends or income thereof, or to sue for and recover such chose in action or interest in respect thereof, either in such person or persons so jointly entitled, or in him or them, together with any other person or

(*r*) 13 & 14 Vict. c. 60, ss. 3—16, 22, 23, 24, 25; 15 & 16 Vict. c. 55, ss. 2, 3, 4, 5.

persons (*s*). And the Lord Chancellor or Lords Justices or the Chancery Division, as the case may be, may in all the preceding cases appoint a new trustee or new trustees (*t*).

So far as the preceding cases refer to lunatics or persons of unsound mind, they have, strictly speaking, nothing to do with the Chancery Division, as orders made in pursuance of them are made " in lunacy," and not " in the High Court of Justice" at all (*u*). Where, however, there are other grounds *in addition to lunacy* for asking for any such, they should be asked for in the High Court of Justice, Chancery Division, and not in lunacy (*x*).

It may be here mentioned, that when a decree has been made by the Chancery Division, directing the sale of any lands for the payment of the debts of a deceased person, every person seised or possessed of such lands, or entitled to a contingent right therein as heir or devisee, will be deemed to be so seised, possessed or entitled as " a trustee" within the meaning of the Trustee Acts, and if he refuses to convey, the court may make a vesting order, vesting such lands in the purchaser, and may also discharge any contingent right of any unborn person under the will of the debtor (*y*). And in all other cases of sales ordered by the court, every person so seised, possessed or entitled, who is a party to the suit or proceeding in which the order for sale was made, or who is otherwise bound by such order, is deemed a trustee within the meaning of the above-mentioned

(*s*) 15 & 16 Vict. c. 55, s. 5.

(*t*) Ib. s. 10.

(*u*) *Re Ormerod*, 3 De G. & J. 249.

(*x*) *Re Arrowsmith*, 4 Jur. 1123; *Re Gardner*, L. R., 10 Ch. D. 29; *Re Currie*, ib. 93.

(*y*) 13 & 14 Vict. c. 60, s. 29.

acts (z). Applications, however, for the purpose of vesting lands in purchasers, do not properly come in here, as they are applications in *actions*, and are made by summons (a).

The Trustee Acts also provide, that wherever it is expedient to appoint a new trustee or trustees, and it is found inexpedient, difficult or impracticable to do so without the assistance of the court, the Chancery Division may make an order appointing a new trustee or new trustees, who have the same rights and powers as if appointed in a suit, either in substitution for, or in addition to, any existing trustee or trustees; and such order may be made, whether there be any existing trustee or not (b); and upon making any order for the appointment of new trustees or a new trustee, the court may either by the same (as is most usual), or by any subsequent order, direct that any lands subject to the trust, and the right to call for a transfer of stock subject to the trust, or to receive the dividends and income thereof, or to sue for or recover any chose in action subject to the trust, or any interest in respect thereof, shall vest in the person or persons who, upon the appointment, shall be the trustee or trustees, and as to the lands for such estate as the court may direct (c); and upon such order, the legal right to transfer such stock will vest accordingly (d).

Petition. Orders for the appointment of new trustees and vesting orders under the Trustee Acts, (except vesting orders made in an action,) are obtained

---

(z) 15 & 16 Vict. c. 55, s. 1.

(a) Cons. Ord. XXXV. r. 1.

(b) 13 & 14 Vict. c. 60, ss. 32, 33 ; 15 & 16 Vict. c. 55, s. 9.

(c) 13 & 14 Vict. c. 60, ss. 34, 35.

(d) 15 & 16 Vict. c. 55, s. 6.

on petition. The petition is headed, " In the High Court of Justice, Chancery Division," and the name of the judge to whom it is intended to be assigned must be mentioned. It is intituled, " In the matter of the Trustee Act, 1850," and also where it is applicable, " In the matter of the act 15 & 16 Vict. c. 55, intituled, ' An Act to extend the provisions of the Trustee Act, 1850,' " and also in the matter of the particular trust, and is addressed to " Her Majesty's High Court of Justice." In general all *cestuis que trusts* (infants by their next friends) must be petitioners, or else the petition must be served upon them (*e*) ; but where they are very numerous, the service will be dispensed with (*f*) ; and, in a recent case in which I was counsel, V.-C. Hall made an order for the appointment of a new trustee, and the vesting of real estate on the petition of the continuing trustees and without service or any *cestui que trust;* the continuing trustees having power to appoint a new trustee, and the petition being only necessitated by the fact of one of the trustees having gone abroad, and not having been heard of for some years (*g*).

The petition contains a concise statement of the trust instrument, the present condition of the trusts and property, showing who are the *cestuis que trusts*, and which if any of them are *sui juris*, and which not, and stating the several facts which make the application necessary or desirable ; and where new trustees are to be appointed, must state that the petitioners are desirous that the persons nominated should be appointed, and that they are fit and proper persons, and are willing to act. The petition must then pray for the order desired,

(*e*) *Re Fellowes*, 2 Jur. 62.
(*f*) *Re Smyth*, 2 De G. & S. 781 ; *Re Sharpley*, 1 W. R. 271.

(*g*) *Re Brettle*, V.-C. Hall, 1st July, 1881.

and end with the usual note as to whether it is intended to serve it on any person, and if so, upon whom.

Where it is necessary to appoint a new trustee of several distinct settlements, in place of a person who was trustee of each of them, an order may be made on one petition intituled in all the settlements where all the settlements are sufficiently connected, as in the case of the marriage settlements of several sisters (h).

Persons to be appointed new Trustees. With regard to the persons whom the court will appoint new trustees, the reader is referred to works on trusts and trustees.

Evidence. The petition is presented, answered, set down, and served, and heard in the usual way. At the hearing it must be verified by affidavit; and certificates of the deaths of the various deceased persons must be produced, also duly verified by affidavit, and an affidavit of fitness of the proposed new trustees, and their written consent to act, also verified by affidavit, must be produced.

Where a vesting order of copyholds is asked for, the written consent of the lord of the manor should be obtained if possible, and duly verified by affidavit and produced (i). By doing so, the lands will vest without any surrender or admittance; but otherwise a person must be appointed to convey or assign the lands (i). The lord should not, however, be served with the petition, as the order is made subject to his rights, if he does not consent to it (k).

(h) *Re Brettle*, V.-C. Hall, 1st July, 1881.

(i) 13 & 14 Vict. c. 60, s. 28; *Ayles* v. *Cox*, 17 Bea. 584; *Cooper* v. *Jones*, 25 L. J., Ch. 240.

(k) *Re Flitchcroft*, 1 Jur., N. S. 418; *Paterson* v. *Paterson*, L. R., 2 Eq. 31; *Re Lane*, 12 W. R. 710.

Hearing. On the hearing of the application, the court may make an order in conformity to the acts, or may order the case to stand over for further evidence, or to enable notice or any further notice of the application to be served, or may refer the matter to chambers, or may dismiss the application either with or without costs (*l*).

The Order. The order is drawn up, passed, and entered, in the usual way like a judgment.

A vesting order made under the acts, is conclusive evidence of the truth of the allegations as to the disqualification of the trustee or mortgagee who is divested by the order; but upon an action by such trustee or mortgagee, the court may direct a reconveyance or reassignment of any lands conveyed or assigned by the vesting order, or a redisposition of any contingent rights conveyed or disposed of by the order, and may order the petitioners to pay the costs occasioned by their having improperly obtained such an order (*m*).

Vesting orders under the act may be made in the case of charity trustees, however appointed (*n*).

Orders under the Trustee Acts require to be stamped like deeds for effectuating the same object; thus, an appointment of new trustees requires a 10*s*. stamp, and if accompanied by a vesting order, another 10*s*. stamp will be needed, but not when the vesting order is of stock only. Where it is a vesting order of any kind of security coming under the head of "mortgage" in the Stamp Act, it must be stamped *ad valorem* as a transfer of mortgage (*o*).

(*l*) 13 & 14 Vict. c. 60, ss. 41, 42.

(*m*) Ib. s. 44.

(*n*) Ib. s. 45.

(*o*) 15 & 16 Vict. c. 55, s. 13.

Where a mortgagee is an infant, or person of unsound mind, and a vesting order is asked for by the mortgagor, he must pay the principal, interest and costs into court in trust in any cause then depending concerning such money; and if there be none, then to the credit of such infant or person of unsound mind, subject to the order and disposition of the court. The money is paid in on the direction of the paymaster-general, obtained on a written request in the ordinary way (*p*).

Costs. The order on a petition under the acts should mention the way in which the costs are to be paid, which will be out of the *corpus* of the fund, when the application is for the benefit of the estate, and out of the income where for the benefit of the life tenant; and where it is only for the benefit of those in remainder, they must pay the costs themselves (*q*).

Lastly, the court may order the petition to stand over, until the rights of the petitioner may be declared in an action, to be instituted for that purpose.

(*p*) 13 & 14 Vict. c. 60, s. 48. Jur. 62 ; *Re Brackenbury*, L. R.,
(*q*) Ib. s. 51; *Re Fellowes*, 2 10 Eq. 45.

Matters relating to Settled Property.

—◆—

CHAPTER I.

THE SETTLED ESTATES ACT, 1877.

Objects of the Act. As in the case of the Trustee Act, so also before explaining the practice under the Settled Estates, it is necessary to give a short summary of the objects of the act. The act, then, is a consolidation, with amendments, of several prior acts, the objects of which were, in certain cases, to give the Chancery Division power to authorize leases and sales of settled estates where it may consider that such leases or sales would be proper and consistent with due regard for the interests of all parties entitled under the settlement; and also to give persons in possession of land for certain limited estates or interests, power (without the consent of the court) to grant agricultural or occupation leases at rack rents for reasonable periods. In fact, the intention of the legislature was to make all real property (except a few estates which are entailed by act of parliament) as saleable as if proper powers for that purpose were inserted in all settlements (a).

(a) See *Re Shepheard's Settled Estates*, L. R., 8 Eq. 573; *Re Clark*, L. R., 1 Ch. Ap. 291; *Beioley* v. *Carter*, L. R., 4 Ch. Ap. 240.

Leases. The court has power to grant or renew leases of the whole or any parts of settled estates, or of any rights or privileges over them, for any purpose, whether involving waste or not; provided (1) That every lease be made to take effect in possession at or within one year from the making of it, and do not exceed in duration twenty-one years for an agricultural or occupation lease, forty years for a mining lease, or lease of water mills, way leaves, water leaves or other rights or easements, sixty years for a repairing lease, or ninety-nine years for a building lease; but such leases (except agricultural leases) may be for longer periods than those above specified, if the court be satisfied that it is the usual custom of the district and beneficial to the inheritance (b). (2) That on every such lease the best rent, or reservation in the nature of a rent, either uniform or not, that can be reasonably obtained, be reserved, payable half-yearly or oftener, without taking any premium, with certain specific provisions with regard to mining leases. (4) That no such lease shall authorize the felling of timber, except for clearing spaces for buildings or works. (5) That every such lease be by deed, executed in counterpart, and containing a condition for re-entry on nonpayment of the rent for a period of twenty-eight days after it becomes due, or for some less period. The act also contains certain provisions authorizing the insertion of such covenants, &c., as the court shall think desirable, and also in relation to the surrender of leases for the purposes of renewal.

The court also has power to authorize preliminary contracts to grant leases, any of the terms of which

(b) Sect. 4.

may be varied in the leases themselves (c) ; and also power to authorize the lords of settled manors to give licences to their copyhold or customary tenants to grant leases of lands held by them of such manors (d). The power to authorize leases may be exercised by the court, either by approving of particular leases, or by ordering that powers of leasing in conformity with the provisions of the act shall be vested, either in the existing trustees of the settlement, or in any other persons ; and such powers when exercised by such trustees take effect in all respects as if the power so vested in them had been originally contained in the settlement, and so as to operate (if necessary) by way of revocation and new appointment of uses, or otherwise as the court may direct. And in every case the court, if it thinks fit, has power to impose any conditions as to consents or otherwise on the exercise of the power, and to authorize the insertion of provisions for the appointment of new trustees from time to time for the purpose of exercising the powers of leasing (e).

Sales. The court has power, if it deems it proper and consistent with a due regard to the interests of all parties entitled under the settlement, to authorize a sale of the whole or any parts of any settled estate, or of any timber (not being ornamental timber) growing on a settled estate (f) ; and when land is so sold for building purposes, the whole or part of the consideration may consist of a chief rent (g). Minerals may be excepted from any such sale, and any rights or privileges reserved ; and the purchaser may be required to enter into

(c) Sect. 8.   (f) Sect. 16.
(d) Sect. 9.   (g) Sect. 18.
(e) Sects. 10, 13.

covenants or submit to any restrictions which the court may deem advisable (*h*).

The court may also direct that any part of any settled estate be laid out for streets, or roads, paths, squares, gardens or open spaces, sewers, drains or watercourses, either to be dedicated to the public or not; and may direct that the parts so laid out, remain vested in the trustees, or be conveyed to or vested in other trustees upon trusts for continuing the appropriation thereof to such purposes (*i*) ; and may also direct that the expense of carrying out such works be defrayed by means of a sale or mortgage of, or charge upon, all or any part of the settled estate ; or be received and paid out of the rents, or out of moneys liable to be invested in the purchase of lands to be settled to the like uses, or out of the income of such moneys, or out of accumulations of rents, and may also give directions as to the repair of such works out of such rents or accumulations (*k*).

Protection of Settled Estates. The court, if it consider it proper and consistent with a due regard for the interests of all parties, may sanction any action, defence, petition to parliament, parliamentary opposition or other proceedings appearing to the court necessary for the protection of any settled estate, and may order that all or any part of the costs be raised and paid by any of the means above mentioned for defraying the costs of laying out streets, &c. (*l*).

Such, then, is a short account of the powers conferred on the Chancery Division by the Settled Estates Act, 1877, but as they are only mentioned in this work in order to make an account of the *practice* under them in-

---

(*h*) Sect. 19.　　　　(*k*) Sect. 21.
(*i*) Sect. 20.　　　　(*l*) Sect. 17.

telligible, the reader is referred to works treating of the
act itself for an account of the *law* relating to it, and of
the cases which have been decided in reference to the
construction of the powers given to the court by the
act (*m*).

Practice. Applications to the court to exercise any
of the powers conferred by this act are made by petition, headed " In the High Court of Justice, Chancery
Division," mentioning the name of the judge to whose
court they are to be assigned, and intituled " In the
matter of the estates settled by the settlor or settlors"
(naming one of them), and referring to the instrument
by which the settlement was created, and mentioning
the parish, place or county in which the hereditaments
to be dealt with are situated, and also "In the matter
of the Settled Estates Act, 1877 " (*n*). For example,
take the following title of a petition :—

In the High Court of Justice.
  Chancery Division.
    Vice-Chancellor Hall.
      In the matter of estates settled by John Smith by will dated
        the 12th day of November, 1842, consisting of messuages
        and hereditaments situate in Queen Square, Wolverhampton,
        in the county of Stafford,
            and
    In the matter of the Settled Estates Act, 1877.
  To Her Majesty's High Court of Justice.

A petition is absolutely necessary, as an order under
the act cannot be made on summons or motion in an
action (*o*). But, of course, if an administration action is
pending, the petition should be intituled both in the
action and in the above matters.

(*m*) See Middleton's Settled
Estates Act, 1877.

(*n*) Settled Estates Act Orders,
1878, Ord. II.

(*o*) *Taylor* v. *Taylor*, L. R., 1
Ch. D. 131.

Petitioners. With regard to the parties, some person entitled legally or equitably to the possession, or to the receipt of the rents and profits of the settled estate, for a term of years determinable on his death, or for an estate for life, or any greater estate, or as assignee of any such person, *must* be a petitioner (*p*), and all other persons interested *may* be joined as petitioners. If there be no person in existence falling within the description above given of a necessary petitioner, it would seem that the court cannot be set in motion (*q*), although it is difficult to reconcile this statement with one case in which a petition was presented by a widow entitled *during widowhood*, and by her children entitled in remainder, and allowed (*r*).

Mortgaged Property. The fact that the property is mortgaged, does not prevent the petition being presented; although, of course, the order made will be subject to the rights of the mortgagee (*s*).

Contents of Petition. The petitioner's full name, address and description must be stated (*t*).

The petition must contain (1) a short statement of the settlement; (2) an account of the devolutions (if any) of the property under the trusts of the settlement, showing who are entitled in possession and who in remainder; (3) a detailed description of the property intended to be dealt with, either in the body of the petition, or by way of a schedule, or annexed plan (*u*); (4) a statement of the grounds upon which the applica-

---

(*p*) Sect. 23; and *Taylor* v. *Taylor*, L. R., 3 Ch. D. 145.

(*q*) *Taylor* v. *Taylor*, L. R., 1 Ch. D. 431.

(*r*) *Williams* v. *Williams*, 9 W. R. 888.

(*s*) Sect. 54.

(*t*) Settled Estates Act Orders, 1878, Ord. XXXI.

(*u*) Ib. Ord. II.

tion is made, stating any provisional contract that may
have been entered into for letting or selling the property ; (5) a statement that no application has been
made to either house of parliament for the purpose of
effecting the object of the petition, or any similar object ;
or if such application has been made, that it was not
rejected on its merits (*x*) ; (6) an address within three
miles from Temple Bar, where the petitioner may be
served with any order of the court relating to the object
of the petition.

The petition then prays for the order which is desired,
and ends with a note, stating whether it is or is not
intended to serve it on any person. Service is commonly made upon all parties interested other than petitioners : but it would seem that service of the petition
is not required, although, as we shall see presently,
service of *notice* of it is (*y*).

Infants. Where a petitioner is an infant, he petitions in the first instance by his next friend; but
although the petition is presented and answered in this
form, it is nevertheless necessary to apply at once for
the appointment of a special guardian to represent him ;
and when such guardian is appointed, if he be the same
person as the next friend (as is usual), the words "next
friend" are struck out of the petition, and the word
"guardian" substituted ; and if the guardian be not the
same person as the next friend, the latter's name is
struck out, and the guardian's name substituted (*z*).

The application for the appointment of the guardian
is made by summons at chambers, taken out by the
next friend, intituled like the petition, and served on

(*x*) Sect. 32.
(*y*) Seton, 4th ed. 1483.

(*z*) Settled Estates Act Orders,
1878, Ord. V.

the infant's parent, testamentary guardian, or guardian appointed by the court, unless the court or judge dispenses with such service (*a*).

This summons must be supported by an affidavit stating (1) the age of the infant; (2) whether he has any parent, testamentary guardian, or guardian appointed by the court, and if so, whether such parent or guardian has any interest in the application, and if he has, the nature of such interest; (3) where, and under whose care, the infant is residing, and at whose expense he is maintained; (4) in what way the proposed guardian is connected with the infant, and why proposed, and how qualified; (5) that the proposed guardian has no personal interest in the application, or if he has, the nature of his interest, and that it is not adverse to that of the infant; and (6) the consent of the guardian to act (*b*).

Where the infant is tenant in tail, the mere appointment of a guardian is not of itself sufficient; for the guardian cannot act when appointed, without the special direction of the court. This direction is obtained on summons issued by the next friend, and served on the guardian or proposed guardian, and may be, and usually is, combined with the application for the appointment of the guardian. On the hearing of this application, the guardian or proposed guardian must make an affidavit, stating that it is proper and consistent with a due regard to the infant's interest that such direction should be given (*c*).

Lunatics.   In the case of a lunatic, he petitions by

(*a*) Settled Estates Act Orders, 1878, Ord. VIII.
(*b*) Ib. Ord. X.
(*c*) Sect. 49; and Settled Estates Act Orders, 1878, Ords. VI., IX., XII.

his committee ; but before doing so, the committee must
get the assent of the Lord Chancellor or Lords Justices,
as the judges entrusted with the care of lunatics (*d*).
This is obtained by applying to the Master in Lunacy
for a special report, which he makes and submits to one
of the judges in question, who indorses it. But in
addition to this, where the lunatic is tenant in tail, the
committee must also apply after the petition is presented for the special direction of the judge of the
Chancery Division to whose court the petition is
assigned; but the production to such judge of the
authority granted by the judges in lunacy is sufficient
evidence upon which he may issue his directions (*e*),
unless he requires more.

Persons of Unsound Mind. In the case of a
person of unsound mind not so found, the court has no
jurisdiction to appoint a guardian either to petition or
consent, and consequently it would seem that no such
person can be a *petitioner* until he is " found a lunatic"
by inquisition (*f*) ; but the court may, in a fit case, dispense with the consent of a person of unsound mind.

Married Woman. A married woman may be a
petitioner, whether of full age or not (*g*), and whether
restrained from anticipation or not (*h*); but (even where
the property is settled to her separate use (*i*)) she must
be examined apart from her husband touching her
knowledge of the nature and effect of the application,
and her free desire to make a consent to it. The ex-

(*d*) Seton, 4th ed. 1480 ; *Re
Woodstock*, L. R., 3 Ch. App.
229.

(*e*) Sect. 49; and Settled Estates
Act Orders, 1878, Ord. XI.

(*f*) *Re Clough*, L. R., 15 Eq.
248 ; *Re Woodstock*, sup.

(*g*) Sect. 52.

(*h*) Sect. 50.

(*i*) Ib.

amination may take place at any time after the petition is presented and answered (*k*), and may be taken before the judge, either in court or in chambers. If taken in court, the registrar takes a note of it, which is sufficient evidence of the examination having been taken; if taken in chambers, the chief clerk indorses a memorandum of it on the petition (*l*). The examination may also take place before a special examiner, appointed on the application of the petitioner. A solicitor who is a perpetual commissioner to take acknowledgments of deeds by married women may be appointed to take the examination, by a judge at chambers, without summons or order, upon the request of the petitioner, and a certificate of the solicitor for the petitioner that the person to be appointed is not a solicitor for the petitioner or for any party whose concurrence or consent to the application is required. This request and certificate need not be served on any person. Where an examination by such solicitor will cause unreasonable expense, delay or inconvenience, or where the married woman is resident out of the jurisdiction, an application may be made by summons *ex parte* by the *petitioner* to appoint, as examiner, a solicitor (if the woman is within the jurisdiction), or any other person (if she be not within the jurisdiction) (*m*).

The request and certificate for the appointment of an examiner is intituled the same as the petition, and then proceeds as follows (*n*) :—

The petitioners, Sarah Perry and Mildred Clarke, in a petition presented in these matters on the 20th day of January, 1881, request

---

(*k*) Settled Estates Act Orders, 1878, Ord. XIII.
(*l*) Ib. Ord. XXVIII.

(*m*) Ib. Ord. XIV.
(*n*) Ib. Appendix, Form 7.

that Clifford Jones, of No. 300, Holland Road, Kensington, in the county of Middlesex, being a solicitor and a perpetual commissioner to take the acknowledgment of deeds by married women, may be appointed for the purpose of examining the above-named petitioners, Sarah Perry, the wife of Thomas Perry, of No. 500, High Street, Kensington, aforesaid, grocer, and Mildred Clark, the wife of Charles Clark, of No. 650, Earl's Court Road, in the said county of Middlesex, draper, respectively, touching their knowledge of the nature and effect of the application intended to be made by the petition, and to ascertain whether they, the said Sarah Jones and Mildred Clark, respectively, freely desire to make such application [*or where the married woman is not a petitioner, to consent to such application*].

We, the solicitors for the petitioners, hereby certify that the said Clifford Jones is not the solicitor for the petitioners or for any party whose concurrence or consent to the application is required.

Dated this 25th day of January, 1881.

SEYMOUR & Co.,

Solicitors for the petitioners,

150, Bedford Row, W.C.

When the application is granted, the chief clerk will append a memorandum to this, to the effect that the judge appoints the party proposed.

A summons for the same purpose is prepared in a way so similar as to need no explanation.

The married woman, on being examined before the examiner, must sign an acknowledgment (intituled like the petition) to the following effect (*o*):—

> The examination of the petitioners, Sarah Perry, the wife of Thomas Perry, of, &c., and Mildred Clark, the wife of Charles Clark, of, &c.

We, the said Sarah Perry and Mildred Clark, having been this day respectively examined, apart from our respective husbands, touching our knowledge of the nature and effect of an application intended to be made to the High Court of Justice, by a petition presented in these matters on the 20th day of January, 1881, by us [*or by   *], for answer thereto severally say that we are aware of the nature and

---

(*o*) Ib. Appendix, Form 9.

effect of the said intended application, and we severally hereby desire
to make [*or* to consent to] such application.

As witness our hands this 10th day of February, 1881.

Witness to the signature of the said ⎫
    S. Perry and M. Clark,   ⎪ SARAH PERRY.
        JOHN SMITH,   ⎬ MILDRED CLARK.
        180, Elsham Road,   ⎪
          Kensington.   ⎭

At the foot of the acknowledgment the examiner
makes the following certificate (*p*) :—

I, the undersigned Clifford Jones, being the person appointed by
the Master of the Rolls for the purpose of examining the above-named
Sarah, the wife of Thomas Perry, and Mildred, the wife of Charles
Clark, hereby certify that I have, this 10th day of February, 1881,
examined the said Sarah Perry and Mildred Clark apart from their
respective husbands, touching their knowledge of the nature and
effect of the application intended to be made by the petition above
referred to, and I have taken such examination in writing as above
set forth ; and I further certify, that at the time of such examination
I explained to them the nature and effect of the said application, and
I am satisfied that they were aware of the nature and effect of such
application, and that they freely desire to make [*or* to consent to] the
said application.

CLIFFORD JONES.

Witness,
    JOHN SMITH.

The witness to the signatures of the married women
must make an affidavit verifying the fact that he saw
the married women sign the acknowledgment, and the
examiner sign the certificate, and that " the signatures
Sarah Perry and Mildred Clark attached to the paper
writing now produced to me, and marked A, are respectively the proper handwritings of the said Sarah, the
wife of Thomas Perry, of, &c., and of the said Mildred,
the wife of Charles Clark, of, &c.; and that the signa-

p) Settled Estates Act Orders, Appendix, Form 10.

ture, Clifford Jones, attached to the paper writing now produced to me, and marked B, is the proper handwriting of Clifford Jones, of, &c.; and I further say that the signature, John Smith, attached to the said paper writings as a witness is my handwriting" (q).

Naming Day for Hearing.　At the time of presenting the petition, the petitioner should name a day for bringing it on for hearing, which must be not sooner than eight clear days after the presentation.　If the petitioner is not ready on the day named, the petition will be ordered to stand over, either to a day named or generally; and in the latter case will be restored to the paper on the application to the secretary of petitions by the petitioner, without the necessity of mentioning the matter to the judge; but two clear days' notice of the restoration must be given to all parties interested (r).

Consent of Interested Parties.　Before presenting a petition under the act, it is desirable to see whether the consent of all parties entitled to object can be secured; as in general such consent will not be dispensed with, except as hereafter mentioned.　The parties whose consent must be sought are the following:— Where there is a tenant in tail, or successive tenants in tail, of full age, then such tenant in tail, or if more than one, the first tenant in tail, and all persons claiming prior to him, and the trustees of unborn persons claiming prior to him, are the proper parties to consent. In all other cases, all other persons in existence having any beneficial interest under or by virtue of the settlement, and the trustees of unborn persons having any

(q) See *Re Clough*, L. R., 15　(r) Settled Estates Act Orders, Eq. 281 ; *Re Woodstock*, sup.　1878, Ord. III.

such interest, are the proper parties (*s*). Where there is an infant tenant in tail, the above parties are still the parties to consent, and also persons entitled *subsequently* to such tenant in tail, unless the court (as it may do if it think fit) dispenses with the consent of such subsequent persons (*t*).

Where the concurrence and consent of any such persons has not been obtained, a notice must be served on each such person, requiring him to notify within a specified time whether he assents to or dissents from the application, or submits his rights or interests, so far as they may be affected by the application, to be dealt with by the court; and such notice must specify to whom, and in what manner, such notification is to be delivered or left. In case no answer is made to such notice, the person to whom it has been given will be taken to have submitted his rights to the court (*u*).

The giving of this notice (save where given to a person of unsound mind not so found, or a person out of the jurisdiction, in which cases an *ex parte* summons for directions must be taken out by the petitioner) requires no order or direction of the court, but should be in the form No. 3, in the Appendix to the Settled Estates Orders, 1878; and the time to be specified in the notice for the answer thereto to be given is, in the case of an infant, to be such time as directed in the order appointing a guardian to such infant (of which we shall treat a few lines further on); and in the case of a married woman or committee of a lunatic not less than twenty-eight clear days after service; and in any other case not less than fourteen days after service (*w*).

(*s*) Sect. 24.
(*t*) Sect. 25.
(*u*) Sect. 26.

(*w*) Settled Estates Act Orders, 1878, Ord. IV.

The court may dispense with notice where (1) the person cannot be found; or (2) where it is uncertain whether he be living or dead; or (3) in case it appears that such notice cannot be given without expense disproportionate to the value of the subject-matter of the application, either on the ground of such person's interest being small or remote, or being similar to those of any other person or persons, or on any other ground; and in that case such person will be deemed to have submitted his interest to be dealt with by the court (*x*).

In the case of infants and lunatics and married women who are not petitioners, the same rules apply as if they were petitioners. But it must always be borne in mind that *in the appointment of a guardian and obtaining special directions, or getting an examiner appointed, the petitioner has the conduct of the proceedings*, and takes out the necessary summons or makes the necessary requests, even where the person with regard to whom they are taken out or made is not a petitioner.

Notice must also be given to all trustees who are seised or possessed of any estate in trust for any person whose consent or concurrence to or in the application is required, and on any other parties whom the court considers ought to be served (*y*).

Any person served with notice, whether as a person interested or as a trustee, may, upon reasonable notice to the petitioner's solicitor, inspect the petition without payment of any fee, and is entitled to be furnished with a copy on the usual terms as to copies (*z*).

On the hearing of the petition, affidavits must be filed

(*x*) Sect. 27; and see *Re Spurway*, L. R., 10 Ch. D. 230.

(*y*) Sect. 30.

(*z*) Settled Estates Act Orders, 1878, Ord. XXII.

showing that it is in fact proper and consistent, with a due regard for the interests of all parties, that the order asked for should be made; and that notice of the application has been served on all trustees; and that an application to a similar effect has not been made to parliament, and rejected or reported against (*a*).   And where leasing powers or a lease are prayed for, evidence must be produced sufficient to enable the court to ascertain the nature, value and circumstances of the estate, and the terms and conditions on which the leases thereof ought to be authorized (*b*).

Hearing. At the hearing the order will be made, or the petition dismissed, or ordered to stand over for further evidence, or sometimes, but rarely, referred to chambers.   As a general rule, a sale for less than twenty-five years' purchase is not sanctioned.

Dispensing with Consent. On the other hand, if all parties are not present, or do not consent, the court may dispense with their consent; (1) where their interests are subsequent to the estate of an infant tenant in tail; or (2) where, having regard to their number, or their estates, or interests, it considers that an order may be properly made notwithstanding the want of such consent (*c*). Or (as is often the case where a party interested cannot be found) it will, either at the hearing or before, order that notice of the application be inserted in certain newspapers, in a special form given in the schedule to the orders ; in which case any person may, within the time named in the advertisement, or even after by special leave, apply by motion, *ex parte* or on notice, for leave to be heard on the petition, and if

---

(*a*) Settled Estates Act Orders,   (*b*) Sect. 11.
1878, Ords. XV., XVI., XVII.   (*c*) Sects. 25, 28.

such leave be granted, the order must be forthwith served on the petitioner's solicitor, when he may, on payment of 13s. 4d., inspect the petition, and also obtain a copy of it on payment of the usual costs (d).

The court may also make the order subject to, and so as not to affect, the rights, estate or interest of any person where concurrence or consent has been refused, or who has not submitted, or is not deemed to have submitted, his rights and interests to be dealt with by the court, or whose rights, estate or interest, ought in the opinion of the court to be excepted (e).

The Order.   With regard to the form of the order made on a petition under the act, it must state the names of the petitioners, of the parties who consent, of the persons on whom notice has been served, and of the persons who have obtained leave to be heard.   It must also state whether any notification has been received from the persons to whom notice has been given, and, if any has been received, the purport thereof; and also the names of the persons with regard to whom notice has been dispensed with; and whether the order is made subject to any and what rights, estate, or interest of any person whose concurrence or consent has been refused, or who may not, or may not be deemed to have submitted his rights or interests to be dealt with by the court, or whose rights or interests ought in the opinion of the court to be excepted (f).

In cases where the court authorizes a lease, the order must also direct that the lease shall contain such con-

---

(d) Settled Estates Act Orders, 1878, Ords. XVIII., XIX., XX., XXI., XXVI., XXVII., LVII. r. 6.

(e) Sect. 29.

(f) Settled Estates Act Orders, 1878, Ord. XXIV.

ditions as are required by the act, and such other covenants, conditions and stipulations, as the court deems
expedient with reference to each particular case, or may
direct the same to contain such covenants, conditions
and stipulations, as may be approved by the judge at
chambers, without directing the lease to be *settled* by the
judge, which is expressly forbidden (*g*).

The order must also state whether or not any record
or notice of the order is to be made, for preventing fraud
or mistake, by indorsing a memorandum of the order
on the settlement, or registering a memorial of it in a
register county or otherwise (*h*). The order is drawn
up, passed, and entered, in the usual way.

Payment of Purchase-money. Unless the order
specifies to the contrary, the purchase-money received
on a sale under the act, and a certain proportion of the
rents or payments reserved in any lease of earth, coal,
stone or minerals, must be paid into court, *ex parte* the
applicant in the matter of the act, and is to be applied
to some of the purposes mentioned in the 34th section
of the act; viz., the redemption of land tax, or incumbrances, the purchase of other lands, or the building of
houses on other land comprised in the settlement, or in
payment to any person absolutely entitled. Where the
order so specifies, the application of the money in
manner above indicated, may be made by the trustees
without the leave of the court; but where the money is
paid into court, a new petition is necessary, and must
be presented by the person who would be entitled to
the possession or receipt of the rents and profits of the
land if the money had been invested in the purchase of

(*g*) Settled Estates Act Orders,
1878, Ord. XXV.; and ss. 14, 15.

(*h*) Sect. 33; and Settled Estates
Act Orders, 1878, Ord. XXIII.

land. Where purchase-money is paid into court in respect of a lease for a life, or lives and years, or years
only, or for any estate less than the fee simple, or in
respect of any reversion dependent on any such lease, or
estate, the money may be laid out in such manner as
the court may consider will give to the parties interested,
the same benefit as they would lawfully have had from
the lease, estate or reversion, in respect of which the
money in question may have been paid (i).

The application of the money under this section, is
made under an order obtained on the petition of any
party interested.

Money in court, under the act, is invested like cash
under the control of the court, and the dividends paid
to the person who would be entitled to the rents of the
settled estate (k).

Rules and Orders. Before preparing any document under the act, the practitioner should consult
the forms appended to the orders, as those forms _must_
be followed where applicable (l). However, the orders
may be dispensed with by the judge in his discretion,
whenever he thinks it desirable (m).

Costs. With regard to costs under the act, the
court has power to order the costs of all parties to be a
charge on the hereditaments the subject of the application, or on others in the same settlement, and may direct
the costs to be varied by sale or mortgage, or out of the
rents or profits (n).

Leasing of Infants' Estates. In addition to the
powers given by the Settled Estates Act, certain powers

(i) Sect. 37.

(k) Sect. 36.

(l) Settled Estates Act Orders,

1878, Ord. XXVII.

(m) Ib. Ord. XXXII.

(n) Sect. 41.

of leasing, and for surrendering and renewing renewable leases are given to the court in cases of infants and married women, by the act 11 Geo. 4 & 1 Will. 4, c. 65. Such powers are exerciseable on summons.

———◆———

CHAPTER II.

THE LANDS CLAUSES CONSOLIDATION ACT, 1845.

WHEN a railway, a dock, a canal, or a street, or any other public work affecting the lands of more than one landowner has to be carried out, the purchase of all the land required by means of agreement with persons entitled to sell it is impracticable; because, in the first place, some portion of it is most probably so settled as to prevent the sale of the fee simple, and in the next place, some of the owners would refuse to sell, at least at a reasonable price. Under these circumstances, it was formerly the practice to insert in all acts of parliament authorizing public works, divers powers of compulsory purchase; but, for the sake of convenience, these powers were, in the year 1845, consolidated in one public act, called the Lands Clauses Consolidation Act; and private acts, passed for the purpose of authorizing public undertakings, now merely "incorporate" the Lands Clauses Consolidation Act, and the promoters thereby acquire the powers specified in the latter act.

So far as the subject of this Work is concerned, it suffices to say—

    (1) That under sect. 69, where vendors, or some of them, are under disability, or have only a partial or qualified interest, and are not entitled to sell

except under the powers vested in them by the act, the purchase-money is to be assessed in one of several ways pointed out by the act; and if it exceeds 200*l.* it *must*, and if under 200*l.* but exceeding 20*l.* it may, be paid into court. In the latter case, however, the promoters have the option of paying it to trustees.

(2) That under sect. 76, where the owner of any land taken, or of any interest therein, on tender of the purchase-money or compensation, refuses to accept it, or fails to make a satisfactory title, or refuses to convey, or is absent from the kingdom, or cannot be found, the purchase-money is paid into court, and the promoters may by deed poll vest the property in themselves.

(3) That under sect. 85, the promoters may enter on lands required before the purchase-money has been assessed or agreed on, when such entry is very urgent, upon first paying into court the amount claimed, or the estimated value of the lands computed in a certain way mentioned in the act 30 & 31 Vict. c. 127, s. 36, and giving a bond for payment of the purchase-money when it shall be assessed or finally agreed on.

The mode of paying money into court in all three cases is by leaving a request for a direction at the pay-office, as explained in the chapter relating to proceedings in that office. Money paid in under sects. 69 or 85 is to be paid to the credit of *ex parte* the promoters in the matter of the special act; that paid in under sect. 76 must be paid to the credit of the parties interested, describing them as nearly as the promoters can do so, subject to the control and disposition of the court.

Money paid in under Sect. 69. Money paid in under this section may be applied in any one or more of five several ways, viz.—(1) in the purchase or redemption of land tax on land settled to the same uses as the land purchased; (2) in the discharge of incumbrances on the land purchased, or land settled to the same uses; (3) in the purchase of other lands to be settled to the same uses; (4) if the money is paid in respect of buildings taken or injured by the promoters, then it may be applied in removing or replacing such buildings, or substituting others in their stead, in such manner as the court may direct; or (5) in payment to any party becoming absolutely entitled (o), including trustees with power of sale (p). And until the money can be applied for any of the foregoing purposes, it may be temporarily invested in government or real securities, and the dividends and interest paid to the person who would have been entitled to the rents and profits of the land sold (q).

Petition. In order to get the money applied, or to obtain an interim investment of it, a petition must be presented by the person who would have been entitled to the rents and profits of the land sold. This petition headed, like other petitions, with the name of the court, division and judge, and is intituled in the matter of the will or settlement in question, and in the matter of the Lands Clauses Consolidation Acts, 1845, 1860 and 1869 (where the two latter are applicable), and in the matter of the special act. The petition should state shortly the claimant's title, the special act, and the purchase and payment into court by the promoters, and should pray for the order which is desired.

(o) Sect. 69.   (p) *Re Hobson*, L. R., 7 Ch. D. 708.
(q) Sect. 70.

The petition must be served on the promoters and on persons having charges on the lands (*r*), but not on the remainderman, unless the money was paid in in respect of an estate less than a fee simple, or unless it seeks permanent re-investment in investments other than lands (*r*) : nor where payment of a share is asked need the parties entitled to the other shares be served (*s*). Chargees, however, if not affected by the order asked for, should be tendered two guineas for their costs (*t*).

By sect. 74, where money is paid in in respect of an estate less than the whole fee simple, all persons interested *must* be served, and any person interested *may* petition ; and the court may order that the money be laid out, invested, accumulated and paid in such manner as it may consider will give to the parties interested, the same benefit as they would have lawfully had from the estate sold, or as near thereto as may be.

Hearing and Evidence.   The petition is presented, answered, set down and heard in the usual way, and must be supported by an affidavit of the petitioner verifying his title, and also stating that he is not aware of any right in any other person, or of any claim made by any other person, to the sum mentioned in the petition or any part thereof; or, if he is aware of any such right or claim, he must state, and refer to, and except the same (*u*).

Payment out.   With regard to parties absolutely entitled, it must be remembered, that except where the sum is small, it will not be paid out to a tenant in tail

(*r*) *Re Browne*, 1 De G., M. & G. 294 ; *Re Leigh*, L. R., 6 Ch. App. 887.

(*s*) *Melling* v. *Bird*, 17 Jur. 155.

(*t*) *Re Gore Langton*, L. R., 10 Ch. App. 328.

(*u*) Cons. Ord. XXXIV. r. 3.

without he executes a disentailing deed (*x*), nor to a married woman without she is separately examined (*y*).

The Order. The order is drawn up, passed and entered, and the money invested or paid out in the usual way.

Subsequent Applications. It should be observed, that where one application has been made in a matter, all future applications should be made to the same judge (*z*) ; but where money paid in to two separate credits is desired to be invested in one purchase, one petition may be presented, intituled in both matters, and if the two funds have been temporarily invested on the order of two different judges, the leave of both judges should be obtained to the setting down of the petition before one of them (*a*).

Costs. With regard to costs, the court orders the promoters to pay the costs, (1) of the purchase and incidental expenses ; (2) of the investment of the money in government or real securities; (3) of the re-investment thereof in the purchase of other lands ; (4) of obtaining the proper orders in that behalf, and of the orders for payment of the dividends of the interim investments, and of the order for payment of the money out of court, and of all proceedings relating thereto, except such as arise between adverse claimants. The costs of one application only, for the re-investment in land are allowed, except where it appears to the court that it is for the benefit of the parties interested that the money should be re-invested in different sums, and at different times (*b*). The costs may, of course, be

(*x*) *Re Reynolds*, L. R., 3 Ch. D. 61.

(*y*) *Re Hayes*, 9 W. R. 769.

(*z*) *Re Browne*, 14 W. R. 298.

(*a*) *Re Gore Langton*, sup.

(*b*) Sects. 80, 81, 82.

taxed on petition of course, but the promoters bear the cost of taxation, unless they get one-sixth taken off (c).

Payment in under Section 76. Any person claiming to be entitled to money paid in under sect. 76, or to the lands purchased, or to any estate or interest therein, or to any part thereof, may present a petition for the investment or distribution of the money or payment of the dividends (d). The court will ascertain the interest of the claimant or claimants, and pay the money or part of it accordingly; and where the whole absolute interest in the land is not claimed by any one, the court will pay the proper proportion of the money due to the claimants for their several interests, and will order the balance to be paid to the promoters (e). The evidence is, of course, similar to the evidence in petitions under the 69th section; and in cases of disputed title, the onus of proof rests on the person who was out of possession at the date of the purchase by the promoters (f).

The costs under this section are the same as those under sect. 69, except that no costs will be allowed where the money has been paid in in consequence of the wilful and capricious refusal of the party entitled, to receive it, or to convey or release the land, or in consequence of his wilful neglect to make out a good title (g).

Payment in under Section 85. Money paid into court under this section may be invested in bank annuities or government securities, on the petition of

(c) Sect. 83.
(d) Sect. 78.
(e) *Brandon* v. *Brandon*, 2 Dr. & Sm. 365.

(f) Sect. 79.
(g) Sect. 80; and see *Ex parte Lawson*, 17 W. R. 186.

the *promoters ;* and on the bond being performed, will also, on their petition, served on the vendor, be paid out of court to the promoters (*h*).

If, however, the bond is not performed, the court may, on the petition of the vendor, order the money to be applied in payment of the purchase-money, or otherwise for the benefit of the parties for whose security it was paid in (*i*). The costs are the same as in the case of money paid in under sect. 69.

The Artizans and Labourers' Dwellings Acts. Certain sections of the Lands Clauses Acts are incorporated with this act; and in applying it, the Artizans Act is to be considered the special act, and the local authority to be the promoters. It is, however, the practice of some equity draftsmen to intitule petitions, not only in the matters of the settlement, and of the Artizans Act and the Lands Clauses Act, but also in the Local Government Provisional Orders Confirmation Act, under which the Artizans Act was in the particular case brought into play.

(*h*) Sect. 85. (*i*) Sect. 87; *Re Mutlow*, 27 W. R. 245.

Matters relating to Infants.

———

CHAPTER I.

CUSTODY OF INFANTS.

BY a recent statute (a), provision has been made for giving the court power to settle differences as to the custody of, and access to, infants, as between their mother on the one hand, and their father or legal guardian on the other. Formerly, in case of a separation between a husband and wife, and a refusal on the part of the husband to allow the wife to have custody of, or access to, the children, the latter had no remedy; and a clause in a deed of separation providing that the husband should give up the custody and control of the children was considered to be void.

Under the above act, however, the wife may present a petition to the Chancery Division by her next friend, intituled, in the matter of the infant or infants, and in the matter of "the Act 36 Vict. c. 12, intituled, 'An Act to amend the Law as to the Custody of Infants,'"

(a) 36 Vict. c. 12.

stating the grounds for the application, and praying for access to the children, or that they may be delivered up to her and remain under her control until they attain such age not exceeding sixteen years, as the court may direct.

The order may be made upon such terms as to the father's or guardian's right of access, as the court may think fit.

The act also provides that a clause in a separation deed, giving the wife the custody and control of the children shall not be invalid; but the court will not enforce such a clause where it considers that to do so would be detrimental to the child (*b*).

The petition is prepared, presented, answered and heard, and the order drawn up, passed, entered and enforced in the usual way; and the petition should be served on the father or guardian of the infant.

——◆——

CHAPTER II.

GUARDIANS OF INFANTS.

THE Chancery Division is the guardian of all infants who have none other, that is to say, supposing that the court is invoked.

How Infants are made Wards of Court. An infant may be made a ward of court in several ways; as, for instance, by a suit regarding his property or person; although when he has no property the court

(*b*) Sect. 2; and see *Re Besant*,   order, see *Re Taylor*, L. R., 4
40 L. T. 469; and for form of   Ch. D. 157.

will not interfere (c). An infant may also be made a ward of court by paying trust money into court under the Trustee Relief Act, in which money the infant is interested (d); or by an order for maintenance (e).

Of course the court cannot exercise a personal control over its wards, and consequently it will appoint a guardian of the estate and also of the person of an infant : the same person is usually appointed to both offices.

Mode of applying for Appointment and Removal of Guardian. All applications to the court, concerning the appointment and removal of guardians (whether appointed by the court or otherwise) are made by summons, intituled "In the matter of A. B. an infant."

This summons must be served on the father, or mother, or testamentary guardian of the infant, and supported by an affidavit of the facts, and of the fitness of the proposed new guardian, and of his willingness to accept the office. The proposed guardian will almost invariably have to give security.

A guardian of a ward of court, may apply to the court by summons from time to time with reference to the management of the infants' property. The office of a guardian appointed by the court, if holden by two persons jointly, ceases on the death of one, or on the marriage of a female guardian (f).

(c) Re Fynn, 2 De G. & S. 481; Clayton v. Clark, 3 De G. F. & J. 682.

(d) Re Bernand, 16 W. R. 538.

(e) See Chapter IV. of this Sub-division.

(f) Bradshaw v. Bradshaw, 1 Russ. 528; Jones v. Powell, 9 Bea. 315.

CHAPTER III.

MARRIAGE OF WARDS OF COURT.

Marriage without Consent a Contempt of Court. It is a contempt of court to marry a female ward of court without the consent of the court.

Consent, how obtained. This consent is obtained on summons or by petition, the latter being the proper course where the infant's property is considerable, and it is desired to effect a settlement under the provisions of the statute 18 & 19 Vict. c. 43, mentioned in the next chapter. The petition or summons is intituled in the matter of the infant, and (in the case of the petition) states the material facts, namely, the infant's age, the fact of the proposed marriage, and the name, age, rank, fortune and occupation of the proposed husband; and prays for an inquiry as to whether the proposed marriage is a proper one, and that if so, proposals for a settlement may be received, and that on the execution of a settlement the marriage may take place. The petition is generally presented by the infant by her next friend, but sometimes by the intended husband, or by both of them, and is presented, answered and set down, in the usual way; but on being called on it is usually adjourned at once into chambers, without any order being made in court, and is proceeded on in chambers in the usual way. The petition or summons must of course be supported by affidavit of the facts.

Preparation of Settlement. If the marriage, and the proposals for a settlement, are approved, the latter is prepared by the solicitor of the ward, and left at chambers, where it is settled in the usual way; but evidence of the fitness of the proposed trustees must be adduced. The settlement being finally approved, the chief clerk sends a minute of the order approving the settlement, and giving the leave of the court to the parties to marry on the execution of it, to the registrar, by whom it is drawn up in the usual way.

Marriage without Consent. If a person marries a female ward of court, without consent of the court, he is guilty of contempt even where he did not know of the wardship, and had the consent of the guardian. Any person may move or petition the court, in such a case, for an inquiry as to the validity of the marriage, and for a proper settlement.

Proceedings under the Marriage Act. Under this act (g), the marriage of a bachelor or spinster infant requires the consent of its father if living, or if dead, of certain other persons. But if the father be *non compos mentis*, or if the other persons be so or be beyond the seas, or unreasonably, or from undue motives, refuse their consent, an application may be made by petition to the Chancery Division for a declaration that the proposed marriage is proper, which declaration has the same effect as the required consent. Such a petition is intituled in the matter of the infant, and in the matter of the act of parliament, 4 Geo. 4, c. 76, intituled, "An Act for amending the Laws respecting the Solemnization of Marriage in England," and is presented, answered and heard in the usual way, its statements being supported by proper evidence.

If a valid marriage of an infant, without such consent as is required by the Marriage Act, has been obtained

---

(g) 4 Geo. 4, c. 76, ss. 16, 17.

by false or fraudulent means, an action at the suit of
the attorney-general, on the relation of the parent or
guardian, may be commenced for forfeiture of all the
estate accruing to the offending party by reason of the
marriage; and such estate will be directed to be secured
for the benefit of the innocent party, and of the issue of
the marriage, or if neither party be innocent, then for the
issue only.   Such an action must be commenced within
one year, and the attorney-general will not sanction
such an action unless the circumstances are verified by
affidavit of the relator, intituled in the matter of the
marriage of the parties, and in the matter of the act.

CHAPTER IV.

INFANTS' PROPERTY.

As to what a guardian may or may not do in relation
to his ward's property, the reader is referred to treatises
on equity jurisprudence; but when it is desirable to
apply to the court for directions, the application is
made by summons intituled in the matter of the infant.

Mode of Applying. Whether the infant is a
ward of court or not, a summons may be taken out by
the guardian, for the allowance of maintenance out of
the income of property belonging to the infant.   The
summons, if original, is intituled in the matter of the
infant; but if taken out in a pending action, is of
course intituled in the action.   It must be served on
the trustees (if any), or other persons interested in the
property, and supported by an affidavit showing the

necessity for the maintenance, the means of the father, the amount of the infant's property, and proposing a scheme for the application of the desired maintenance.

Settlement by Infants. An infant is incapable of settling his or her property, except with the aid of the court; but by 18 & 19 Vict. c. 43, a male of twenty years, and a female of seventeen, may upon marriage, with the sanction of the court, make a valid settlement; except that no power of appointment can be exercised by an infant if the donor has declared an intention to the contrary, and except that a disentailing deed, or a power of appointment executed by the infant under the act, is void if the infant dies under age.

The application must be made in all cases by petition (h) of the infant or his or her guardian, intituled in the matter of the infant and of the act. The petition must be served on all persons appearing to be interested in the property, and should set forth the facts, and pray "that a proper settlement of the property may under or by virtue of the said act of parliament be sanctioned by this honorable court, and that your petitioner may be at liberty upon or in contemplation of the said marriage to execute such settlement."

If the infant is a ward of court, the application should be joined with the application for leave to marry.

As in the case of a petition for leave to marry, so a petition to sanction an infant's settlement, is usually at once adjourned into chambers, and proceeded on there in the usual way.

The evidence in such cases is prescribed by the Rules of 8th August, 1857, r. 20, and must show (1) the age

(h) *Pearcth* v. *Marriott*, W. N. 1866, p. 48.

of the infant; (2) whether the infant has any parents or guardians; (3) with whom or under whose care the infant is living, and if the infant has no parents or guardians, what near relations he or she has; (4) the rank of the infant and parents; (5) the infant's property; (6) the age, rank and position of the other party; (7) such other party's property and income; (8) the fitness of the proposed trustees and their consent to act. It would seem that the mother of the infant with regard to the first five points, and the other party's father with regard to the residue, should make the affidavit if possible; but if not, the ages of the parties must be proved by certificates of birth duly verified (*i*).

The proposed settlement being sanctioned, it is proposed and settled in chambers, and the order drawn up in the usual way (*k*).

(*i*) Daniell's Ch. Pr. 670.　　(*k*) Sup. p. 280.

SUB-DIVISION IV.

Miscellaneous Matters.

CHAPTER I.

ADMINISTRATION SUMMONSES.

UNDER the Chancery Procedure Act, 1854, a method was introduced, by which an order for the administration of the *personal* estate of a deceased person might be obtained in chambers by any person claiming as creditor, legatee or next of kin. The matter is commenced by an originating summons, intituled in the matter of the deceased person, and between the applicant as plaintiff, and the executor or administrator as defendant, and calling on the latter to attend on a day named, at the judge's chambers, to show cause why an order for the administration of the personal estate of the deceased should not be made (a).

When applicable to Real Estate. No order for the administration of real estate can be made on summons, except where all the testator's real estate is devised to trustees for sale (b), or although not *devised* to them where they are empowered to sell it (c), or (which is the same thing), where it is devised subject to payment of debts (d) ; in all of which cases, an order for administration of the realty may be obtained. In other cases, however, an action must be instituted if administration of real estate is desired.

Procedure on Summons. The summons is served like a writ of summons, and the defendant must enter an appearance to it, if he wishes to be heard, and give notice of his appearance (e) ; and, save that there are no pleadings, and no hearing in court, the matter is to all intents and purposes governed as to parties, service of order, appointment of guardians *ad litem*, and so on, by the rules applicable to actions.

On the day fixed for the return of the summons, the defendant may attend, and show cause against it, or consent to the order asked for.

Evidence. It is necessary that on the return of the summons, the plaintiff should prove (1) his title to sue as creditor, legatee, or next of kin ; and (2) that the defendant is the executor or administrator of the deceased ; and, where administration of realty is required, that he is devisee in trust for sale of all the realty, or devisee

(a) 15 & 16 Vict. c. 86, s. 45.

(b) Ib. sect. 47.

(c) *Colman* v. *Turner*, L. R., 10 Eq. 230.

(d) *Ogden* v. *Lowry*, 4 W. R. 156.

(e) Cons. Ord. XXXV. r. 9.

subject to debts, or donee of a power of sale over the whole of the realty. These facts about the defendant, must be proved by production of the probate, or letters of administration, as the case may be, and notice should be given to the defendant to produce them, and if he fails to do so, the summons must be adjourned for the production of office copies.

If the order for administration is made, the subsequent proceedings for taking accounts, and making inquiries, under the order, are had in chambers, in the same way as if the order had been a judgment made in an administration action instituted in the usual way.

----◆----

CHAPTER II.

CHARITIES.

In this chapter, it is not intended to include any case in which there is a dispute between the persons representing charitable property on the one hand, and some third party who claims that property for himself on the other hand. The following procedure only refers to cases in which the *administration* of the charity is concerned.

Actions by Attorney-General. The most formal method of commencing proceedings for the administration of charitable property, is an action by the attorney-general; and in heavy and important matters, this course is still adopted. But the questions for decision may be brought before the court in a cheaper and more expeditious way as " a matter," under the provisions of several acts of parliament.

Consent of Charity Commissioners. Before any proceeding can be commenced, however, concerning any charity by any one except the attorney-general, he must obtain the order or certificate of the Board of Charity Commissioners authorizing the proceedings (*f*): but of course this only relates to the administration of the charity, and not to questions touching its property arising between the charity, and third parties, as, for instance, the getting out of court of funds paid in under the Trustee Relief Act, or the Lands Clauses Consolidation Act (*g*).

The Charity Commissioners do not by any means give their certificate, as a matter of course, and the application for it has to be made to them in a certain form, which can be obtained at their office.

Romilly's Act. One mode of applying to the court for the administration of any charitable trust, is under the statute 52 Geo. 3, c. 101 (known as Romilly's Act), which authorizes any two or more persons interested in the charity (*h*), with the previous sanction of the attorney-general, to obtain relief by petitioning the court. Such a petition is intituled in the matter of the particular charity, and of the act in question; it must be signed by the petitioners in the presence of their solicitor; and their counsel must certify on it, that it is in his opinion a proper petition to be presented under the act, and the solicitor must also certify on it that the petitioners are capable of paying the costs. The petition is then left with the attorney-general's clerk for his sig-

---

(*f*) 16 & 17 Vict. c. 137, ss. 17, 18.

(*g*) *Re Poplar Free School*, 39 L. T. 88 ; *Re Lister's Hospital*, 6 De G., M. & G. 184.

(*h*) *Re Bedford Charities*, 2 Swan. 518.

nature after which it is presented, answered and heard in the usual way.

Romilly's Act is, however, limited in its operation, being confined to plain and simple cases, where the opinion or direction of the court is required (i).

The Charitable Trusts Act, 1853. By this act, applications relating to any charity, of which the gross annual income exceeds 30l., were authorized to be made by summons, by any person, subject, however, to the certificate of the Charity Commissioners. The summons must (except where it is merely for the appointment of new trustees and a vesting order), be served on the attorney-general, and on all parties affected by the order sought for. The copy served on the attorney-general, should be sealed for service. The judge has a discretion to refuse to proceed on the summons, if he thinks the case would be more fitly dealt with by an action or petition.

Applications under this act are not now of frequent occurrence, because by the Charitable Trusts Act, 1860, very large powers were given to the Charity Commissioners themselves, authorizing them on the application of parties interested on behalf of a charity, to make such orders as might be made by a judge in chambers, such orders to be subject to an appeal to the Chancery Division (k). But the commissioners may decline to exercise their powers, in any case which, by reason of its contentious nature, or of any special questions of law or fact involved in it, may seem to them more suitable for the adjudication of the court (l).

(i) See *Phillipott's Charity*, 8 Sim. 389; *Re Manchester New College*, 16 Bea. 610; *Corporation of Ludlow v. Greenhouse*, 1 Bli., N. S. 17.

(k) 23 & 24 Vict. c. 136, s. 8.

(l) Ib. sect. 5.

U

Appeals from Charity Commissioners. With
regard to appeals from orders of the commissioners, the
attorney-general or any person authorized by him, or by
the commissioners themselves, and where the gross
annual income of the charity (exclusive of lands and
buildings actually used by it), exceeds 50*l.*, any trustee
or person acting in its administration, or any two inhabitants of the parish or district in which it (having
such gross income), is specially applicable, may, within
three calendar months after the definitive publication of
such order, present a petition to the Chancery Division,
appealing against it, and praying such relief as the case
may require.   Any school master or mistress, or other
officer, removed by order of the board without the concurrence of the trustees or governors of the charity, or
the majority of them, and without the approval of a
special visitor (if any) of the charity, may within two
calendar months next after such removal, appeal in like
manner; and the court may, if it shall think fit at any
stage of the proceedings, require the commissioners'
reasons for their order, and may remit the order to them
for reconsideration with or without a declaration in
relation to it, or may make a substitutive or other
order in relation to the matter of the appeal as it shall
think just.   And the court may also make any order
as to the costs of the appeal, and, before hearing or proceeding with it, require the appellant (other than the
attorney-general) to give security for costs (*m*).

No petition of appeal can be presented by any one
except the attorney-general before the expiration of
twenty-one days after written notice, under the appel-

(*m*) 23 & 24 Vict. c. 136, s. 8.

lant's hand, of his or her intention to appeal shall have been delivered to the commissioners at their office (*n*).

The attorney-general, or any person authorized by him, or by the commissioners, may appear on such petition as respondent (*o*), and the court may make any order concerning the costs of such respondent (*o*).

Form of Appeal. The petition of appeal is intituled in the matter of the particular charity, and in the matter of "The Charitable Trusts Acts, 1853 to 1869," and must state the circumstance which gives the appellant a *locus standi*, the creation and state of the charity, the order appealed against, the publication of notice of the order by the commissioners, the fact that the order has been definitively published, the reasons why the petitioner is aggrieved by the order, and the fact of the twenty-one days' notice having been given of the petitioner's intention to appeal; and should pray for the discharge or variation of the order, or that it may be remitted for further consideration with a declaration, or for a specific declaration, and that the costs may be provided for (*p*).

Charities to which Charity Acts apply. The charities to which the Charity Acts apply are limited (*q*), and do not include many cases which are generally looked upon as charitable trusts; such as the universities and their colleges and halls, Eton and Winchester colleges, *bonâ fide* meeting-houses, the British Museum, friendly and benefit societies, savings banks, Queen Anne's Bounty, societies for religious or charitable purposes wholly supported by voluntary contributions,

(*n*) Ib.

(*o*) Ib. sect. 9.

(*p*) See Daniell's Forms, 3rd

cd. 1157.

(*q*) See 16 & 17 Vict. c. 137, s. 66.

missionary societies whose funds or property are without the jurisdiction, and some others; but as this does not concern the question of procedure, the reader is referred to works treating of charities, and the Charitable Trusts Acts.

However, the commissioners may order that the acts shall extend to any such charities, on the application of the trustees or other administrators of the charity (s).

The subject of charities is too large to be treated of fully in a small work of this kind, which relates merely to the ordinary business of the court, and the reader is therefore refered for further information to Daniell's or Evans's Chancery Practice, and to works treating exclusively of charities.

CHAPTER III.

MARRIED WOMEN'S PROPERTY.

UNDER the Married Women's Property Act, 1870 (t), in any question arising between a husband and wife in relation to property which is declared by the act to be the separate property of the wife, either party may apply to the Chancery Division by summons or motion, or to the judge of the county court of the district in which either party resides; and on such application the judge may make such order, and direct such inquiries, and award such costs, as he shall think proper.

If either party requires it, the judge may hear the application in his private room (t). The application is usually made by summons intituled in the matter of

(s) 32 & 33 Vict. c. 110, s. 4.   (t) 33 & 34 Vict. c. 93, s. 9.

extended by 45 & 46 Vict c 75 s. 97. M. W. P. Act 1882

"A. B., the wife of C. B.," and in the matter of the act, and should be supported by evidence of the facts relied on.

Life Policies under the Act. Under the same act a married man may effect a policy on his own life for the benefit of his wife, or of her and his children, or any of them. When the sum assured by the policy becomes payable, the court, or the county court judge, will appoint a trustee of the money, whose receipt will be a good discharge to the office (*u*).

The application for the trustee should be by petition (*v*) intituled like the above-mentioned summons, and should ask, not merely for the appointment of the trustee, but, where the policy does not express the respective interests of the wife and children, should ask for directions as to the distribution of the fund, which will in general be made on the lines of the Statute of Distributions, *i. e.*, one-third to the widow, and the residue amongst the children.

———◆———

CHAPTER IV.

VENDORS AND PURCHASERS.

UNDER the Vendors and Purchasers Act, 1874 (*x*), certain questions arising between vendors and purchasers may be settled on summons in chambers, without the necessity of commencing an action. The summons is entitled "In the matter of a contract for the sale of real [*or* leasehold] estate, made between John Smith and Thomas Arnold. And in the matter

(*u*) Ib. sect. 10.   L. R., 6 Ch. D. 127.
(*v*) *Re Mellor's Policy Trusts,*   (*x*) 37 & 38 Vict. c. 78, s. 9.

By s. 11. 45 & 46 Vict c 75 the wife may ... the benefit of her husband — children ... may appoint a trustee

of the Vendors and Purchasers Act, 1874;" and states that the summons is an application, that it may be declared that the applicant's contention (stating it shortly) is correct, and that a good title has or has not (as the case may be) been shown in accordance with the particulars and conditions of sale. And that the other party may pay the costs of the application.

The summons is served, returned, and heard, or adjourned into court (w), and the order made thereon, or the application dismissed, in the usual way. In one case (x), decided in January, 1877, Lord Justice James said that the act " was never intended to apply to cases where there were questions of controverted facts. Their lordships could not go into the question as to who was entitled to the land, since the settlement of that question would necessitate a perusal of the abstracts of title, and they were not before the court. Any strict point of law or construction arising upon the abstract or upon the purchaser's requisitions, or in respect of the contract, might be properly brought before the court in a summary way as provided by the act." In a case decided in March of the same year (y), however, his lordship said, " My opinion is, that upon the true construction of this act of parliament, whatever could be done in chambers upon a reference as to title under a decree *where the contract was established*, can be done upon proceedings under this act; and that what this act has done is this, it has enabled the parties to dispense with the form of a bill and answer (writ and judgment), and at once to

---

(w) *Re Brown and Sibley's Contract*, L. R., 3 Ch. D. 156.

(x) *Popple and Barratt's Contract*, 25 W. R. 248.

(y) *Burroughs, Lynn and Sexton's Contract*, L. R., 5 Ch. D. 601.

put themselves in chambers in exactly the same position in which they would have been, and with all the rights which they would have had under the old form of decree. The order, therefore, must be varied by entering the evidence as read, and omitting the clause relating to its rejection." These two cases would appear to be scarcely reconcileable, but it is apprehended that the latter is the statement which has been since acted upon, and that evidence of controverted facts is now clearly admissible.

An order under this act must be appealed from within twenty-one days (z).

CHAPTER V.

MATTERS RELATING TO SOLICITORS.

It is not intended to give any account here of the means by which gentlemen are admitted to practise the profession of solicitors. Information in relation to such matters is given in many manuals written for the purpose, and forms no part of the practice peculiar to the Chancery Division.

It is proposed in this work merely to treat shortly of the mode in which a solicitor who has misconducted himself in the *practice of his profession* can be brought before the court, and punished for his misconduct ; and also to give some account of the manner in which a solicitor's bill of costs may be taxed, and how a solicitor may obtain a lien for his costs upon the subject-matter of his professional labours.

(z) *Re Blyth and Young's Contract*, L. R., 13 Ch. D. 116 ; 28 W. R. 266 ; 41 L. T., N. S. 746.

Section 1.

Striking a Solicitor off the Roll.

Every solicitor is an officer of the Supreme Court of Judicature, and as such is liable to be summarily suspended or dismissed from his office for professional misconduct. An application for that purpose may be made by the Incorporated Law Society, or by a private individual who has been injured by the misconduct; and fourteen days' notice of the application must, together with all affidavits intended to be used, be given and delivered to the registrar of solicitors, and an affidavit of such service and delivery must be produced when the application is made (*b*). The affidavits and notice are intituled, in the matter of the solicitor, thus: "In the matter of Percival Brooks, a solicitor of the Supreme Court of Judicature," and are headed in the usual way, with the name of the court, division and judge.

Mode of Application. The application is made by *ex parte* motion, for an order *nisi*, calling on the solicitor to show cause to the contrary on a day named. If the order is granted, it must be personally served on the solicitor, unless an order for substituted service is obtained. If cause is shown on the day named, the case is then and there determined, and the order *nisi* dismissed, or made absolute, or varied; but if no cause is shown, the applicant subsequently moves *ex parte* to make the order absolute, on an affidavit of service of the order *nisi*, and production of the registrar's certificate that no cause has been shown against it. The court being once set in motion, the applicant

(*b*) 37 & 38 Vict. c. 68, ss. 7, 8.

cannot by retiring from the case put an end to it, as the registrar of solicitors may attend and ask for the order to be made absolute; and if made absolute, he may see that it is drawn up and put in force (c).

Re-admission. A solicitor who has been struck off the roll may apply to be re-admitted, by petition to the Master of the Rolls; but must, six weeks before making the application, give the same notices as if he were applying to be admitted for the first time, and the affidavits in support must be filed at the Petty Bag Office, together with a copy of them for the use of the registrar of solicitors (d); and an affidavit of these regulations having been complied with must be produced on the hearing of the petition (d). The petition is presented at the Petty Bag Office, and must be served on the registrar of solicitors, at least fourteen days before the hearing (d). The order if made, is drawn up, passed and entered in the usual way, and must be filed with the clerk of the Petty Bag (d).

———

SECTION 2.

Taxing a Solicitor's Bill of Costs.

A solicitor's bill may be taxed, *i. e.* criticised with a view to its reduction, either by his own client or by a third party who has been ordered to pay the costs of the client; but, save as is subsequently stated, the procedure is the same in either case.

The initiatory procedure is different according to the

(c) Ib. sects. 10, 11.   (d) Regulations as to Re-admission, Nov. 1875.

date at which the application is made, and is as follows :—

(1) If made within one calendar month from the delivery of the bill, it is by petition or motion of course.

(2) If made after the expiration of that period, but within twelve calendar months, it is by *ex parte* motion.

(3) If after that period, *or* within that period after a verdict given, or writ of inquiry issued, for the amount (except payment by a defendant of costs indorsed on a writ (*h*)), the application is by summons duly served on the solicitor, and supported by affidavit setting forth the reasons for the application, and will only be granted under special circumstances; and the applicant will usually have to pay the costs of the application (*i*).

When the application under the third of the above sets of circumstances is made by a third party, the judge, in considering it, may take into account any special circumstances applicable to the applicant, although not to the client (*k*) ; the solicitor may also be ordered to deliver a copy of his bill to the third party, on payment of a proper charge for the same.

All applications for taxation are intituled in the matter of the solicitor in question.

The order for taxation being obtained, the costs are taxed in the usual way, as upon a judgment (*l*).

(*h*) R. S. C., Ord. III. r. 7.

(*i*) Daniell's Forms, 3rd ed. 1142 : *Re Hair*, 11 Bea. 96.

(*k*) 6 & 7 Vict. c. 73, s. 38 ; and see as to applications by cestuis que trustent, sect. 39.

(*l*) Infra, Division III. Chapter II.

SECTION 3.

Obtaining Lien in favour of a Solicitor.

Where any property has been recovered or preserved in any action or matter, through the instrumentality of a solicitor, the judge before whom the action or matter is pending, or was heard (*m*), may, on the petition of the solicitor, declare that he is entitled to a charge on the property for his costs and charges (*n*). The petition is intituled in the action or matter in question, and also in the matter of the Solicitors Act, 1860, and must be served on the parties interested, and is presented, answered and heard, and the order drawn up, passed and entered in the usual way, and must be supported by affidavit.

CHAPTER VI.

DISTRINGAS NOTICES, AND STOP ORDERS.

THE Bank of England, and most public companies, refuse to take any notice of trusts or equities, and always permit a transfer of stock standing in their registers by the person therein registered as the owner. The court will, however, interfere to protect parties equitably entitled by a proceeding called distringas, or by a restraining order: and where funds are in court it will issue what is known as a stop order to prevent their being paid out.

Distringas. Up to the year 1880, this process consisted of a fictitious writ addressed to the sheriffs of

(*m*) *Owen v. Henshaw*, L. R., 7 Ch. D. 385; *Henrick v. Sutton*, L. R., 6 Ch. D. 865.
(*n*) 23 & 24 Vict. c. 127, s. 28.

London, or of the county where the company carried on business, commanding them to distrain on the Bank of England or other public company (o) to compel them to appear to an action said to have been commenced against them.

No action was, however, in reality commenced, and the writ was never delivered to the sheriffs, and the only effect of it was, that the bank or company could not transfer the stock without first giving notice to the person suing out the distringas.

The writ of distringas is now, however, abolished (p), and the practice made more rational by the substitution of a notice verified by affidavit.

New Practice. Under the new practice the party desiring to effect a distringas, makes an affidavit in the following form (q) :—

> In the matter of an indenture of settlement, dated the 3rd day of May, 1878, and made between John Ball, of the one part, Selina Williams, of the second part, and Thomas Ball and Arthur Clifford, of the third part,
> and
> In the matter of the act of parliament, 5 Vict. c. 5.
>
> I, the above-named John Ball, of No. 105, High Street, in the city of Exeter, grocer, make oath and say, that according to the best of my knowledge, information and belief, I am beneficially interested in the stock comprised in the settlement above mentioned, which stock, according to the best of my knowledge and belief, now consist of the stock specified in the notice hereto annexed.
>
> Sworn, &c.
>
> This affidavit is filed on behalf of John Ball, whose address for service is 105, High Street, Exeter, aforesaid.

(o) Although 5 Vict. c. 5 only refers to the bank, it has been the practice that a distringas may issue against any public company. Seton, 4th ed. 285, and R. S. C., Ord. XLVI. r. 3 (1880), seems to confirm this practice.

(p) R. S. C., Ord. XLVI. r. 2a (1880).

(q) Form B. 28, Sched. R. S. C., 1880.

To this affidavit a notice in the following form (*r*) must be annexed :—

To the London and North Western Railway Company.

Take notice, that the stock comprised in and now subject to the trusts of the settlement, referred to in the affidavit to which this notice is annexed, consists of the following, that is to say [*here specify the stock*].

This notice is intended to stop the transfer of the stock only, and not the receipt of dividends [*or*, the receipt of the dividends on the stock, as well as the transfer of the stock].

(Signed)   John Ball.

The affidavit and notice are filed at the central office, and an office copy of the affidavit and duplicate of the notice sealed with the seal of the office is procured and served on the company (*s*).

This service has the same effect as the old writ of distringas, for a period of five years (*t*) ; and that period may be extended from time to time, for further periods of five years at a time, by a notice of renewal signed by the person by whom or on whose behalf the original notice was given. But such notice must be served before the expiration of the five years secured by the last preceding notice, or a new affidavit will be neces- sary (*u*).

The affidavit and notice are usually served by being taken to the solicitors for the bank, or to the secretary of the public body, as the case may be, together with the notice. If any application for transfer or payment be afterwards made to the bank or other public body, they will not comply with such application for eight

---

(*r*) Form B. 23, Sched. R. S. C., 1880 ; and R. S. C., Ord. XLVI. r. 5.

(*s*) R. S. C., Ord. XLVI. r. 4.
(*t*) Ib. r. 7.
(*u*) Ib. r. 8.

days, and will at once send notice of it by post to the person who obtained the distringas at the address for service (x).

These eight days give time to institute an action, in which, if desirable, the bank or other public body may be made co-defendants, and restrained by injunction in the ordinary way; otherwise, at the expiration of the eight days, the stock will be transferred, or the dividends paid to the person applying for such transfer or payment (y).

The person obtaining the distringas, may at any time discharge it by a request in writing, signed by him and sent to the bank or other company; but if any other person claiming an interest in the stock wishes to discharge it, he must apply by motion on notice, or by petition duly served (z). And upon the hearing of such motion or petition, the court may award costs against the person obtaining the distringas, or against the party applying.

In case of any change in the address for service the same should be at once notified to the bank or other company by a memorandum to that effect sent in a pre-paid letter (a). So, also, if it is found necessary to correct the description of the stock, this may be effected by filing and serving an amended notice, sealed with the central office seal. The amended notice takes effect only from the day of its service (b).

Restraining Orders. A restraining order is similar in its effect to a distringas, except that the bank or other public body cannot transfer the stock or pay the

---

(x) R. S. C., Ord. XLVI. r. 4.
(y) Cons. Ord. XXVII. r. 4;
and R. S. C. Ord. XLVI. r. 10.
(z) R. S. C., Ord. XLVI. r. 9.
(a) Ib. r. 6.
(b) Ib. r. 11.

dividends at the expiration of eight days' notice, but are restrained until the order is discharged by a subsequent order of the court.

Restraining orders are granted on *ex parte* motion, or *ex parte* petition, intituled "In the matter of the act of parliament, 5th Vict. c. 5, intituled, ' An Act to make further provisions for the Administration of Justice,' and in the matter of Matthew Brown" (the applicant). The petition (if the application is made in that form) should set forth special grounds to induce the court to grant the application, and should pray that the bank, or other public company, may be restrained from permitting the transfer of the stock in question (describing it), and from paying any dividends due or to become due in respect thereof until further order.

The application must be supported by an affidavit showing the special circumstances relied on.

The order, if granted, is drawn up, passed and entered in the usual way, and served on the chief accountant of the bank, or the secretary of any other public body ; and it remains in force until discharged or varied by an order of the court, obtained on motion of any party interested, of which notice must be given to the party who has obtained the order. A person who has obtained a distringas, may also apply for a restraining order.

Stop Orders. Wherever money, or stock, or securities are standing, or are deposited in the name of the paymaster-general, to the credit of an action or matter, and any party entitled to the money or stock or securities, or any of them, assigns or mortgages his interest, the assignee or mortgagee may obtain what is known as " a stop order;" the effect of which is to prevent the fund in question being paid or transferred out of court, or otherwise dealt with, until the stop order is discharged or another order made, directing the fund to be paid or transferred, notwithstanding the stop order.

Stop orders are obtained on summons, intituled in the action or matter to the credit of which the fund is in court, and duly served on the assignor or mortgagor. Evidence in support must be produced, showing the title of the assignor, and (unless admitted) of the assignee, to the fund. The proceedings in the action usually furnish sufficient evidence of the first, and the assignment or mortgage should be produced and duly verified to prove the second. If a person who has obtained a stop order assigns his interest, his assignee may obtain a stop order in the usual way, but he need only produce the original stop order and evidence of the assignment. On the application for a stop order, the certificate of the paymaster-general that the fund is in court, must also be produced.

The order, or an office copy of it, must be left at the pay office.

Notice of any application to deal with the fund, must be served on the party who has obtained a stop order; and, on the hearing of the application, the order may be discharged, or payment, or transfer out, ordered to the person in whose favour it was made; or such payment or transfer may be delayed, to enable him to take steps to assert his right.

CHAPTER VII.

MATTERS NOT BEFORE SPECIFIED.

In addition to the several matters before specified there are many of which it would be outside the province of this Work to give a detailed account, but one or two of which will be shortly noticed in this chapter.

Registration of Trade Marks. By the Trade Marks Registration Acts, 1875 and 1876 (*f*), a register of trade marks was instituted, and no action can be commenced for infringement, unless registration of the trade mark in question has been made or refused.

Any person aggrieved by the wrong entry on the register of the name of some one else, or the omission of his own name as proprietor of a trade mark, or by the registration of a mark not authorized by the act, may apply to rectify the register (*g*). The subject of trade marks is a special one, forming almost a distinct branch of practice, and the reader is, therefore, referred to books on the subject, and to the rules under the Trade Marks Act, for further information.

Municipal Corporations. Under the statutes 5 & 6 Will. 4, c. 76, s. 71, and 16 & 17 Vict. c. 137, s. 65, the court may on petition appoint new trustees of property held by a municipal corporation for charitable purposes.

The application is made by petition, intituled in the matter of the charity or charities in question, (shortly describing them,) and in the matter of the act 52 Geo. 3, c. 101, and in the matter of the Municipal Corporations Act, 1835, and of the Charitable Trusts Act, 1853.

(*f*) 38 & 39 Vict. c. 91 ; 39 & 40 Vict. c. 33.

(*g*) *Ex parte Stephens*, 24 W. R. 819.

Production of Cestui que Vie. By the statute
6 Anne, c. 18, it was enacted, that where a person is in
possession of land for the life of another (called the
cestui que vie), the reversioner, upon affidavit that he has
cause to believe that the *cestui que vie* is dead, may obtain an order for his production; and, in default of such
production, may enter upon and hold the land. The
application under the act is by *ex parte* motion, founded
on an affidavit of the facts, and the order is, in the first
instance, for production of the *cestui que vie* out of court,
at a particular place and time named. The order is
served on the tenant *pur autre vie.* If the production is
not made according to the order, a second application
must be made *ex parte*, for the production of the *cestui
que vie* in court, or before commissioners, and must be
supported by an affidavit of the service of the first order,
and non-production at the time and place named in it.
The second order is served on the tenant *pur autre
vie* personally. Sometimes this second order provides
that in default of production the *cestui que vie* shall be
presumed to be dead; but if it does not, then a third
application is necessary for that purpose. Where the
tenant for life or *cestui que vie* is abroad the party presenting the order may apply to send over commissioners
appointed by the order to view such person. The return
of the commissioners is filed at the Petty Bag Office.
If it appears to the court on affidavit or otherwise, that
the person ordered to produce the *cestui que vie* cannot do
so, from no fault of his own, and that the *cestui que vie*
is in fact alive, no order for production will be made.

Mortgage Debenture Acts. Under the statutes
28 & 29 Vict. c. 78, and 33 & 34 Vict. c. 20, a *mortgagor*
of a registered security may, upon default by the com-

pany in doing so, apply by summons for an order for the discharge of the security in the company's register, and a holder of a mortgage debenture may, upon default in payment of principal or interest, apply by summons or petition for the appointment of a receiver. Proceedings under these acts are intituled in the matter of the particular company, and in the matter of "The Mortgage Debenture Acts, 1865 and 1867" (*h*).

Executors and Administrators' Accounts.

By the 19th section of the statutes 13 & 14 Vict. c. 35, and the 23 & 24 Vict. c. 38, s. 14, executors or administrators are enabled immediately, or at any time, after probate or grant of administration, to obtain an order to have an account taken in chambers of the debts and liabilities affecting the personal estate of the deceased. The order may be obtained either on *ex parte* summons, or on motion or petition of course, intituled "In the matter of the estate of the deceased" (describing him). On the order being made, a summons to proceed is taken out, and the account taken in the usual way. The account may be *ordered* to be taken in a district registry.

Sales of Ships or Shares therein under the Merchant Shipping Acts.

Under these acts a ship or a share therein, vested by transmission in an unqualified owner, may be ordered to be sold. The application is by petition, intituled in the matter of the particular ship, and of the Merchant Shipping Act, 1854, and it must be duly served.

Protectorship by the Court of certain Settlements.

Under the statute 3 & 4 Will. 4, c. 74,

(*h*) See Daniell's Forms, 3rd ed. 1232.

the Chancery Division becomes in certain cases protector of settlements. When this is the case, and it is desired to bar the entail, the leave of the court becomes necessary, and this may be obtained on petition of the tenant in tail, intituled in the matter of the person who would be protector if it were not for some disability vesting his office in the Court, and in the matter of the above act. This petition should be served on all persons interested in remainder.

Registration of Titles Act. By the statute 25 & 26 Vict. c. 53, a land registry was constituted, with a staff of officers, whose duty it is to investigate titles submitted to them for registration as indefeasible, and any question or dispute which may arise in the process of registration may be referred to a judge of the Chancery Division. Under another part of the act, the Chancery Division is empowered, upon the application of any person empowered by the act to apply for registration of title, to carry out sales of land with an indefeasible title.

The application is made by petition or summons, intituled in the matter of the party applying, and in the matter of the act. The sale, if ordered to be carried out under the act, is effectuated by a vesting order. Such applications, however, are very rare.

Declaration of Titles Act. Under the statute 25 & 26 Vict. c. 67, any person claiming to be entitled to freeholds in possession in fee, or to have a power of disposing of the fee, or any person entitled to apply for the registration of an indefeasible title under the act for registration of titles, may apply to the court by petition, for a declaration that the petitioner has an indefeasible title to the hereditaments in question.

The petition is intituled in the matter of the party applying, and in the matter of "The Declaration of Title Act, 1862." On the hearing of the petition, the court, if satisfied that the petitioner has *proved such a possession*, and has *stated such a title* as, if established, would entitle him to a declaration under the act, will make an order for the investigation of the petitioner's title in chambers, in the same way as if he had obtained, as vendor, an order for specific performance of an agreement for sale of the land in question (*i*).

The proceedings are thereupon taken in chambers on a summons to proceed in the usual way.

However, as proceedings under the act are of very rare occurrence, owing to the great expense and trouble involved in the investigation, the reader is referred for further information to Daniell's Chancery Practice, where the subject is fully treated of.

(*i*) 25 & 25 Vict. c. 67, s. 6.

Division III.

OF PROCEEDINGS COMMON TO ACTIONS AND MATTERS.

Sub-div. I.—Taxation of Costs.

II.—Enforcing Judgments and Orders.

III.—Appeal.

IV.—Miscellaneous Regulations relating to Procedure.

Taxation of Costs.

IT is outside the object of this work, to treat of the principles which govern the court in awarding the costs of actions and matters, but when the order has awarded those costs, a further proceeding becomes necessary in order that the amount of them may be determined.

This proceeding is called "taxation," and costs are either taxed as between "party and party," or as between "solicitor and client;" the latter being taxed far more liberally for the solicitor than the former, in which no costs are allowed except such as were strictly necessary. Whenever a party to an action is ordered to pay the costs of another party without more being said, such costs are deemed to be costs between party and party.

Higher and Lower Scale. There are two scales of costs, one called the lower scale and the other the higher scale, and solicitors are entitled to charge and be allowed their fees according to one scale or the other, under certain rules set forth in Ord. VI. of the R. S. C. (Costs) of the 12th August, 1875, in which the different items under both scales are set out in detail, and to which the reader is referred; but the court or a judge may, in any cause, direct the fees in either scale to be allowed to all, or either, or any of the parties, and as to all or any part of the costs, notwithstanding the rule in question (*a*).

(*a*) R. S. C. (Costs), 1875, Ord. VI. r. 3. And see infra, Sub-div. IV.

Procedure. Assuming, then, that a bill of costs has to be taxed before it is paid, the solicitor of the party claiming payment of the costs causes a fair copy of the bill to be made on foolscap paper bookwise, with a space or margin on the left-hand side for the purpose of noting any deductions which may be made on the taxation. This copy, together with a copy of the judgment or order under which the costs are to be taxed, also written or printed on similar paper, bearing in the margin a certificate of the solicitor that it is a true copy of the judgment or order as passed and entered, is taken to the office of the taxing master who has taxed any previous costs in the same action or matter; or if there have been no costs previously taxed, the solicitor makes a certificate of the fact in the margins both of the *original* judgment or order and of the copy, and takes them and the bill to the office of the sitting taxing master, who will insert the name of the taxing master on the rota in a certificate in the margin of the *original* judgment or order, which certificate should be prepared in blank by the solicitor. This certificate is then copied on the copy judgment or order, and the latter, and also the bill, left with the clerk of the taxing master to whom it is referred, with all vouchers and papers in respect of which charges are made in the bill. At the same time a warrant to proceed, with an appointment for that purpose, is obtained from the clerk, and must be duly served on the parties interested in the taxation.

The parties served may, on undertaking to pay proper costs therefor, require and, on paying such costs, obtain from the solicitor, within forty-eight hours after demand (unless the time is extended by the court), copies of the bill, so written as to correspond page for page with the copy left with the master (b). The charge is 4d. per folio, or in causes *in formâ pauperis* 1½d. per folio (c). The folios in the copies should be numbered in the margin, and the copies should be properly and legibly written, and indorsed with the name and address of the solicitor or party (d).

If a solicitor refuses or neglects to comply with a request for a copy of the bill, the copy may be obtained from the master's chambers; and in that case, not only will the solicitor be disentitled to the costs of such copy, but an additional two clear days will be added to the period which must elapse before any further proceeding can be taken (c).

In order to relieve the master of frivolous points, the bill is generally first gone through by his clerk in the presence of the parties; and then any points which are intended to be contested are reserved for an adjourned appointment before the master himself. The master will require evidence that the business charged for has actually been done, that it was reasonably necessary that it should be done, and that the amount charged is reasonable. The papers in the action or matter are usually the evidence that the work has actually been done, and one document will often prove several distinct items; for instance, the order or judgment proves the steps necessary to get it passed and entered (f).

Where a party entitled to appear on the taxation does not do so, an affidavit of service of the warrant must be indorsed on the original warrant, and sworn before the master.

(b) Cons. Ord. XXXVI. rr. 4, 5, 6, 7, 8.

(c) Cons. Ord. IV. rr. 1, 2, 3.

(d) Cons. Ord. XXXVI. rr. 8, 11.

(e) Ib. rr. 12, 16.

(f) Hunter's Suit, 204.

With regard to what costs are allowed on taxation, and what between solicitor and client, and what between party and party, such questions are matters of law and not of procedure, and the reader is referred to Messrs. Morgan and Davey's learned treatise on Costs, where all such points are carefully discussed and elucidated.

In going through the bill, if the master considers that any item ought to be struck out or reduced, he enters the deduction in the margin. These deductions being added up, are finally deducted from the total amount of the original bill, and if a client is taxing his own solicitor's bill, and the bill has been reduced by more than one-sixth, the solicitor will have to bear the costs of the taxation.

The master signs the bill when taxed; and if it is desired to issue execution for the costs, his certificate must be obtained and filed, and an office copy produced on the sealing of the writ of execution.

Review. If any party be dissatisfied with the decision of the master, he should, before the certificate is signed, deliver his objection in writing to the other party, specifying the item or items to which he objects, but not giving the reasons for his objection (*g*), and should apply to the master for a warrant to review the taxation (*h*); and thus any such objections are brought a second time before the master, who may allow further evidence, and will state the grounds of his decision and any special circumstances either in the certificate or otherwise (*i*). If dissatisfied with this review by the master, any party may apply for a summons of review

(*g*) *Simmons* v. *Storer*, L. R., 14 Ch. D. 154.

(*h*) R. S. C., Costs (special al-

lowances and general provisions), r. 30.

(*i*) Ib. r. 31.

before the judge in chambers, on the hearing of which no other evidence can in general be used than what was produced before the master (*k*).

The certificate of the master, however, is conclusive as to items not objected to (*l*).

Payment of Costs. If the costs are payable out of a fund in court, a cheque for the amount will be drawn up at the Pay Office on the production of the judgment or order and the taxing master's certificate; but otherwise the payment, if not made, must be enforced by execution in some of the modes stated in Sub-division II. of this Part.

District Registry. Where an action is commenced and proceeds in a district registry, the costs are calculated and allowed as if it had been a London case (*m*); and where judgment is entered in the district registry, the costs are to be taxed there, unless the court or judge orders to the contrary; but such order will always be made except in simple cases (*n*).

(*k*) Ib. r. 33.
(*l*) Ib. r. 32.
(*m*) Ib. r. 34.

(*n*) R. S. C., Ord. XXXV. r. 3; *Day* v. *Whitaker*, L. R., 6 Ch. D. 734.

SUB-DIVISION II.

Enforcing Judgments and Orders.

CHAPTER I.

INTRODUCTORY.

AT one time, the old Court of Chancery had no means of enforcing its decrees, except by "process of contempt"; *i. e.*, by imprisonment and sequestration. Its powers, however, were from time to time extended, and although imprisonment and sequestration may be considered to be the most appropriate method of enforcing obedience to judgments and orders in the Chancery Division, yet there are divers other methods which require to be shortly noticed.

The court, then, possesses the following weapons for enforcing its authority, viz. :—

1. Writs of execution, viz. :—
    (A.) For enforcing judgments and orders in all cases except the payment of money.
       (1) Writ of attachment.
       (2) Writ of sequestration.
    (B.) For enforcing judgment of actual delivery of property.
       (3) Writ of possession with regard to lands.
       (4) Writ of delivery with regard to lands.
    (C.) For enforcing judgment for the payment of money.
       (5) Writ of *fieri facias*.
       (6) Writ of *elegit*.
2. Execution of judgments otherwise than by writ, viz. :—
    (1) Orders attaching debts due to a judgment debtor.
    (2) Orders charging stock or shares held by a judgment debtor.
    (3) Order of committal to prison.
    (4) Vesting orders transferring the *legal* estate in property from a person ordered to convey the same and who refuses to obey that order.

CHAPTER II.

ENFORCING JUDGMENTS AND ORDERS BY WRITS OF EXECUTION.

BEFORE examining each particular kind of writ of execution it is desirable that we should first consider the practice relating to *all* writs of execution indiscriminately, and then we can afterwards consider the nature of, and practice peculiar to, each particular kind of writ.

Section 1.

Writs of Execution generally.

How prepared and issued. All writs of execution are prepared by the party prosecuting them, and, like writs of summons, are issued by being sealed by the master of the Supreme Court, or the district registrar (*a*), as the case may be.

No writ of execution will be issued without the production to the sealing officer, of the judgment or order, or an office copy thereof, showing the date of entry; and the officer must satisfy himself that the proper time has elapsed, to entitle the applicant to have execution (*b*). The applicant must also file a *præcipe* or request on a slip of paper in the following form :—

1880.   S.   No. 100.

In the High Court of Justice.

Chancery Division.

V.-C. Hall.

Between John Smith . . . . . . Plaintiff,

and

William Jones . . . . Defendant.

Seal a writ of *fieri facias* directed to the sheriff of Devonshire to levy against William Jones the sum of 100*l.*, and interest thereon at the rate of 5*l.* per centum per annum, from the   day of   ,
1880, and 20*l.* costs.

Judgment dated the 20th day of January, 1881.

George Robinson,

Solicitor for the Plaintiff.

(*a*) R. S. C., Ord. XXXV. r. 3.   (*b*) R. S. C., Ord. XLII. r. 9.

Writs of execution, like writs of summons, may be obtained printed in blank at the law stationers; and such a form, appropriately filled in, must be taken, with the *præcipe* and judgment, and the taxing master's certificate for costs (if they are to be included in the writ), to the central office or district registry, where it will be sealed, and the *præcipe* filed (c).

The writ must be indorsed with the name and place of abode, or office of business, of the solicitor suing out the same; and, also, if he is acting as agent, the name and similar address of his principal, or where no solicitor is employed, then with a memorandum expressing that it has been sued out by the plaintiff or defendant in person, and mentioning the city, town, or parish, and also the name of the hamlet, street, and number of the house of such plaintiff's or defendant's residence, if any such there be (d). The writ must also bear date the day of its issue (e).

Writs of execution are tested like writs of summons (f).

Against whom a Writ may be sued out. Writs of execution are not confined to the parties to the action, but may be sued out by, or against, any person, whether a party or not, in whose favour, or against whom, any order is made (g).

Costs. A party is not bound to include his costs in the writ by which he seeks to enforce the rest of the judgment, but may issue separate writs for the costs, and the rest of the judgment, even if the latter is for the recovery of money only; but the writ for costs

(c) Ib. r. 10.
(d) Ib. r. 11.
(e) Ib. r. 12.

(f) Ib. Ord. II. r. 8.
(g) Ord. XLII. r. 21.

U.   Y

cannot be sued out less than eight days after the first writ (h).

Applicable to Orders as well as Judgments. Writs of execution are not confined to the enforcement of judgments only, but are applicable for enforcing every order of the court or a judge, whether in an action, cause or matter (i).

Where Leave required. As between the original parties to an action, execution may be issued at any time within six years from the recovery of the judgment (k); but where that period has elapsed, or any change has taken place by death or otherwise in the parties entitled, or liable, to execution, application for leave to issue execution must be made to a judge or to the district registrar by summons, and on such application, leave may be granted or refused, or any question or issue necessary to determine the rights of the parties may be ordered to be tried, and terms as to costs or otherwise may be imposed (l); and the same remark applies to cases where judgment has been had against a firm in the firm's name, and it does not appear on the record that an alleged partner is in fact one (m).

Leave must also be obtained where the judgment is to take effect only on the happening of a condition or contingency (n).

Where a party desires to appeal from a judgment, he should apply to the court from whose decision he desires to appeal (o), to stay execution pending the appeal. The court or a judge may grant this at the time

(h) R. S. C., Ord. XLII. r. 15a.
(i) Ib. r. 20.
(k) Ib. r. 18.
(l) Ib. r. 19; and Ord. XXXV. r. 3a.
(m) Ib. r. 8.

(n) Ib. r. 7.
(o) R. S. C., Ord. LVIII. r. 17; *Att.-Gen.* v. *Swansea Co.*, L. R., 9 Ch. D. 46; *Goddard* v. *Thompson*, 38 L. T. 166.

of giving judgment, or afterwards on motion, of which due notice must be given (*p*).

A writ of execution remains in force for one year only, but may be renewed for an additional six months by leave obtained on summons (*q*).

Lastly, it need scarcely be said, that a writ of execution, obtained irregularly or wrongly, will be set aside on motion or summons supported by affidavit.

SECTION 2.

The different kinds of Writs of Execution.

Having now considered the general principles applicable to all writs of execution, let us examine them in detail.

SUBSEC. 1.—*The Writ of Attachment.*

Where applicable. The writ of attachment cannot now be issued for enforcing mere money claims (*r*), even where they consist of costs (*s*), but is available in all other cases where a party refuses or neglects to do or to omit to do some act which he is ordered to do or omit by a judgment or order, including disobedience in refusing to deliver up real or personal property (*t*).

Leave required in all Cases. As, however, attachment means the imprisonment of the party proceeded against, it is not left to the discretion of the suitor, like the writs of *fieri facias*, *elegit* and possession, but can only be issued by special leave of the court or

---

(*p*) R. S. C., Ord. LVIII. r. 16; *Republic of Peru v. Weguelin*, 24 W. R. 297.

(*q*) R.S.C.,Ord. XLII. rr.16,17.

(*r*) *Phosphate Sewage Co. v. Hartmont*, 25 W. R. 743; *Lewis*

(*Earl) v. Barnett*, L. R., 6 Ch. D. 252.

(*s*) *Jackson v. Manby*, L. R., 1 Ch. D. 86.

(*t*) R. S. C., Ord. XLII. r. 4; and Ord. XLIV. r. 1.

judge or district registrar (*u*), the granting of which is quite discretionary (*v*).

Service of Judgment or Order. The first step towards getting an attachment, is to serve the party implicated, with a copy of the judgment or order, indorsed with a notice to the effect, that if he neglects to obey the judgment or order by the time named therein (where he is ordered to do something), he will be liable to have his property sequestrated, and himself arrested and committed to prison (*x*).

The service of the copy judgment or order must be made *personally ;* but where personal service cannot be made, the court will, on *ex parte* motion (in case of a judgment), or a summons (in case of an order in chambers), order substituted service ; but the application must be supported by affidavit, stating what efforts have been made to effect personal service, and also the mode of substituted service suggested by the applicant (*y*).

Where personal service is made, it is effected by giving to the person intended to be served, a true copy of the judgment or order, and at the same time showing to him the original, or an office copy, sealed with the report office seal, and signed by a master of the Supreme Court.

Time for applying for an Attachment. When the judgment orders an act to be done, no further step can be taken, until the expiration of the time within which it is ordered to be done ; but when an act is ordered to be omitted, steps for enforcing it may be taken immediately that the party ordered to desist does any act in contravention of the order.

(*u*) R. S. C., Ord. XLIV. r. 2 :   5 Ch. D. 943.
and Ord. XXXV. r. 3a.
  (*x*) Cons. Ord. XXIII. r. 10.
  (*v*) *Ashworth* v. *Outram*, L. R.,   (*y*) See Daniell's Ch. Pr. 905.

Motion for Attachment. Supposing that the party served with the judgment or order disobeys it, the next step is to serve him, or his solicitor (z), with notice of motion, or with a summons, for a writ of attachment (a), and for the costs occasioned by the application (b). It is sufficient to leave the notice at the residence of the party affected (c). The motion or summons is brought on in the usual way, and must be supported by an affidavit, showing—(1) service of the judgment or order; (2) default in obedience to it; and (3) service of the notice of motion or summons.

The Writ. If the court grants the application, the party applying prepares a writ of attachment on judicature paper in the following form :—

1881. S. No. 100.

In the High Court of Justice.

 Chancery Division.

  V.-C. Hall.

    Between John Smith . . . . Plaintiff,

        and

    Peter Jones . . . . Defendant.

  Victoria, &c.

  To the sheriff of Staffordshire, greeting.

We command you to attach A. B. so as to have him before us in our High Court of Justice, Chancery Division, immediately after the receipt of this writ, wheresoever the said court shall then be, there to answer to us, as well touching a contempt which he as is alleged has committed against us, as also such other matters as shall be then and there laid to his charge ; and further to perform and abide such order, as our said court shall make in this behalf ; and hereof fail not, and bring this writ with you.

Witness, Roundell Baron Selborne, Lord High Chancellor of Great Britain, the ——— day of ——— 1881.

(z) *Browning* v. *Sabin*, L. R., 5 Ch. D. 511.

(a) R . S. C., Ord. XLIV. r. 2.

(b) See *Abud* v. *Riches*, L. R., 2 Ch. D. 528.

(c) *In re a Solicitor*, L. R., 11 Ch. D. 152.

The writ thus prepared, is taken to the registrar's office, together with two "*præcipes*" in the form indicated in subsection 1. One of these *præcipes* is filed in the registrar's office, and the other is marked by the entering clerk there, after which the writ and the marked *præcipe* are taken to the central office or district registry and filed there, and the writ is then sealed by the master of the Supreme Court or registrar, and by that means issued. The writ thus issued is sent to the under-sheriff, by whom it is executed.

Return of the Writ. Where a day is named in the writ for its return, the sheriff must, on pain of contempt, return it on that day; and where no time is named, he should return it in a reasonable time. The return consists in giving back the writ to the solicitor of the party suing it out, with an indorsement, signed by or on behalf of the sheriff, stating the result of his action in the matter.

If successful, the return is what is technically called "*cepi corpus*," and if unsuccessful, "*non est inventus.*"

Duties of Sheriff. Contempt is, it would seem, no longer bailable, and the sheriff has no right to bail the person arrested; and if he does so, an *ex parte* motion should be made that the tipstaff of the court arrest the person bailed.

The ordinary course is for the sheriff to arrest the party, and lodge him in gaol, where he may be left until he "purges his contempt," by doing the act required of him, or promising to omit to do that which the order has restrained him from doing (*d*).

Non est inventus. Where a return of *non est inventus* is made, and the prosecuting party does not

(*d*) Daniell's Ch. Pr. 908.

know in what place the offender is to be found, the next step is to move *ex parte*, that the serjeant-at-arms do arrest him; which will be granted on the production of the writ, and the return thereto. The registrar draws up the order, and delivers it to the proper officer, who arrests the offender, and (unless he is already in prison) brings him before the court, whence he is committed to prison. If, however, he is already in prison, the serjeant-at-arms leaves the order for his arrest with the gaoler, who thereupon detains him in the prison in which he then is. A person against whom a serjeant-at-arms has been ordered, cannot escape arrest, even by consent of the prosecuting party, until the fees of the serjeant-at-arms are certified by him to have been duly paid (e).

Discharge. When a person in custody under an attachment desires to be discharged, he must apply to the court for his discharge, which is done by "petition of course" where his compliance with the order can be certified by an officer of the court, and by motion (for which due notice must be given to the other side) founded on affidavit (or consent) in all other cases.

SUBSEC. 2.—*Writ of Sequestration.*

What it consists of. Sequestration is a process by which a person is deprived of the use and enjoyment of all his real and personal property within the jurisdiction of the court; and consists of a writ directed to commissioners, usually four in number, nominated by the prosecuting party, commanding them to enter the lands and seize the goods of the offender (*f*).

(e) Cons. Ord. XXX. r. 2.   (f) Hunter's Suit, 6th ed. 170.

Requires no Leave. This writ, unlike the writ of attachment, in general requires no order, but may be issued wherever any person is, by any judgment or order (*g*), directed to pay money into court, or to do any other act in a limited time, and, after due service of such judgment, refuses or neglects to obey the same (*h*). A sequestration cannot be issued merely to enforce payment of costs, without an order (*i*), nor is it a proper remedy for mere nonpayment of a debt or damages (*k*). It is also to be observed, that the order only mentions the case of refusal or neglect to *do an act*, and makes no reference to cases where a person disobeys an injunction restraining him from doing an act.

The Writ. The writ is prepared and issued by the party prosecuting it, in the same way as a writ of attachment, but should be engrossed on parchment (*l*).

Effect of Writ. When issued it is delivered to the commissioners, who may then take possession of the offender's goods and chattels in possession (but they cannot sell them without an order of court), and also of the rents of his real estate; and if the tenants will not pay them, an order may be obtained on motion, compelling them to pay them (*m*). An order may also be obtained to let the offender's lands, but not to sell them (*n*).

Sequestrators must account. The sequestra-

(*g*) *Sprunt* v. *Pugh*, L. R., 7 Ch. D. 567; R. S. C., Ord. XLII. r. 20.

(*h*) R. S. C., Ord. XLVII. r. 1; *Sprunt* v. *Pugh*, L. R., 7 Ch. D. 567.

(*i*) R. S. C., Ord. XLVII. r. 2; but in a proper case an order will be made on motion: *Snow* v. *Bolton*, L. R., 17 Ch. D. 433.

(*k*) See *Ex parte Nelson*, W. N. 1880, p. 42; but cons. *Wilcock* v. *Terrell*, L. R., 3 Ex. D. 323.

(*l*) Dan. Ch. Pr. 913.

(*m*) Ib. 916.

(*n*) Ib. 915.

tors cannot, however, pay over the property to the prosecutor, but are in the nature of receivers appointed by
the court, and must from time to time accordingly
make returns to the court of their receipts, and may be
ordered to pay the balances into court, and to pass their
accounts from time to time. If the prosecutor wishes a
money claim to be discharged out of the sequestered property, he must obtain an order for that purpose on motion.

Discharge. When an offender has purged his
contempt, he should take out a summons to have the
sequestration discharged, and calling upon the commissioners to pass their accounts (o).

SUBSEC. 3.— *Writ of Possession.*

This is a writ commanding the sheriff to put the
person who has recovered judgment for the recovery or
for the delivery of possession of land into actual possession of it (p), and is essentially a common law writ,
having been used under the old practice in actions of
ejectment. Formerly, if by a decree in chancery, a
defendant was required to deliver up possession of lands,
and refused to do so after service of the decree upon him,
an order might have been obtained on motion, for what
was called a " writ of assistance." By this writ the
sheriff was commanded to eject the defendant in possession. The new practice supersedes this (q), and the
person in whose favour the judgment is given, may,
without any order for that purpose, sue out a writ of
possession on filing an affidavit showing due service of
the judgment, and that it has not been obeyed (r).

(o) Seton, 1586.

(p) R. S. C., Ord. XLII. r. 3;
and Ord. XLVIII. r. 1.

(q) *Hall* v. *Hall*, 47 L. J., Ch.
680.

(r) R. S. C., Ord. XLVIII. r. 2.

SUBSEC. 4.—*Writ of Delivery.*

This is a writ for the delivery up of any property other than land or money. The practice is governed by the 78th sect. of the Common Law Procedure Act, 1854 (*s*), by which it was enacted, that the court or a judge might, upon the application of the plaintiff in any action for the detention of any chattel, order that execution should issue for the return of the chattel detained, and that if such chattel could not be found, and unless the court or a judge should otherwise order, the sheriff should distrain the defendant by all his lands and chattels in his bailiwick, till the defendant should render such chattel; or, at the option of the plaintiff, that the sheriff should cause the assessed value of the chattel to be distrained out of the defendant's goods; and that the plaintiff should also, either by the same or a separate writ of execution, be entitled to have the defendant's goods distrained for damages, costs and interest in the action.

Leave. It is apprehended, that before this writ can be issued, an order for that purpose will be required.

SUBSEC. 5.—*Writ of Fieri Facias.*

This writ is solely used for the purpose of recovering money (*t*), whether in the nature of damages or costs, or otherwise; and is, in form, a command to the sheriff, to seize and sell the goods of the person against whom it is issued. Although sometimes used in the Chancery Division, especially for enforcing payment of costs, it is nevertheless essentially a common law writ, and as

---

(*s*) R. S. C., Ord. XLII. r. 4;   (*t*) R. S. C., Ord. XLII. r. 15.
and Ord. XLIX.

such, its nature, and the mode of issuing it, will be found treated of in books relating to common law practice. All that need be said here on the subject is, that any person to whom any sum of money, or any costs are payable under a judgment, may, immediately after the judgment shall be duly entered, and without serving the judgment on the defendant, sue out a writ or writs of *fieri facias* to enforce payment thereof, unless the judgment is for payment within a specified period, when the writ cannot be issued until after the expiration of such period, unless the court or judge, at the time of giving the judgment, or a judge afterwards, shall order otherwise (*n*). The court or a judge may also stay execution for any period (*x*).

SUBSEC. 6.—*Writ of Elegit.*

This writ is also solely used for the purpose of recovering money, and is in form a command to the sheriff, to deliver to the judgment creditor, the whole of the judgment debtor's lands (*y*), and the judgment creditor is then placed in the position of a mortgagee in possession, and is obliged to account for the rents and profits, and he may apply to the court by petition for a sale of the lands (*z*), the writ having been first duly registered. This writ, like that of *fieri facias*, is essentially a common law writ, and the reader is therefore referred to books on common law practice for a detailed exposition of the method of suing it out and enforcing it.

The consideration of writs of *Fieri facias de bonis ecclesiasticis* and of *Sequestrari de bonis ecclesiasticis* scarcely come within the scope of this Work.

(*n*) R. S. C., Ord. XLII. r. 15.   (*y*) 1 & 2 Vict. c. 110, s. 11.
(*x*) Ib.   (*z*) 27 & 28 Vict. c. 112.

CHAPTER III.

ENFORCING JUDGMENTS AND ORDERS OTHERWISE THAN
BY WRITS OF EXECUTION.

SECTION 1.

Attachment of Debts.

Examination of Judgment Debtor. Where a
judgment is for the recovery by, or payment to, any
person, of money, the party entitled to enforce it may
apply to the court, or a judge, or the district registrar,
for an order for the oral examination of the judgment
debtor with respect to debts owing to him. The examination takes place before an officer of the court, or
a special examiner; and the court, or a judge, or district
registrar may make an order for such examination, and
for the production of any books or documents (*a*). The
examination is in the nature of a strict cross-examination, and the debtor is bound to answer all questions
relevant to the subject-matter (*b*).

Order attaching Debts. The court, or a judge,
or a district registrar may also on the *ex parte* application of a judgment creditor, either before or after any
such examination, and upon affidavit by himself or his
solicitor, stating that judgment has been recovered, and
is still unsatisfied, and to what amount, and that *any other
person is indebted to the judgment debtor, and is within the
jurisdiction,* order that all debts "owing or accruing" from
such third person (who is called the garnishee) to the
judgment debtor, shall be attached to answer the judg-

(*a*) R. S. C., Ord. XLV. r. 1;
and Ord. XXXV. r. 3a.

(*b*) *Republic of Costa Rica* v.
Strousberg, L. R., 16 Ch. D. 8.

ment debt; and by the same or any subsequent order, it may be ordered that the garnishee shall appear before the court or judge, or an officer of the court, to show cause why he should not pay to the judgment creditor the debt due to the judgment debtor, or so much thereof as may be sufficient to satisfy the judgment debt (c).

What Debts may be attached. The question as to what debts are " owing and accruing," and therefore attachable, is very frequently a source of great difficulty. For instance, a salary or allowance to accrue *in futuro* is not attachable (d), although a debt certain but payable *in futuro* is (e). Again, money in the hands of an officer of a court; as, for instance, a receiver, trustee in bankruptcy, a registrar, or under the control of the court or the like, is not attachable (f) ; nor are seamen's (g) or workmen's wages (h), or naval or military half-pay (i), although a pension for purely past services is attachable (k).

How attached Debts are bound. The service of an order that debts due or accruing due shall be attached, or notice of it to the garnishee in such manner as the court or judge may direct, binds such debts in his hands (l) ; and if he does not forthwith pay them, or so much of them as will satisfy the judgment debt,

(c) R. S. C., Ord. XLV. r. 2 ; and Ord. XXXV. r. 3a.

(d) *Hall* v. *Pritchett*, L. R., 3 Q. B. D. 215; *Innes* v. *East India Co.*, 17 C. B. 351.

(e) *Sparkes* v. *Young*, 8 Ir. C. L. R., Q. B. 261.

(f) *Russell* v. *East Anglian Railway Co.*, 3 M. & G. 104 ; *Ex parte Hunter*, L. R., 8 C. P. 24 ; *Dawson* v. *Malley*, Ir. Rep., 1 C.

L. 207; *Ex parte Hawkins*, L. R., 3 Ch. 787 ; *Dolphin* v. *Layton*, L. R., 4 C. P. D. 130 ; *Stevens* v. *Phillips*, L. R., 10 Ch. 417.

(g) 17 & 18 Vict. c. 104, s. 233.

(h) 33 & 34 Vict. c. 30.

(i) *Dent* v. *Dent*, L. R., 1 P. & D. 366.

(k) *Wilcock* v. *Terrell*, L. R., 3 Ex. D. 323.

(l) R. S. C., Ord. XLV. r. 3.

into court, and dispute the debt alleged to be due from him to the judgment debtor, or if he does not appear upon summons, the court or judge may order execution to issue against him (*m*).

Garnishee disputing the Debts. If, however, the garnishee shows reasonable grounds (*n*) for disputing his liability, the court or judge, instead of ordering execution to issue, may order that any question or issue necessary for determining his liability shall be tried or determined, in any manner in which any issue or question in an action may be tried and determined (*o*). And if the garnishee suggests that a third party is entitled to, or has a charge or lien on the debt, such party may be ordered to appear (*p*) ; and the court or judge may, after hearing his allegations, or in case of his non-appearance when ordered, order execution to issue against the garnishee, or order any question or issue to be tried as above mentioned, and may bar the claim of such third party or make such other order, and upon such terms with regard to the lien or charge (if any) of such third party, and as to costs, as the court or judge shall think just and reasonable (*q*).

Payment by, or execution levied upon, a garnishee, is a valid discharge to him as against the judgment debtor *quà* the amount paid or levied, even though the attachment is afterwards set aside or the judgment reversed (*r*).

Costs. The costs of garnishee orders are in the discretion of the court or judge (*s*).

(*m*) R. S. C., Ord. XLV. r. 4.

(*n*) *Newman* v. *Rooke*, 4 C. B.; N. S. 434.

(*o*) R. S. C., Ord. XLV. r. 5.

(*p*) Ib. r. 6.

(*q*) Ib. r. 7.

(*r*) Ib. r. 8.

(*s*) Ib. r. 10.

Only applicable to Judgments. Execution by attachment of debts is only applicable to *judgments*, and not to mere *orders* (*t*).

___

Section 2.

Charging Orders on Stock.

How obtained. Where a judgment is for the recovery by, or payment to, any person of money, and the judgment debtor has any interest, whether in possession, remainder or reversion, vested or contingent, in any government stocks, funds or annuities, or in any stock or shares of any public company in England (whether incorporated or not), or in the dividends, interests or annual proceeds thereof, his interest may be ordered to stand charged with the payment of the amount for which judgment is recovered and interest thereon ; and such order entitles the judgment creditor to all such remedies as he would have been entitled to if such charge had been made in his favour by the judgment debtor. But no proceedings can be taken to realize the charge (which must, of course, be by action), until after the expiration of six calendar months from the date of the charging order (*u*).

The application for a charging order is made on petition or summons, supported by affidavit ; but in order to prevent the judgment debtor parting with the property sought to be charged, the application is *ex parte* in the first instance, and an order *nisi* is made, which restrains the bank or company from allowing a transfer of the stock or shares unless and until the order *nisi*

___

(*t*) *Best* v. *Pembroke*, L. R., 8 Q. B. 363 ; *Sunderland Board* v. *Frankland*, ib. 18 ; *Cremetti* v.

Crom, L. R., 4 Q. B. D. 225.

(*u*) R. S. C., Ord. XLVI. r. 1 ; and 1 & 2 Vict. c. 110, ss. 14, 15.

is discharged, on good cause being shown by the judgment debtor (x). No order will be made unless the judgment has been entered for a specific and ascertained amount; but it is not material that the date fixed for payment has not arrived (y).

A time is mentioned in the order *nisi* within which the judgment debtor must show-cause against it, and if he fails to do so, the order will, on proof of notice to the judgment debtor, or his solicitor or agent, be made absolute, subject to a power vested in the judge to discharge or vary such order (z).

Notice of a charging order should be at once given to the bank or the company, as the case may be; and if the stock charged is in court, the order should be lodged at the Chancery Pay Office (a).

An order *nisi* may be made by a district registrar, but an order absolute cannot (z).

Section 3.

Committal under the Debtors Act.

A simpler method of coercing an obstinate party than that afforded by writ of attachment, is by moving to commit him to prison for contempt of court. No person can, however, be arrested or imprisoned for making default in *payment of money* recovered by judgment, save only:—

(1.) For default in payment of a penalty or penal sum not arising out of contract.

(2.) For default by a trustee or person acting in a fiduciary capacity, and ordered to pay by a court

---

(u) 1 & 2 Vict. c. 110, s. 15.

(x) *Widgery* v. *Tepper*, L. R., 6 Ch. D. 364; *Bagnall* v. *Carlton*, ib. 130.

(y) 1 & 2 Vict. c. 110, s. 15.

(z) R. S. C., Ord. XXXV. r. 3a.

(a) *Haly* v. *Barry*, L. R., 3 Ch. 452.

of equity any sum in his possession or under his control.

(3.) For default by a solicitor when ordered to pay costs for misconduct as such, or in payment of a sum of money when ordered to pay the same in his character of an officer of the court.

(4.) Default in payment of any debt, or instalment of any debt, due from any person in pursuance of any judgment or order of a competent court, where it is proved to the satisfaction of the court that the defaulter has had means to pay since the date of the judgment or order (b).

No person can, however, be imprisoned for more than one year under the first three exceptions, or for more than six weeks under the fourth (c). And with respect to exceptions two and three, the court or judge making the order for payment, or having jurisdiction in the action or proceeding in which the order for payment is made, may inquire into the case, and subject to the proviso as to imprisonment for not more than one year, may grant or refuse, either absolutely or on terms, any application for a writ of attachment (see *supra*) or other process or order of arrest or imprisonment, and any application to stay the operation of any such writ, process or order, or for discharge from arrest or imprisonment thereunder (d).

When it is desired to imprison a person for contempt of court or non-payment of money, the application should be by motion (on notice), founded on an affidavit setting forth the contempt, or where the application is made in consequence of non-payment of money, showing

(b) 32 & 33 Vict. c. 62, s. 4.   (d) 41 & 42 Vict. c. 54.
(c) Ib.

V.   z

the debtor's means of payment (*e*), and his neglect or refusal to pay; but the court may direct an inquiry or require further evidence as to this (*f*). The order, where made in consequence of non-payment of money, may be for committal until the whole debt and costs are paid or until some instalment and costs are paid (*g*); but upon payment of the amount mentioned in the order, and of the costs and fees, the debtor will be entitled to a certificate of payment, signed by the creditor or his solicitor, and upon such order will be entitled to be discharged (*h*). In other cases he must apply for his discharge by motion.

When made, an office copy of the order, indorsed with the master's direction to the sheriff to execute it, must be delivered to the sheriff (or sheriffs, where it is uncertain in what county the debtor is), for execution (*i*); and the sheriff must within two days after the arrest indorse the date thereof on the order, and return it to the creditor or his solicitor (*k*).

It must be observed that committal is only in aid of, and not in substitution for, other modes of execution, and therefore a debtor does not, by enduring his imprisonment, become released from his liability to pay the debt (*l*); and where the order is for payment by instalments, and on payment of the first instalment the debtor gets discharged from prison, but makes default in payment of a subsequent one, he will become liable to be attached by writ of attachment (for which see

(*e*) Cons. Ord. XLII. r. 2, and 32 & 33 Vict. c. 62, s. 5; Gen. Ord. Jan. 1870, r. 10.

(*f*) Gen. Ord. Jan. 1870, rr. 11, 12.

(*g*) Ib. r. 13.

(*h*) Ib. r. 17.

(*i*) Ib. r. 15.

(*k*) Ib. r. 16.

(*l*) 32 & 33 Vict. c. 62, s. 5; Gen. Ord. Jan. 1870, r. 14.

supra), and will not then be entitled to be discharged at the end of the year or six weeks, as the case may be (*m*).

SECTION 4.

Vesting Orders.

It is convenient in this place to mention another means possessed by the court of enforcing obedience to a particular class of orders, viz., those in which the execution of a deed or conveyance is required by the court in order to vest the legal estate in property in the person equitably entitled to it. Formerly, a contumacious person, if he chose to lie in prison, or submit to have his property sequestered, might defeat the plaintiff of his rights. In such cases the obstinate person is considered a trustee of the legal estate, and on his refusal or neglect to convey it a vesting order will be made under the provisions of the Trustee Acts, which are more particularly treated of in the second part of this work. The application is by summons.

SECTION 5.

Receiver.

It would seem that where a writ of execution is inapplicable a receiver will be appointed on motion in the usual way (*n*).

(*m*) Ib. r. 18.

(*n*) *Salt* v. *Cooper*, L. R., 16 Ch. D. 544.

Sub-division III.

Appeal.

When any party is dissatisfied with a judgment or order of the Chancery Division, he may in general appeal from it to the Court of Appeal, where, if the appeal is from an interlocutory order, it will be heard by not less than two judges; or, if a final judgment or order, by not less than three (a). A person not a party to an action, but interested in it, may obtain leave to appeal on *ex parte* motion (b).

Time. A party is, however, not permitted to keep an appeal hanging over his opponent's head for an indefinite time, and if his appeal is from an interlocutory order in an *action*, or any order made in a *matter*, he cannot, except by leave of the Appeal Court, serve notice of motion of appeal (c) after twenty-one days, and, in the case of a final judgment in an *action*, after one year from the date at which the judgment is entered; or where an action is dismissed or a judgment refused, with or without costs, then from the date of such dismissal or refusal (d). A refusal to give leave to amend at the hearing forms part of the final judgment, and is not an interlocutory proceeding (e).

(a) 38 & 39 Vict. c. 77, s. 12.

(b) *Markham* v. *Markham*, L. R., 16 Ch. D. 1.

(c) *Ex parte Viney*, L. R., 4 Ch. D. 794; *Ex parte Saffery*, L. R., 5 Ch. D. 365.

(d) R. S. C., Ord. LVIII. rr. 9, 15; and see *Swindell* v. *Birm. Syndicate*, L. R., 3 Ch. D. 127; *International Society* v. *City of Moscow Gas Co.*, L. R., 7 Ch. D. 241.

(e) *Land* v. *Briggs*, L. R., 16 Ch. D. 663.

If these periods have expired, special leave to appeal must be applied for by motion, of which notice must be given to the other side (*f*); and leave will not be given unless the appellant has been misled, either by his opponents, or an officer of the court, or has been the victim of unavoidable accident. Mere mistake, whether of fact, procedure or law, is no ground for granting leave (*g*).

Mode of Appealing. The mode of appealing is by serving fourteen days' notice of motion in the case of a judgment (final or interlocutory), and four days in case of an interlocutory order (*h*), upon all parties *directly* affected by the appeal (*i*); and it is not necessary to serve any other parties, although the Court of Appeal may order that notice shall be served on any person, whether parties to the action or matter or not, and may adjourn the hearing of the appeal for that purpose upon terms (*k*).

Irregular Notice. If a notice of appeal is irregular, or does not cover the whole ground of appeal, or is otherwise defective, it may be amended by the Court of Appeal (*l*); and where considered desirable, a notice of appeal may be withdrawn, and a new one substituted;

(*f*) *Everett* v. *Lawrence*, L. R., 4 Ch. D. 139.

(*g*) *International Society* v. *City of Moscow Gas Co.*, supra; *Highton* v. *Treherne*, 39 L. T. 411 ; *Rhodes* v. *Jenkins*, L. R., 7 Ch. D. 711 : *Craig* v. *Phillips*, ib. 249 ; *Re Hankey*, L. R., 10 Ch. D. 613

(*h*) R. S. C., Ord. LVIII. r. 4.

(*i*) Where a person served with notice of the decree in an administration action does not get leave

to attend the proceedings, he must, nevertheless, be served with notice of appeal, if directly affected. *Re Rees*, L. R., 15 Ch. D. 490.

(*k*) R. S. C., Ord. LVIII. r. 3; *Hunter* v. *Hunter*, 24 W. R. 527 ; *Purnell* v. *G. W. Railway Co.*, L. R., 1 Q. B. D. 636.

(*l*) Ib.; *Re Duchess of Westminster, &c. Co.*, L. R., 10 Ch. D. 307.

but the latter must of course be given within the time limited for giving an original notice of appeal (*m*). Where, however, both parties have agreed that the appeal shall be withdrawn neither party can change his mind and prosecute the appeal without leave (*n*).

Form of Notice. No precise form is required for the notice (*o*), but of course it is desirable, that the notice should be correct, both in form and substance. Such a notice should be in the following form :—

In the Court of Appeal.

1881. S. No. 100.

Between John Styles . . . . . Plaintiff,

and

Samuel Crane. . . . . Defendant.

Take notice, that this honorable court will be moved on Thursday, the 26th day of May, 1881, or as soon thereafter as counsel can be heard, by Mr. A. B. as counsel on the part of the above-named defendant Samuel Crane, that the judgment made in this action and dated the 20th day of March, 1881, may be reversed [*or if only part is appealed from, so far as it directs that (stating the part appealed against)*]. And that it may be adjudged that [*stating the order desired.*]

Dated this   day of   1881.

George Smith,

Solicitor for the above-named Defendant.

To Mr. Francis Jones,

Solicitor for the above-named Plaintiff.

Setting down. Although notice of motion is given, the appeal is not brought on like a motion in the High Court, but must be set down for hearing. This is done where a judgment or order is appealed against, by taking the judgment or order, or an office copy of it, together with a copy of the notice of motion, to the proper officer

---

(*m*) *Norton* v. *L. & N. W. Railway Co.*, 40 L. T. 597.

(*n*) *Watson* v. *Cave*, L. R.

Ch. D. 23.

(*o*) *Ex parte Laws*, L. R., 7 Ch. 160.

of the Court of Appeal, who thereupon sets down the appeal, by entering it in the proper list of appeals; and it comes on to be heard according to its order in that list, unless the Court of Appeal, or a judge of that court, directs otherwise; but it must not come into the paper for hearing before the day named in the notice (p). Where the appeal is from the *refusal* of a judgment or order, of course the notice of appeal only need be taken to the officer (q). In entering the appeal, it must be borne in mind that it must be entered before the day named in the notice for bringing it on, otherwise it will be treated as abandoned; unless indeed that day falls in vacation, in which case the appeal should be entered before the next day of the sitting of the court (r).

Ex parte Appeals. Where an application to the High Court is *ex parte*, an appeal from its refusal is also *ex parte* (s); and in that case, it is made by motion without setting it down or entering it for hearing, but such appeal motion must be made within four days, unless a judge of the court below, or of the Appeal Court, extends the time (t).

Urgent Appeals. It is obvious that certain classes of appeals require prompt hearing, in order to prevent a miscarriage of justice. Such are appeals from interlocutory orders in urgent cases. Accordingly such appeals are set down in a separate list, and are heard quickly. Appeals of this kind are either (1) in cases of injunction, prohibition, *ne exeat regno*, or stop orders; (2) in cases relating to the appointment of receivers,

---

(p) R. S. C., Ord. LVIII. r. 8.

(q) *Smith* v. *Grindley*, L. R., 3 Ch. D. 80.

(r) *Re National Funds Co.*, L. R., 4 Ch. D. 305; *Shoelensack* v. *Price*, W. N. 1880, p. 69.

(s) R. S. C., Ord. LVIII. r. 10.

(t) Ib.

managers, or liquidators; (3) in cases in which enlarged
time is asked for redemption, or for payment into court,
or any other question of enlarging time; (4) questions
relating to wards or infants; (5) questions in relation to
contempt, or enforcing execution; (6) questions relating
to discovery of documents; (7) questions relating to procedure or practice (*u*). In setting down an appeal in
this list, the solicitor must certify at the bottom of the
notice of motion the class in the above list under which
the appeal falls.

Rehearing. When the appeal comes on for hearing
it is *reheard* (*w*), and the Court of Appeal has all the
powers and duties of the High Court, and full discretion
to hear further evidence *vivâ voce*, or by affidavit or deposition. This further evidence may be given without
any leave or interlocutory applications, or in any case as
to matters which have occurred after the date of the
decision appealed against. In other cases, special leave
must be obtained, which is usually asked for *at the hearing of the appeal*, where it is to be given by affidavit,
notice of the intention to make the application having
been previously given to the other side (*x*). But where
it is *vivâ voce*, a special notice must be previously made
and an order obtained (*y*).

How Evidence used. Where a question of fact
is appealed against, and the evidence was taken by affidavit in the court below, those affidavits are used in the
Court of Appeal. If the evidence in the court below
was *vivâ voce*, then the judge's notes of the evidence are

(*u*) Registrar's Notice, January,
1877; W. N. 1877, pt. ii., p. 162.
(*w*) R. S. C., Ord. LVIII. r. 2.

(*x*) See *Hastie* v. *Hastie*, L. R.,
1 Ch. D. 562.
(*y*) *Dicks* v. *Brooks*, L. R., 13
Ch. D. 652.

used in the Court of Appeal, or such other materials may be used as the court may direct (z). Short-hand notes may be referred to, but the judge's notes are the ultimate test of what was said, and the Court of Appeal does not encourage short-hand notes of evidence (a).

Where evidence has not been printed in the court below, that court, or the Court of Appeal, or a judge of either court, may order it to be printed for the purpose of the appeal (b).

Procedure on Hearing. The appeal being by way of rehearing, is heard like the original case, with the exception that the judge's notes of *vivâ voce evidence* are read instead of the evidence being again given *vivâ voce*. The court has power to give any judgment, or make any order, which ought to have been made, even though the notice of appeal does not ask for it; and it also has power to give relief to any of the parties, although *they* may not have appealed, and it has absolute discretion over the costs (c).

Where a respondent to an appeal also wishes to appeal himself, he need not give the ordinary notice of appeal; but he should within eight or four days (according as the appeal is from a final judgment or interlocutory order), give notice of his intention to appeal(d). The omission to give this notice does not diminish the powers of the court, but is ground for an adjournment and for a special order as to costs (e). However, a respondent who seeks to have an order varied on a

---

(z) R. S. C., Ord. LVIII. r. 11; and see as to short-hand notes, *Laming* v. *Gee*, 26 W. R. 217.

(a) *Kelly* v. *Byles*, L. R., 13 Ch. D. 693.

(b) R. S. C., Ord. LVIII. r. 12.
(c) Ib. r. 5.
(d) Ib. rr. 6, 7.
(e) Ib. r. 6.

point in which the appellant has no interest, cannot proceed in this way, but must give notice of appeal (e).

An interlocutory order which has *not* been appealed, does not bar or prejudice the Court of Appeal on an appeal from the *final* order in the action (f).

Wherever an application may be made, either to the court below or to the Appeal Court, it should be made in the first instance to the court below (g). Every application to the Appeal Court, or a judge of it, must be made by motion (h).

An appeal does not operate as a stay of execution, unless ordered by the court below or the Court of Appeal (i).

Abandonment of Appeal. Where a notice of appeal is withdrawn, the appeal will on motion be dismissed with costs (k).

Staying Appeals. Vexatious or frivolous appeals may, like frivolous or vexatious actions, be stayed on motion made to the Court of Appeal (l). Under special circumstances, too, the Court of Appeal will order the appellant to give security for the costs of the appeal (m); as, for instance, where he is insolvent or has not paid the costs incurred in the court below (n). If the security is not given in a reasonable time the respondent may move to dismiss the appeal.

(e) *Re Cavander*, L. R., 16 Ch. D. 270.

(f) R. S. C., Ord. LVIII. r. 14.

(g) Ib. r. 17.

(h) Ib. r. 18.

(i) Ib. r. 16.

(k) *Charlton* v. *Charlton*, L. R., 16 Ch. D. 273 ; and see *Harrison*

v. *Leutner*, ib. 559.

(l) *Vale* v. *Oppert*, L. R., 5 Ch. D. 969.

(m) R. S. C., Ord. LVIII. r. 15.

(n) *Waddell* v. *Blockey*, L. R., 10 Ch. D. 416; *Plimpton* v. *Spiller*, 21 S. J. 668.

Miscellaneous Regulations with regard to Procedure.

———◆———

CHAPTER I.

SITTINGS, VACATIONS AND TIME.

BOTH the High Court and the Court of Appeal have periodical vacations, which are the same for both courts. The periods during which the court transacts business in court used to be called terms, but they are now designated " sittings."

There are four sittings and four vacations in every year. The Michaelmas Sittings commence on the 2nd of November, and terminate on the 21st of December; the Hilary Sittings commence on the 11th of January, and end on the Wednesday before Easter; the Easter Sittings commence on the Tuesday after Easter week, and end on the Friday before Whitsuntide; and the Trinity Sittings commence on the Tuesday after Whitsun week, and end on the 8th of August (*a*).

As to the vacations, the Long Vacation opens on the 10th of August, and terminates on the 24th of October; the Christmas Vacation commences on the

(*a*) R. S. C., Ord. LXI. rr. 1, 2.

24th of December, and closes on the 6th of January; the Easter Vacation begins on Good Friday, and ends on Easter Tuesday ; and the Whitsun Vacation commences on the Saturday before Whitsunday, and terminates on the Tuesday following.

During the vacations, two judges (*b*) and one chief clerk in each set of chambers, take any *urgent* business. The central office and district registries are, however, open all the year round except on certain days (*c*).

Pleading. No pleadings can be amended or delivered in the long vacation unless directed by a judge (*d*); and the time of the long vacation is not reckoned in the computation of the times appointed or allowed for filing, amending, or delivering any pleading, unless otherwise directed by a judge (*e*).

Time. As to time generally ; month means calendar month (*f*) ; and where any limited time less than six days from or after any date is appointed for any purpose, Sunday, Christmas Day and Good Friday do not count (*g*).

So, where the time for doing anything expires on a Sunday (or other *dies non*), it may be done on the next day (*h*) ; and generally, in the absence of a written consent of the opposite party (which is binding (*i*)), a judge or the court has full power to enlarge or abridge the times appointed for doing any act or taking any proceeding upon terms or otherwise as justice may require (*k*).

(*b*) R. S. C., Ord. LXI. r. 5.

(*c*) Ib. r. 4.

(*d*) R. S. C., Ord. LVII. r. 4.

(*e*) Ib. r. 5.

(*f*) Ib. r. 1.

(*g*) Ib. r. 2.

(*h*) Ib. r. 3.

(*i*) Ib. r. 6a.

(*k*) Ib. r. 6.

It may be mentioned that service of proceedings must be made before 6 p.m. on ordinary days, and before 2 p.m. on Saturdays, or they will be taken to have been served on the next day on which they are capable of being served (*l*).

———◆———

CHAPTER II.

COURT FEES.

ON almost every proceeding taken in the offices of the court, fees have to be paid; and these fees are called court fees.

How paid. Court fees are invariably paid in the central office by means of stamps either impressed or adhesive, according to the nature of the proceeding (*m*): but in the district registries (except at Manchester and Liverpool (*n*)) they are at present paid in money (*o*).

No document requiring to be stamped will be received, filed, used, or admitted in evidence, without being properly stamped; but if such a document has been filed or received through inadvertence, the Lord Chancellor or the court may order that the same shall be properly stamped (*p*).

Higher and Lower Scales. The fees are calculated upon two scales; the higher scale being applicable to actions for special injunctions to restrain the commission or continuance of waste, nuisances, breaches of covenant, injuries to property, and infringement of

---

(*l*) Ib. r. 8.

(*m*) Ord. 28th Oct. 1875, r. 1.

(*n*) Ord. 24th Oct. 1877, r. 2.

(*o*) Ord. 28th Oct. 1875, r. 1.

(*p*) Jud. Act, 1875, s. 26.

rights, easements, patents, copyrights and other similar cases, where the procuring of the injunction is the principal relief sought for (*q*). The higher scale is also applicable to all cases to which the lower scale is inapplicable.

The lower scale is applicable to liquidated demands, to administration actions, partnership actions, foreclosure or redemption actions, actions for specific performance, proceedings under the Trustee Acts or the Trustee Relief Acts, proceedings relating to the guardianship or maintenance of infants, proceedings relating to funds carried to separate accounts, and proceedings under any railway or private act of parliament, or under any summary or statutory jurisdiction, in any of which cases the estate or fund to be dealt with does not exceed 1,000*l.* in value; and generally, in all other cases where the estate or fund does not exceed that sum (*r*).

The court or a judge may, however, in any case direct that either scale shall be charged.

Certificate of Scale. The solicitor (or suitor) must, on any action or proceeding in which he claims to pay the lower scale of fees, file with the proper officer a certificate that "to the best of his judgment and belief the lower scale of fees of court is applicable to this case." A copy of this is sealed, and its production to all officers of the court is sufficient authority to them to accept the lower scale (*s*).

Payment on improper Scale. In any case in which the lower scale has been erroneously or improperly certified, the deficiency in fees paid must be

(*q*) Add. R. Aug. 1875. Ord. VI. r. 2.

(*r*) Ib. r. 1.

(*s*) Ord. 28th Oct. 1875, r. 3.

made good (*t*) ; and, on the other hand, where the higher scale has been erroneously paid, the excess may be allowed by the taxing master on taxation of the costs (*u*).

Deposit. A deposit on account of expenses may be required by an official referee before proceeding with a reference (*x*) ; and, in such case, the solicitor or party making the deposit, must present to the officer requiring the deposit, a certificate duly stamped for the amount of such deposit. Forms of these certificates may be obtained at Somerset House. When the fees are afterwards ascertained, the referee indorses the amount of them on the certificate, and if the amount exceed the deposit, the certificate must be stamped up to the excess before he will give his award. If, on the other hand, the deposit exceed the amount of the fees, the excess will be repaid at Somerset House on production of the certificate and indorsement (*y*).

Amount of Fees. As every practitioner possesses a copy of the Rules and Orders under the Judicature Acts, it is not considered needful to reproduce here the schedule to the order as to costs of the 28th October, 1875, which sets forth the amount of the fees payable in different proceedings ; nor the schedule to the order as to fees and percentages of the 22nd April, 1876, which specifies the form of stamp (*i. e.* whether adhesive or impressed) applicable to each such proceeding.

(*t*) Ord. 28th Oct. 1875, r. 3.　　(*x*) Ord. 24th April, 1877.
(*u*) Ib.　　　　　　　　　　　　(*y*) Ord. 22nd April, 1876, r. 3.

CHAPTER III.

SUPPLEMENTAL ACTIONS.

SOMETIMES after a judgment has been passed and entered, it is found that the judgment ought to have been extended, so as to give some further relief; or that the relief ordered by the judgment will be incomplete without something further. In such cases it would seem that the old practice will prevail, and that a new writ may be issued claiming the new relief, and also claiming that the new action may be taken as supplemental to the former one, and that the proceedings already had in the old action may be adopted. For instance, in a foreclosure action, it may be found after judgment, that some other property was included in and liable under the mortgage, although not included in the judgment for foreclosure. In such a case it is apprehended that a supplemental action might be commenced for foreclosure of this property.

INDEX.

CHAMBERS,

PLEADINGS—*continued.*
(6.) *Amendment of*—continued.
how made, 104.
effect of, on adversary's pleadings, *ib.*
(7.) *Default of pleading.* See JUDGMENT.
by plaintiff, 106.

POLICIES OF ASSURANCE, applications as to, granted under Married Women's Property Act, 1870..293.

POSSESSION, WRIT OF, 329.

PRESERVATION of property. *See* INJUNCTION.

PRINTING of pleadings, 79.

PROCEEDINGS, obtaining leave to attend, 47.

PRODUCTION OF CESTUI QUE VIE, 306.

PRODUCTION OF DOCUMENTS. *See* EVIDENCE.

PROTECTOR OF SETTLEMENT, when court is the, 307.

QUESTIONS OF FACT. *See* TRIAL.

QUESTIONS OF LAW. *See* DEMURRER and SPECIAL CASE.

RAILWAY COMPANIES. *See* LANDS CLAUSES ACT.

RECEIVER,
mode of application for, 216.
should be claimed by writ, *ib.*
inquiry as to fitness of, *ib.*
giving security, *ib.*
appointment of party to the action, 217.
refusal to hand over property to, *ib.*
interfering with, *ib.*
powers of, 218.
accounts of, *ib.*
procedure, *ib.*
failure to deliver, 219.
discharge of, *ib.*
will sometimes be appointed by way of execution where sequestration inapplicable, 339.

RECOVERY OF LAND,
what claim can be joined with claim for, 52.
service of writ of summons in action, 62.

U.   C C

C. F. ROWORTH, PRINTER, BREAM'S BUILDINGS, CHANCERY LANE.

CATALOGUE

OF

𝕷𝖆𝖜 𝖂𝖔𝖗𝖐𝖘

PUBLISHED BY

MESSRS. BUTTERWORTH,

𝕷𝖆𝖜 𝕭𝖔𝖔𝖐𝖘𝖊𝖑𝖑𝖊𝖗𝖘 𝖆𝖓𝖉 𝕻𝖚𝖇𝖑𝖎𝖘𝖍𝖊𝖗𝖘

TO THE QUEEN'S MOST EXCELLENT MAJESTY,

AND TO

H.R.H. THE PRINCE OF WALES.

" *Now for the Laws of England (if I shall speak my opinion of them without* " *partiality either to my profession or country), for the matter and nature of* " *them, I hold them wise, just and moderate laws: they give to God, they give to* " *Cæsar, they give to the subject what appertaineth. It is true they are as mixt* " *as our language, compounded of British, Saxon, Danish, Norman customs.* " *And surely as our language is thereby so much the richer, so our laws are like-* " *wise by that mixture the more complete.*"—LORD BACON.

LONDON:

7, FLEET STREET, E.C.

1882.

INDEX TO CATALOGUE.

Law Works published by Messrs. Butterworth.

STEPHEN'S NEW COMMENTARIES.—8th Edit.

Mr. SERJEANT STEPHEN'S NEW COMMEN-
TARIES ON THE LAWS OF ENGLAND, partly founded
on Blackstone. By JAMES STEPHEN, Esq., LL.D., Judge of
County Courts. The Eighth Edition. Prepared for the press
by HENRY ST. JAMES STEPHEN, of the Middle Temple, Barrister-
at-Law. 4 vols. 8vo. 4*l*. 4*s*. cloth. 1880

** The Work selected for the Intermediate Examinations for Solicitors for
1882 and 1883.

From the "Law Times."

"Dr. James Stephen has just brought
out the eighth edition of Mr. Serjeant
Stephen's Commentaries on the Laws
of England (founded on Blackstone).
This edition deserves more attention
than previous editions, for the reason
that it has been revised with a view to
giving full effect to the alterations in
our law and practice introduced by the
Judicature Acts, and with the design of
giving a more scientific classification of
crimes, so as to bring the last book into
harmony with the general structure
of the proposed Criminal Code. Dr.
Stephen has been assisted in his work by
his son, Mr. Henry St. James Stephen.
From our examination of the work
(facilitated by the adoption of the
American plan of cutting the leaves in
the binding), we believe it will be found
to be one of the most valuable text
books which we possess, not only as to
the general law, but as to the new system which has grown up under the
Judicature Acts."

From the "Law Journal."

"It is quite unnecessary for us to
reiterate the praises we have, on many
former occasions, bestowed upon this
excellent work. A new edition has
been rendered necessary, both by reason
of the last edition having been exhausted, and of the recent changes in
the law effected by the operation of the
Judicature Acts; and Dr. Stephen has
not shirked the labour required. The
last edition was published in the year
1874; and, although the changes then
intended to be introduced by the Judicature Act of 1873 were embodied in
it, yet the subsequent Judicature Acts
and new rules of procedure, supplemented by judicial decisions upon them,
have made Dr. Stephen's task of revision no light one."

From the "Articled Clerks Journal."

"We feel bound to state that the
edition (Eighth) before us is certain to
maintain, with greater credit if possible,
the position of its predecessors, which
is that of the Student's best text-book
on the General Laws of England."

PALEY'S SUMMARY CONVICTIONS.—6th Edition.

THE LAW and PRACTICE OF SUMMARY CON-
VICTIONS under the SUMMARY JURISDICTION ACTS,
1848 and 1879, including proceedings preliminary and subsequent to Convictions, and the responsibility of Convicting
Magistrates and their Officers: with Forms. Sixth Edition.
By WALTER H. MACNAMARA, Esq., of the Inner Temple, Barrister-at-Law. In 1 vol. 8vo. 24*s*. cloth. 1879

**POWELL ON EVIDENCE. By CUTLER & GRIFFIN.
—Fourth Edition.**

POWELL'S PRINCIPLES and PRACTICE of the
LAW of EVIDENCE. Fourth Edition. By J. CUTLER, B.A.,
Professor of English Law and Jurisprudence, and Professor of
Indian Jurisprudence at King's College, London, and E. F.
GRIFFIN, B.A., Barristers-at-Law. Post 8vo. 18s. cloth.   1875

"There is hardly any branch of the law of greater interest and importance, not only to the profession, but to the public at large, than the law of evidence. On this branch of the law, moreover, all well as on many others, important changes have been effected of recent years. We are, therefore, all the more inclined to welcome the appearance of the Fourth Edition of this valuable work."—*Law Examination Journal.*

**DENISON AND SCOTT'S HOUSE OF LORDS APPEAL
PRACTICE.**

APPEALS TO THE HOUSE OF LORDS: Procedure
and Practice relative to English, Scotch and Irish Appeals; with
the Appellate Jurisdiction Act, 1876; the Standing Orders of
the House; Directions to Agents; Forms, and Tables of Costs.
Edited, with Notes, References and a full Index, forming a
complete Book of Practice under the New Appellate System.
By CHAS. MARSH DENISON and CHAS. HENDERSON SCOTT, of the
Middle Temple, Esqs., Barristers-at-Law. 8vo. 16s. cloth.   1879

"The most important portion of the work, viz., that concerning the Procedure and Practice on Appeal to the House of Lords, contains information of the most important kind to those gentlemen who have business of this nature; it is well and ably compiled, and the practitioner will find no difficulty in following the various steps indicated.

"The whole book is well and carefully prepared, and is unusually readable in its style."—*Justice of the Peace.*

"This is a small volume upon a subject of the greatest practical interest at the present time, for, notwithstanding the changes which have been made in the construction of the ultimate Court of Appeal, there are no two opinions as to the position which it holds in the confidence of the profession and the public. A learned introduction gives a brief but sufficient historical sketch of the jurisdiction of the House of Lords. This is followed by a practical treatise, which is a complete and well-written guide to the procedure by which an Appeal is begun, continued, and ended, including an important chapter on Costs. In an Appendix are given the Act of 1876, the portions of the Supreme Court of Judicature (Ireland) Act, 1877, and the Scotch Statutes, Forms, and Bills of Costs."—*Law Times.*

DAVIS'S LABOUR LAWS OF 1875.

THE LABOUR LAWS OF 1875, with Introduction
and Notes. By J. E. DAVIS, Esq., Barrister-at-Law, and late
Police Magistrate for Sheffield. 8vo. 12s. cloth.   1875

CRUMP'S PRINCIPLES OF MARINE INSURANCE

THE PRINCIPLES OF THE LAW RELATING TO
MARINE INSURANCE AND GENERAL AVERAGE in
England and America, with occasional references to French and
German Law. By F. OCTAVIUS CRUMP, of the Middle Temple,
Esq., Barrister-at-Law. In 1 vol. royal 8vo. 21s. cloth.   1875

HAMEL'S CUSTOMS LAWS.

THE LAWS OF THE CUSTOMS, 1876, consolidated by direction of the Lords Commissioners of her Majesty's Treasury. With practical Notes and References throughout; an Appendix containing various Statutory Provisions incidental to the Customs; the Customs Tariff Act, 1876, and a Copious Index. With Supplement to 1881. By FELIX JOHN HAMEL, Esq. Post 8vo. 3s. 6d. cloth; demy 8vo. 4s. 6d.   1881

SHELFORD'S JOINT STOCK COMPANIES.— Second Edition by PITCAIRN and LATHAM.

SHELFORD'S LAW of JOINT STOCK COMPANIES, containing a Digest of the Case Law on that subject; the Companies Acts, 1862, 1867, and other Acts relating to Joint Stock Companies; the Orders made under those Acts to regulate Proceedings in the Court of Chancery and County Courts; and Notes of all Cases interpreting the above Acts and Orders. Second Edition, much enlarged, and bringing the Statutes and Cases down to the date of publication. By DAVID PITCAIRN, M.A., Fellow of Magdalen College, Oxford, and of Lincoln's Inn, Barrister-at-Law, and FRANCIS LAW LATHAM, B.A., Oxon, of the Inner Temple, Barrister-at-Law, Author of "A Treatise on the Law of Window Lights." 8vo. 21s. cloth.   1870

DREWRY'S FORMS OF CLAIMS AND DEFENCES.

FORMS OF CLAIMS AND DEFENCES IN CASES intended for the CHANCERY DIVISION OF THE HIGH COURT OF JUSTICE. With Notes, containing an Outline of the Law relating to each of the subjects treated of, and an Appendix of Forms of Endorsement on the Writ of Summons. By C. STEWART DREWRY, of the Inner Temple, Esq., Barrister-at-Law, Author of a Treatise on Injunctions, and of Reports of Cases in Equity, temp. Kindersley, V.-C., and other works. Post 8vo. 9s. cloth.   1876

"Mr. Drewry's plan of taking the facts for the forms from reported cases and adapting them to the new rules of pleading, seems the best that can be adopted. The forms we have looked at seem to be fairly correct."—*Solicitors' Journal.*

"The equity draftsmen of the present day, who, however experienced in the niceties of the past system, cannot but need the aid of a work thus compiled, and, trusting to its guidance, benefit in time and labour saved; while to the younger members of the profession especially we cordially recommend the work."—*Irish Law Times.*

ROBERTS' PRINCIPLES OF EQUITY.—Third Edition.

THE PRINCIPLES OF EQUITY as administered in the SUPREME COURT OF JUDICATURE and other Courts of Equitable Jurisdiction. By THOMAS ARCHIBALD ROBERTS, of the Middle Temple, Esq., Barrister-at-Law. Third Edition. 8vo. 18s. cloth.   1877

DAVIS'S COUNTY COURTS PRACTICE & EVIDENCE.
—Fifth Edition.

THE PRACTICE AND EVIDENCE IN ACTIONS IN THE COUNTY COURTS. By JAMES EDWARD DAVIS, of the Middle Temple, Esq., Barrister-at-Law. Fifth Edition. 8vo. 38s. cloth; 43s. calf.   1874

DAVIS'S COUNTY COURT RULES AND ACTS OF 1875 and 1876.

THE COUNTY COURT RULES, 1875 and 1876, with Forms and Scales of Costs and Fees; together with the County Courts Act, 1875, and other recent Statutes affecting the Jurisdiction of the County Courts. Forming a SUPPLEMENT to the Fifth Edition of the COUNTY COURT PRACTICE and EVIDENCE, but entirely complete in itself. By JAMES EDWARD DAVIS, of the Middle Temple, Esq., Barrister-at-Law. In 1 vol. 8vo. 16s. cloth.   1876

DAVIS'S EQUITY AND BANKRUPTCY IN THE COUNTY COURTS.

THE JURISDICTION & PRACTICE of the COUNTY COURTS in Equity (including Friendly Societies), Admiralty, Probate of Wills, Administration, and in Bankruptcy. By J. E. DAVIS, of the Middle Temple, Esq., Barrister-at-Law. 1 vol. 8vo. 18s. cloth; 22s. calf.   1872

CHADWICK'S PROBATE COURT MANUAL.
Corrected to 1876.

EXAMPLES of ADMINISTRATION BONDS for the COURT of PROBATE; exhibiting the principle of various Grants of Administration, and the correct mode of preparing the Bonds in respect thereof; also Directions for preparing the Oaths; arranged for practical utility. With Extracts from Statutes; also various Forms of Affirmation prescribed by Acts of Parliament, and a Supplemental Notice, bringing the work down to 1876. By SAMUEL CHADWICK, of her Majesty's Court of Probate. Roy. 8vo. 12s. cloth.

CHUTE'S EQUITY IN RELATION TO COMMON LAW.

EQUITY UNDER THE JUDICATURE ACT, or the Relation of Equity to Common Law. By CHALONER WILLIAM CHUTE, Barrister-at-Law; Fellow of Magdalen College, Oxford; Post 8vo. 9s. cloth.   1874

MOZLEY AND WHITELEY'S CONCISE LAW DICTIONARY.

A CONCISE LAW DICTIONARY, containing Short and Simple Definitions of the Terms used in the Law. By HERBERT NEWMAN MOZLEY, M.A., Fellow of King's College, Cambridge, and of Lincoln's Inn, Esq., and GEORGE CRISPE WHITELEY, M.A., Cantab, of the Middle Temple, Esq., Barristers-at-Law. In 1 vol. 8vo. 20s. cloth; 25s. brown calf.   1876

"This book is a great deal more modest in its views than the law dictionary we reviewed a little while ago. Its main object is to explain briefly legal terms, both ancient and modern. In many cases, however, the authors have added a concise statement of the law. But, as the work is intended both for lawyers and the public at large, it does not profess to give more than an outline of the doctrines referred to under the several headings. Having regard to this design, we think the work is well and carefully edited. It is exceedingly complete, not only giving terse explanations of legal phrases, but also notices of leading cases and short biographies of legal luminaries. We may add that a very convenient table of reports is given, showing the abbreviations, the date and the court, and that the book is very well printed."—*Solicitors' Journal.*

"This book contains a large mass of information more or less useful. A considerable amount both of labour and learning has evidently been expended upon it, and to the general public it may be recommended as a reliable and useful guide. Law students desirous of cramming will also find it acceptable."—*Law Times.*

"It should contain everything of value to be found in the other larger works, and it should be useful not merely to the legal profession, but also to the general public. Now, the work of Messrs. Mozley and Whiteley appears to fulfil those very conditions; and, while it assists the lawyer, will be no less useful to his client. On the whole, we repeat that the work is a praiseworthy performance which deserves a place in the libraries both of the legal profession and of the general public."—*Irish Law Times.*

DE COLYAR'S LAW OF GUARANTEES.

A TREATISE ON THE LAW OF GUARANTEES and of PRINCIPAL and SURETY. By HENRY A. DE COLYAR, of the Middle Temple, Barrister-at-Law. 8vo. 14s. cloth. 1874

"Mr. Colyar's work contains internal evidence that he is quite at home with his subject. His book has the great merit of thoroughness. Hence its present value, and hence we venture to predict will be its enduring reputation."—*Law Times.*

"The whole work displays great care in its production; it is clear in its statements of the law, and the result of the many authorities collected is stated with an intelligent appreciation of the subject in hand."—*Justice of the Peace.*

TROWER'S PREVALENCE OF EQUITY.

A MANUAL OF THE PREVALENCE OF EQUITY, under Section 25 of the Judicature Act, 1873, amended by the Judicature Act, 1875. By CHARLES FRANCIS TROWER, Esq., M.A., of the Inner Temple, Barrister-at-Law, late Fellow of Exeter College, and Vinerian Law Scholar, Oxford, Author of "The Law of Debtor and Creditor," "The Law of the Building of Churches and Divisions of Parishes," &c. 8vo. 5s. cloth. 1876

"The amount of information contained in a compressed form within its pages is very considerable, and on the whole it appears to be accurate. The work has been carefully revised, and is well and clearly printed."—*Law Times.*

FAWCETT'S LAW OF LANDLORD AND TENANT.

A COMPENDIUM OF THE LAW OF LANDLORD AND TENANT. By WILLIAM MITCHELL FAWCETT, Esq., of Lincoln's Inn, Barrister-at-Law. 1 vol. 8vo. 14s. cloth. 1871

"This new compendium of the law on a wide and complicated subject, upon which information is constantly required by a vast number of persons, is sure to be in request. It never wanders from the point, and being intended not for students of the law, but for lessors and lessees, and their immediate advisers, wisely avoids historical disquisitions, and uses language as untechnical as the subject admits."—*Law Journal*.

"Mr. Fawcett takes advantage of this characteristic of modern law to impart to his compendium a degree of *authenticity* which greatly enhances its value as a convenient medium of reference, for he has stated the law in the very words of the authorities."—*Law Magazine*.

HUNT'S LAW OF FRAUDS AND BILLS OF SALE.

THE LAW relating to FRAUDULENT CONVEYANCES under the Statutes of Elizabeth and the Bankrupt Acts; with Remarks on the Law relating to Bills of Sale. By ARTHUR JOSEPH HUNT, of the Inner Temple, Esq., Barrister-at-Law, Author of "A Treatise on the Law relating to Boundaries, Fences and Foreshores." Post 8vo. 9s. cloth. 1872

"Mr. Hunt has brought to bear upon the subject a clearness of statement, an orderliness of arrangement and a subtlety of logical acuteness which carry him far towards a complete systematization of all the cases. Neither has his industry been lacking; the cases that have arisen under 'The Bankruptcy Act, 1869,' and under the Bills of Sale Act, have been carefully and completely noted up and disposed by him in their appropriate places. The index also is both accurate and careful, and secures much facility of reference to the various matters which are the subjects of the work."—*Law Magazine*.

"Mr. Hunt's book is as readable as a treatise on so technical a subject can well be made. Mr. Hunt's arrangement of his materials follows an orderly and intelligible plan. The index is apparently carefully prepared, and the table of cases shows that none of the recent cases have been overlooked. Mr. Hunt has produced a really useful book unencumbered by useless matter, which deserves great success as a manual of the law of fraudulent dispositions of property."—*Law Journal*.

BUND'S AGRICULTURAL HOLDINGS ACT, 1875.

The LAW of COMPENSATION for UNEXHAUSTED AGRICULTURAL IMPROVEMENTS, as amended by the Agricultural Holdings (England) Act, 1875. By J. W. WILLIS BUND, M.A., of Lincoln's Inn, Barrister-at-Law, Author of "The Law relating to Salmon Fisheries in England and Wales," &c. 12mo. 5s. cloth. 1876

POWELL'S LAW OF INLAND CARRIERS.— Second Edition.

THE LAW OF INLAND CARRIERS, especially as regulated by the Railway and Canal Traffic Act, 1854. By EDMUND POWELL, Esq., of Lincoln College, Oxon, M.A., and of the Western Circuit, Barrister-at-Law, Author of "Principles and Practice of the Law of Evidence." Second Edition, almost re-written. 8vo. 14s. cloth.

FOLKARD ON SLANDER & LIBEL.—Fourth Edition.

THE LAW OF SLANDER AND LIBEL (founded upon Starkie's Treatise), including the Pleading and Evidence, Civil and Criminal, adapted to the present Procedure; also MALICIOUS PROSECUTIONS and CONTEMPTS of COURT. By H. C. FOLKARD, Barrister-at-Law. In 1 thick vol. roy. 8vo. 45s. cloth.   1876

PYE ON CLAIMS TO DEBTORS' ESTATES.

NOTES ON THE CONFLICTING CLAIMS TO THE PROPERTY OF A DEBTOR. By HENRY JOHN PYE, of the Inner Temple, Esq., Barrister-at-Law. Just published, post 8vo. 3s. 6d. cloth.   1880

COOTE'S PROBATE PRACTICE.—Eighth Edition.

THE COMMON FORM PRACTICE OF THE HIGH COURT of JUSTICE in granting Probates and Administrations. By HENRY CHARLES COOTE, F.S.A., late Proctor in Doctors' Commons, Author of "The Practice of the Ecclesiastical Courts," &c. &c. 8th Edit. In 1 vol. 8vo., 26s. cloth; 30s. calf. 1878

. The Forms as printed in this work are in strict accordance with the Orders of Court and Decisions of the Right Hon. Sir James Hannen, and are those which are in use in the Principal Registry of the Probate Divisional Court.

"The above is another name for what is commonly known to the profession as Coote's Probate Practice, a work about as indispensable in a solicitor's office as any book of practice that is known to us. The seventh edition is chiefly distinguishable from the sixth edition in this, that certain important modifications and alterations are effected which have been rendered necessary by the Judicature Acts. Judicial decisions subsequent to the last edition have been carefully noted up. We notice several new and useful forms; and the author has not only attempted, but has in the main succeeded, in adopting the forms and directions under the old Probate practice, as embodied in previous editions of the work, to the new procedure under the Judicature Acts. Solicitors know that the difficulties in the way of satisfying the different clerks at Somerset House are frequently great, and there is nothing so likely to tend to simplicity of practice as Mr. Coote's book."—*Law Times.*

TRISTRAM'S CONTENTIOUS PROBATE PRACTICE.

THE CONTENTIOUS PRACTICE OF THE HIGH COURT OF JUSTICE, in respect of Grants of Probates and Administrations, with the Practice as to Motions and Summonses in Non-contentious Business. By THOMAS HUTCHINSON TRISTRAM, Q.C., D.C.L., Advocate of Doctors' Commons, of the Inner Temple, Chancellor of the Diocese of London. Demy 8vo. 21s. cloth.   1881

TOMKINS & JENCKEN'S MODERN ROMAN LAW.

COMPENDIUM OF THE MODERN ROMAN LAW. Founded upon the Treatises of Puchta, Von Vangerow, Arndts, Franz Möhler, and the Corpus Juris Civilis. By FREDERICK J. TOMKINS, Esq., M.A., D.C.L., Author of the "Institutes of Roman Law," translator of "Gaius," &c., and HENRY DIEDRICH JENCKEN, Esq., Barristers-at-Law, of Lincoln's Inn. 8vo. 14s. cloth.   1870

SHELFORD'S RAILWAYS.—Fourth Edition, by Glen.

SHELFORD'S LAW OF RAILWAYS, containing the whole of the Statute Law for the Regulation of Railways in England, Scotland and Ireland. With Copious Notes of Decided Cases upon the Statutes, Introduction to the Law of Railways, and Appendix of Official Documents. Fourth Edition, by W. CUNNINGHAM GLEN, Barrister-at-Law, Author of the "Law of Highways," "Law of Public Health and Local Government," &c. 2 vols. royal 8vo. 63s. cloth; 75s. calf. 1869

" The work must take its unquestionable position as the leading Manual of the Railway Law of Great Britain."—Law Magazine.

" At any rate we may venture to predict that Mr. Cunningham Glen's edition of Shelford on Railways will be the standard work of our day in that department of law."—Law Journal.

" Far be it from us to under value Mr. Shelford's labours, or to disparage his merits. But we may nevertheless be permitted to observe that what has hitherto been considered as 'the best work on the subject' (Shelford), has been immeasurably improved by the application of Mr. Glen's diligence and learning. . . . Sufficient, however, has been done to show that it is in every respect worthy of the reputation which the work has always enjoyed."—Justice of the Peace.

GRANT'S BANKERS AND BANKING COMPANIES. Fourth Edition. By C. C. M. PLUMPTRE.

GRANT'S TREATISE ON THE LAW RELATING TO BANKERS AND BANKING COMPANIES. With an Appendix of the most important Statutes in force relating thereto. Fourth Edition. By C. C. M. PLUMPTRE, of the Middle Temple, Esq., Barrister-at-Law. 8vo. 26s. cloth.

" Eight years sufficed to exhaust the second edition of this valuable and standard work, we need only now notice the improvements which have been made. We have once more looked through the work, and recognize in it the sterling merits which have acquired for it the high position which it holds in standard legal literature. Mr. Fisher has annotated all the recent cases."—Law Times.

FISHER'S LAW OF MORTGAGE—Third Edition.

The LAW of MORTGAGE and OTHER SECURITIES UPON PROPERTY. By WILLIAM RICHARD FISHER, of Lincoln's Inn, Esq., Barrister-at-Law. 2 vols. roy. 8vo. 60s. cloth; 72s. calf. 1876

" This work has built up for itself, in the experienced opinion of the profession, a very high reputation for carefulness, accuracy and lucidity. This reputation is fully maintained in the present edition. The law of securities upon property is confessedly intricate, and, probably, as the author justly observes, embraces a greater variety of learning than any other single branch of the English law. At the same time, an accurate knowledge of it is essential to every practising barrister, and of daily requirement amongst solicitors. To all such we can confidently recommend Mr. Fisher's work, which will, moreover, prove most useful reading for the student, both as a storehouse of information and as intellectual exercise."—Law Magazine.

" We have received the third edition of the Law of Mortgage, by William Richard Fisher, Barrister-at-Law, and we are very glad to find that vast improvements have been made in the plan of the work, which is due to the incorporation therein of what Mr. Fisher designed and executed for the abortive Digest Commission. In its present form, embracing as it does all the statute and case law to the present time, the work is one of great value."—Law Times.

BOYLE'S PRÉCIS OF AN ACTION AT COMMON LAW.

PRÉCIS of an ACTION at COMMON LAW, showing at a Glance the Procedure under the Judicature Acts and Rules in an Action in the Queen's Bench, Common Pleas and Exchequer Divisions of the High Court of Justice. By HERBERT E. BOYLE, Solicitor. 8vo., 5s. cloth. 1881

" In this little manual, Mr. Boyle has succeeded in exhibiting a succinct and lucid outline of all the ordinary proceedings in actions governed by the practice, under the English Judicature Acts and Orders, of what used to be called the common law courts. Taking the various steps of that procedure in their natural order, he summarises the orders of court relating to each, arranging them under distinct headings, and referring to authorities upon their construction and application. Students preparing for the Final Examination certainly need a guide of this description, and Mr. Boyle has well supplied that need. Indeed, we do not remember having ever before seen the English procedure so well explained within so brief a compass."—*Irish Law Times.*

" A student who is ignorant of procedure, and desires to prepare for his Final Examination, will do well to procure Mr. Boyle's work."—*Law Examination Journal.*

BEDFORD'S FINAL EXAMINATION GUIDE TO PROBATE AND DIVORCE.—2nd Edition.

THE FINAL EXAMINATION GUIDE to the LAW of PROBATE and DIVORCE: containing a Digest of Final Examination Questions with the Answers. By E. H. BEDFORD, Solicitor, Temple, Author of the "Final Examination Guide to the Practice of the Supreme Court of Judicature." In 1 vol. post 8vo. 6s. cloth.

BEDFORD'S FINAL EXAMINATION GUIDE.

THE FINAL EXAMINATION GUIDE TO THE PRACTICE of the SUPREME COURT of JUDICATURE, containing a Digest of the Final Examination Questions, with many New Ones, with the Answers, under the Supreme Court of Judicature Act. By EDWARD HENSLOWE BEDFORD, Solicitor, Temple. In 1 vol. 8vo. 7s. 6d. cloth. 1875

BEDFORD'S PRELIMINARY QUESTIONS AND ANSWERS.

THE PRELIMINARY (No. 53): containing the QUESTIONS of the PRELIMINARY EXAMINATIONS (Solicitors) of October, 1882, with the Answers. By EDWARD HENSLOWE BEDFORD, Solicitor. 8vo., 6d. sewed, by post 7d. 1882

* *Continued each term.*

By the same Author, on a Sheet, 1s.

A TABLE of the LEADING STATUTES for the INTERMEDIATE and FINAL EXAMINATIONS in Law, Equity and Conveyancing.

LEWIS'S INTRODUCTION TO CONVEYANCING.

PRINCIPLES OF CONVEYANCING EXPLAINED and ILLUSTRATED by CONCISE PRECEDENTS. With an Appendix on the Effect of the Transfer of Land Act in Modifying and Shortening Conveyances. By HUBERT LEWIS, B.A., late Scholar of Emmanuel College, Cambridge, of the Middle Temple, Barrister-at-Law. 8vo. 18s. cloth.   1863

"By the diligent and painstaking student who has duly mastered the law of property, this work will undoubtedly be hailed as a very comprehensive exponent of the Principles of Conveyancing."—*Leguleian, or Articled Clerks' Magazine.*

"Mr. Lewis has contributed a valuable

aid to the law student. He has condensed the Practice of Conveyancing into a shape that will facilitate its retention on the memory, and his Precedents are usefully arranged as a series of progressive lessons, which may be either used as illustrations or exercises." *Law Times.*

PHILLIMORE'S INTERNATIONAL LAW.—3rd edit.

Vol. I. 8vo. 24s. cloth ; Vol. II. 26s. cloth.

COMMENTARIES ON INTERNATIONAL LAW. By the Right Hon. Sir ROBERT PHILLIMORE, Knt., P.C., Judge in the Probate, Matrimonial, Divorce and Admiralty Division of the High Court of Justice.   1879

*** *Vol. III., second edition (1875), price 36s.; Vol. IV., second edition (1874), price 34s. cloth, may be had separately to complete sets.*

Extract from Pamphlet on "American Neutrality," by GEORGE BEMIS *(Boston, U.S.).* —"Sir Robert Phillimore, the present Queen's Advocate, and author of the most comprehensive and systematic 'Commentaries on International Law' that England has produced."

"The authority of this work is admittedly great, and the learning and ability displayed in its preparation have been recognized by writers on public law both on the Continent of Europe and in the United States. With this necessarily imperfect sketch we must conclude our notice of the first volume of a work which forms an important contribution to the literature of public law. The book is of great utility, and one which should find a place in the library of every civilian."—*Law Magazine.*

"It is the most complete repository of matters bearing upon international law that we have in the language. We need not repeat the commendations of the text itself as a treatise or series of treatises which this journal expressed upon the appearance of the two first volumes. The reputation of the Author is too well established and too widely known. We content ourselves with testifying to the fulness and thoroughness of the work as a compilation after an inspection of the three volumes. (2nd edition)."—*Boston (United States) Daily Advertiser.*

"Sir Robert Phillimore may well be proud of this work as a lasting record of his ability, learning and his industry.

Having read the work carefully and critically, we are able to highly recommend it."—*Law Journal.*

"The second edition of Sir Robert Phillimore's Commentaries contains a considerable amount of valuable additional matter, bearing more especially on questions of international law raised by the wars and contentions that have broken out in the world since the publication of the first edition. Having upon a former occasion discussed at some length the general principles and execution of this important work, we now propose to confine ourselves to a brief examination of a single question, on which Sir Robert Phillimore may justly be regarded as the latest authority and as the champion of the principles of maritime law, which, down to a recent period, were maintained by this country, and which were at one time accepted without question by the maritime powers. Sir Robert Phillimore has examined with his usual learning, and established without the possibility of doubt, the history of the doctrine 'free ships, free goods,' and its opposite, in the third volume of his 'Commentaries' (p. 302)."—*Edinburgh Review, No. 296, October,* 1876.

UNDERHILL'S CHANCERY PROCEDURE.

A PRACTICAL and CONCISE MANUAL of the PRO-
CEDURE of the CHANCERY DIVISION of the HIGH COURT
of JUSTICE, both in Actions and Matters. By ARTHUR UNDER-
HILL, LL.D., of Lincoln's Inn, Barrister-at-Law, author of
"A Concise Treatise on the Law of Private Trusts and Trustees,"
"A Summary of the Law of Torts," &c. 1 vol. post 8vo., 10s. 6d.
cloth. 1881

"This work, coming from the pen of the author of the well-known works on Torts and Trusts, will be found to be at once concise and readable. We would advise its perusal by all students and young practitioners."—*Justice of the Peace*.

"Mr. Underhill has produced within small compass a very useful work on Chancery Practice." — *Law Students' Journal*.

"This most excellent treatise on Chancery Practice supplies a long existing want. Within a comparatively small space Mr. Underhill, in his usual clear, emphatic and intelligent manner, has supplied the student with all the necessary information respecting the peculiar practice in the Chancery Divi-

sion. The book is divided into *three* parts—the first division treats of *actions* and contains eleven sub-divisions; the second division treats of *matters* and contains four sub-divisions, while the third division treats of proceedings common to both actions and matters, and also contains four sub-divisions. The work cannot fail to be of great service to the student, especially if he aspires for Honors, and he will find it a complete work to his purpose, while to the practitioner such accurate informa-tion as is conveyed in its pages can hardly fail to be of service; and, like its companion the now well-known 'Underhill's Torts,' and 'Underhill's Trustees,' the volume will meet with a ready sale."—*Gibson's Final*.

UNDERHILL'S LAW OF TORTS.—Third Edition.

A SUMMARY OF THE LAW OF TORTS, OR
WRONGS INDEPENDENT OF CONTRACT, including the
Employers' Liability Act, 1880. By ARTHUR UNDERHILL, LL.D.,
of Lincoln's Inn, Esq., Barrister-at-Law; assisted by C. C. M.
PLUMPTRE, of the Middle Temple, Esq., Barrister-at-Law.
Third Edition. Post 8vo. 8s. cloth. 1881

"He has set forth the elements of the law with clearness and accuracy. The little work of Mr. Underhill is inexpen-sive and may be relied on." — *Law Times*.

"The plan is a good one and has been honestly carried out, and a good index facilitates reference to the contents of the book."—*Justice of the Peace*.

UNDERHILL'S LAW OF TRUSTS AND TRUSTEES.

A CONCISE MANUAL OF THE LAW RELATING TO
PRIVATE TRUSTS AND TRUSTEES. By ARTHUR UNDER-
HILL, M.A., of Lincoln's Inn and the Chancery Bar, Barrister-
at-Law. Post 8vo. 8s. cloth. 1878

"The author so treats his subjects that it will not be found a difficult matter for a person of ordinary intel-ligence to retain the matter therein con-tained, which must be constantly ne-cessary, not only to the professional man, but also for all those who may have taken upon themselves the re-sponsibilities of a trustee."—*Justice of the Peace*.

"We recently published a short re-view or notice of Mr. A. F. Leach's 'Digest of the Law of Probate Duty,' and remarked that it was framed after

the model of Sir Fitzjames Stephen's 'Digest of the Criminal Law and Law of Evidence from the Indian Acts,' and which has been followed by Mr. Pollock in his 'Digest of the Law of Partner-ship.' Mr. Underhill has, in the above-named volume, performed a similar task in relation to the 'Law of Trusts.' In seventy-six articles he has summarized the principles of the 'Law of Trusts' as distinctly and accurately as the sub-ject will admit, and has supplemented the articles with illustrations."—*Law Journal*.

SCRIVEN ON COPYHOLDS.—6th Edit., by Brown.

A TREATISE on the LAW of COPYHOLDS and of the other TENURES (Customary and Freehold) of LANDS within Manors, with the Law of Manors and Manorial Customs generally, and the Rules of Evidence applicable thereto, including the Law of Commons or Waste Lands, and also the Jurisdiction of the various Manorial Courts. By JOHN SCRIVEN. The Sixth Edition, thoroughly revised, re-arranged, and brought down to the present time, by ARCHIBALD BROWN, Esq., of the Middle Temple, Barrister-at-Law, B.C.L., &c., Editor of "Bainbridge on the Law of Mines." 1 vol. roy. 8vo. 30s. cloth.   1882

BAINBRIDGE ON MINES.—4th Edit., by Archibald Brown.

A TREATISE on the LAW of MINES and MINERALS. By WILLIAM BAINBRIDGE, Esq., F.G.S., of the Inner Temple, Barrister-at-Law.   Fourth Edition.   By ARCHIBALD BROWN, M.A. Edin. and Oxon, of the Middle Temple, Barrister-at-Law. This Work has been wholly re-cast, and in the greater part rewritten.   It contains, also, several chapters of entirely new matter, which have obtained at the present day great Mining importance. 8vo. 45s. cloth.   1878

"This work must be already familiar to all readers whose practice brings them in any manner in connection with mines or mining, and they well know its value. We can only say of this new edition that it is in all respects worthy of its predecessors." — *Law Times on 3rd edit.*

"It would be entirely superfluous to attempt a general review of a work which has for so long a period occupied the position of the standard work on this important subject. Those only who, by the nature of their practice, have learned to lean upon Mr. Bainbridge as on a solid staff, can appreciate the deep research, the admirable method, and the graceful style of this model treatise.."—*Law Journal on 3rd edit.*

ADAMS'S LAW OF TRADE-MARKS.

A TREATISE ON THE LAW OF TRADE-MARKS; with the Trade-Marks Regulation Act, 1875, and the Lord Chancellor's Rules. By F. M. ADAMS, of the Middle Temple, Esq., Barrister-at-Law. 8vo. 7s. 6d. cloth.   1876

NASMITH'S INSTITUTES OF ENGLISH LAW.

THE INSTITUTES OF ENGLISH LAW.—Part 1, English Public Law.   Part 2, English Private Law (in 2 vols.). Part 3, Evidence and the Measure of Damages. By DAVID NASMITH, LL.B., of the Middle Temple, Barrister-at-Law, Author of the Chronometrical Chart of the History of England, &c. In 4 vols. post 8vo. 30s. cloth.   1873—1879

⁎ The above may be had separately to complete sets at the following prices :—Part 1, 10s. cloth. Part 2, 20s. cloth. Part 3, 10s. cloth.

"Mr. Nasmith has evidently expended much labour and care in the compilation and arrangement of the present work, and so far as we have been able to test it, the bulk of his Treatise, which is confined to a concise exposition of the existing law, appears to merit the praise of accuracy and clearness."—*Law Magazine.*

SIR T. ERSKINE MAY'S PARLIAMENTARY PRACTICE.—Eighth Edition.

A TREATISE ON THE LAW, PRIVILEGES, PROCEEDINGS AND USAGE OF PARLIAMENT. By Sir THOMAS ERSKINE MAY, D.C.L., K.C.B., Clerk of the House of Commons and Bencher of the Middle Temple. Eighth Edition, Revised and Enlarged. 8vo. 42s. cloth. 1879

CONTENTS: Book I. Constitution, Powers and Privileges of Parliament.—Book II. Practice and Proceedings in Parliament.—Book III. The Manner of passing Private Bills, with the Standing Orders in both Houses, and the most recent Precedents.

"A work, which has risen from the position of a text book into that of an authority, would seem to a considerable extent to have passed out of the range of criticism. It is quite unnecessary to point out the excellent arrangement, accuracy and completeness which long ago rendered Sir T. E. May's treatise the standard work on the law of Parliament."—*Solicitors' Journal.*

"We need make no comment upon the value of the work. It is an accepted authority and is undeniably the law of Parliament. It has been brought up to the latest date, and should be in the hands of every one engaged in Parliamentary life, whether as a lawyer or as a senator."—*Law Times.*

FULTON'S Manual of CONSTITUTIONAL HISTORY.

A MANUAL OF CONSTITUTIONAL HISTORY, founded on the Works of Hallam, Creasy, May and Broom: comprising all the Fundamental Principles and the Leading Cases in Constitutional Law. By FORREST FULTON, Esq., LL.D., B.A., University of London, and of the Middle Temple, Barrister-at-Law. Post 8vo. 7s. 6d. cloth. 1875

TUDOR'S LEADING CASES ON REAL PROPERTY.—Third Edition.

A SELECTION of LEADING CASES on the LAW relating to REAL PROPERTY, CONVEYANCING, and the CONSTRUCTION of WILLS and DEEDS; with Notes. By OWEN DAVIES TUDOR, Esq., of the Middle Temple, Barrister-at-Law, Author of "Leading Cases in Equity." Third Edition. 1 thick vol. royal 8vo. 2l. 12s. 6d. cloth. 1879

"The work before us comprises a digest of decisions which, if not exhaustive of all the principles of our real property code, will at least be found to leave nothing untouched or unelaborated under the numerous legal doctrines to which the cases severally relate. To Mr. Tudor's treatment of all these subjects, so complicated and so varied, we accord our entire commendation. There are no omissions of any important cases relative to the various branches of the law comprised in the work, nor are there any omissions or defects in his statement of the law itself applicable to the cases discussed by him. We cordially recommend the work to the practitioner and student alike, but especially to the former."—*Solicitors' Journal and Reporter.*

"In this new edition, Mr. Tudor has carefully revised his notes in accordance with subsequent decisions that have modified or extended the law as previously expounded. This and the other volumes of Mr. Tudor are almost a law library in themselves, and we are satisfied that the student would learn more law from the careful reading of them, than he would acquire from double the time given to the elaborate treatises which learned professors recommend the student to peruse, with entire forgetfulness that time and brains are limited, and that to do what they advise would be the work of a life."—*Law Times.*

MOSELY'S ARTICLED CLERKS' HANDY BOOK.—By Bedford.

MOSELY'S PRACTICAL HANDY-BOOK OF ELE-MENTARY LAW, designed for the Use of ARTICLED CLERKS, with a Course of Study, and Hints on Reading for the Intermediate and Final Examinations. Second Edition, by EDWARD HENSLOWE BEDFORD, Solicitor. Post 8vo., 8s. 6d. cloth.   1878

"This book cannot be too strongly recommended to every one who contemplates becoming a solicitor."—*Law Examination Journal.*

"Mr. E. H. Bedford, indefatigable in his labours on behalf of the articled clerk, has supervised a new edition of Mosely's Handy Book of Elementary Law. It will certainly not be the fault of either author or editor if the years spent under articles are not well spent, and if the work required to lay a sound foundation of legal knowledge is not done with that ' knowledge' of which they so emphatically declare the necessity."—*Law Magazine.*

CUTLER & GRIFFIN'S INDIAN CRIMINAL LAW.

AN ANALYSIS OF THE INDIAN PENAL CODE, including the INDIAN PENAL CODE AMENDMENT ACT, 1870. By JOHN CUTLER, B.A., of Lincoln's Inn, Barrister-at-Law, Professor of English Law and Jurisprudence, and Professor of Indian Jurisprudence at King's College, London, and EDMUND FULLER GRIFFIN, B.A., of Lincoln's Inn, Barrister-at-Law. 8vo. 6s. cloth.   1871

ROUSE'S CONVEYANCER, with SUPPLEMENT, 1871. Third Edition.

The PRACTICAL CONVEYANCER, giving, in a mode combining facility of reference with general utility, upwards of Four Hundred Precedents of Conveyances, Mortgages and Leases, Settlements, and Miscellaneous Forms, with (not in previous Editions) the Law and numerous Outline Forms and Clauses of WILLS and Abstracts of Statutes affecting Real Property, Conveyancing Memoranda, &c. By ROLLA ROUSE, Esq., of the Middle Temple, Barrister-at-Law, Author of "The Practical Man," &c. Third Edition, greatly enlarged. With a Supplement, giving Abstracts of the Statutory Provisions affecting the Practice in Conveyancing, to the end of 1870; and the requisite Alterations in Forms, with some new Forms; and including a full Abstract in numbered Clauses of the Stamp Act, 1870. 2 vols. 8vo. 30s. cloth; 38s. calf.   1871

₊ *The Supplement may be had separately, price 1s. 6d. sewed.*

"The best test of the value of a book written professedly for practical men is the practical one of the number of editions through which it passes. The fact that this well-known work has now reached its third shows that it is considered by those for whose convenience it was written to fulfil its purpose well."—*Law Magazine.*

ROBSON'S BANKRUPT LAW.—Fourth Edition.

A TREATISE on the LAW of BANKRUPTCY; containing a full Exposition of the Principles and Practice of the Law, including the Law as to Bills of Sale under the Bills of Sale Act, 1878, and the Application of the Bankruptcy Rules, as to Proofs by Creditors, under Section 10 of the Judicature Act, 1875; with an Appendix comprising the Statutes, Rules, Orders, and Forms. 4th Edit. By GEORGE YOUNG ROBSON, Esq., of the Inner Temple, Barrister-at-Law. 1 vol. 8vo. 38s. cloth.   1881

CHRISTIE'S CRABB'S CONVEYANCING.— Fifth Edition, by Shelford.

CRABB'S COMPLETE SERIES OF PRECEDENTS in CONVEYANCING and of COMMON and COMMERCIAL FORMS in Alphabetical Order, adapted to the Present State of the Law and the Practice of Conveyancing; with copious Prefaces, Observations and Notes on the several Deeds. By J.T. CHRISTIE, Esq., Barrister-at-Law. Fifth Edition, with numerous Corrections and Additions, by LEONARD SHELFORD, Esq., of the Middle Temple, Barrister-at-Law. 2 vols. roy. 8vo. 3l. cloth.   1859

CUTLER'S LAW OF NATURALIZATION.

THE LAW OF NATURALIZATION as Amended by the Act of 1870. By JOHN CUTLER, B.A., of Lincoln's Inn, Barrister-at-Law, Editor of "Powell's Law of Evidence," &c. 12mo. 3s. 6d. cloth.   1871

"Professor Cutler's book is a useful summary of the law and of the changes which have been made in it. The act is given in full with a useful index."— *Law Magazine.*

COOTE'S ADMIRALTY PRACTICE.—Second Edition.

THE PRACTICE OF THE HIGH COURT OF ADMIRALTY OF ENGLAND: also the Practice of the Judicial Committee of Her Majesty's Most Honourable Privy Council in Admiralty Appeals, with Forms and Bills of Costs. By HENRY CHARLES COOTE, F.S.A., one of the Examiners of the High Court of Admiralty, Author of "The Practice of the Court of Probate," &c. Second Edition, almost entirely re-written; and with a SUPPLEMENT *containing the County Court Practice in Admiralty,* the Act, Rules, Orders, &c. 8vo. 16s. cloth.   1869

*** *This work contains every Common Form in use by the Practitioner in Admiralty, as well as every description of Bill of Costs in that Court, a feature possessed by no other work on the Practice in Admiralty.*

"Mr. Coote, being an Examiner of the Court, may be considered as an authoritative exponent of the points of which he treats. His treatise is, substantially considered, everything that can be desired to the practitioner."— *Law Magazine.*

ORTOLAN'S ROMAN LAW, Translated by PRICHARD and NASMITH.

THE HISTORY OF ROMAN LAW, from the Text of Ortolan's Histoire de la Législation Romaine et Généralisation du Droit (edition of 1870). Translated, with the Author's permission, and Supplemented by a Chronometrical Chart of Roman History. By I. T. PRICHARD, Esq., F.S.S., and DAVID NASMITH, Esq., LL.D., Barristers-at-Law.   8vo. 28s. cloth.   1871

"We know of no work, which, in our opinion, exhibits so perfect a model of what a text-book ought to be. Of the translation before us, it is enough to say, that it is a faithful representation of the original."—*Law Magazine.*

KELLY'S CONVEYANCING DRAFTSMAN.—2nd Edit.

THE DRAFTSMAN: containing a Collection of Concise Precedents and Forms in Conveyancing; with Introductory Observations and Practical Notes. By JAMES H. KELLY. Second Edition. Post 8vo. 12s. 6d. cloth.   1881

"Mr. Kelly's object is to give a few precedents of each of those instruments which are most commonly required in a solicitor's office, and for which precedents are not always to be met with in the ordinary books on conveyancing. The idea is a good one, and the precedents contained in the book are, generally speaking, of the character contemplated by the author's design. We have been favourably impressed with a perusal of several of the precedents in this book, and practitioners who have already adopted forms of their own will probably find it advantageous to collate them with those given by Mr. Kelly. Each set of precedents is prefaced by a few terse and practical observations."—*Solicitors' Journal.*

"Such statements of law and facts as are contained in the work are accurate." —*Law Journal.*

"It contains matter not found in the more ambitious works on conveyancing, and we venture to think that the student will find it a useful supplement to his reading on the subject of conveyancing."—*Law Examination Journal.*

REDMAN ON ARBITRATIONS AND AWARDS.

A CONCISE TREATISE on the LAW OF ARBITRATIONS and AWARDS; with an Appendix of Precedents and Statutes. By JOSEPH HAWORTH REDMAN, of the Middle Temple, Esq., Barrister-at-Law, Author of "A Treatise on the Law of Railway Companies as Carriers." 8vo. 12s. cloth. 1872

"The arrangement is good, the style clear, and the work exhaustive. There is a useful appendix of precedents and statutes, and a very good index."—*Law Times.*

"This is likely to prove a useful book in practice. All the ordinary law on the subject is given shortly and in a convenient and accessible form, and the index is a good one."—*Solicitors' Journal.*

"We have no doubt but that the work will be useful. The precedents of awards are clearly and concisely drawn. The arrangement of chapters is conveniently managed. The law is clearly stated, and, so far as we can judge, all the important cases bearing directly on the subject are given, while the index appears reasonably copious. These facts, combined with the smallness of the volume, ought to make the book a success."—*Law Journal.*

REDMAN'S REFERENCES UNDER THE JUDICATURE ACTS.

The LAW and PRACTICE of REFERENCES under the JUDICATURE ACTS, with an Appendix of Orders and Forms; being a Supplement to "The Law of Arbitrations and Awards." By J. H. REDMAN, of the Middle Temple, Esquire, Barrister-at-Law. 8vo. 2s. cloth.   1881

CLIFFORD & STEPHENS' REFEREES' PRACTICE, 1873.

THE PRACTICE OF THE COURT OF REFEREES on PRIVATE BILLS IN PARLIAMENT; with Reports of Cases as to the Locus Standi of Petitioners decided during the Sessions 1867—72. By FREDERICK CLIFFORD, of the Middle Temple, and PEMBROKE S. STEPHENS, of Lincoln's Inn, Esqs., Barristers-at-Law. 2 vols. royal 8vo. 3l. 10s. cloth.

In continuation of the above,

Royal 8vo., Vol. I. Part I., price 31s. 6d.; Vol. I. Part II., 15s.; Vol. II. Part I. 12s. 6d. sewed; Vol. II. Part II. 12s. 6d. sewed; Vol. II. Part III. 12s. 6d. sewed; Vol. II. Part IV. 15s.; and Vol. III. Part I. 15s.

CASES DECIDED DURING THE SESSIONS 1873 to 1881, by the COURT OF REFEREES on PRIVATE BILLS in PARLIAMENT. By FREDERICK CLIFFORD and A. G. RICKARDS, Esqs., Barristers-at-Law.

"These Reports are a continuance of the series of 'Clifford and Stephens' Reports,' which began in 1867, and seem to be marked by the same care and accuracy which have made these Reports a standard for reference and quotation by practitioners and the Court itself."—*Times.*

"The book is really a very useful one, and will doubtless commend itself to Parliamentary practitioners."—*Law Times.*

"The Reports themselves are very well done. To parliamentary practitioners the work cannot fail to be of very great value."—*Solicitors' Journal.*

SAUNDERS' LAW OF NEGLIGENCE.

A TREATISE on the LAW applicable to NEGLIGENCE. By THOMAS W. SAUNDERS, Esq., Barrister-at-Law, Recorder of Bath. 1 vol. post 8vo. 9s. cloth.   1871

"The book is admirable; while small in bulk, it contains everything that is necessary, and its arrangement is such that one can readily refer to it. Amongst those those who have done a good service Mr. Saunders will find a place."—*Law Magazine.*

"We find very considerable diligence displayed. The references to the cases are given much more fully, and on a more rational system than is common with textbook writers. He has a good index."—*Solicitors' Journal.*

DIXON'S LAW OF PARTNERSHIP.

A TREATISE ON THE LAW OF PARTNERSHIP.

By J. DIXON, of Lincoln's Inn, Esq., Barrister-at-Law, Editor of "Lush's Common Law Practice." 1 vol. 8vo. 22s. cloth.   1866

"He has evidently bestowed upon this book the same conscientious labour and painstaking industry for which we had to compliment him some months since, when reviewing his edition of 'Lush's Practice of the Superior Courts of Law,' and, as a result, he has produced a clearly written and well arranged manual upon one of the most important branches of our mercantile law."—*Law Journal.*

"Mr. Lindley's view of the subject is that of a philosophical lawyer. Mr. Dixon's is purely and exclusively practical from beginning to end. We imagine that very few questions are likely to come before the practitioner which Mr. Dixon's book will not be found to solve. We have only to add, that the value of the book is very materially increased by an excellent marginal summary and a very copious index."—*Law Magazine and Review.*

MICHAEL & WILL'S GAS AND WATER SUPPLY.
Second Edition.

THE LAW RELATING TO GAS AND WATER: comprising the Rights and Duties, as well of Local Authorities as of Private Companies in regard thereto, and including all Legislation to the close of the last Session of Parliament. Second Edition. By W. H. MICHAEL and J. SHIRESS WILL, of the Middle Temple, Esqs., Barristers-at-Law. 8vo. 25s. cloth.   1877

"The Law of Gas and Water, by Messrs. Michael and Will, has reached a second edition, and the authors tell us that they have not only brought the law down to the present time but they have re-written a considerable portion of the text, particularly with reference to gas. When the first edition appeared we expressed an opinion that the work had been executed with care, skill and ability. This edition is a decided improvement on the first, and therefore we need add nothing now. It is a work which has probably found its way into the hands of all interested in the practical application of the Acts of Parliament relating to gas and water supply."—*Law Times.*

DAVIS ON REGISTRATION.—Second Edition. With Supplement.

THE LAW of REGISTRATION, PARLIAMENTARY, and MUNICIPAL, with all the STATUTES and CASES. With a Supplement comprising the Cases decided on Appeal on the Parliamentary and Municipal Registration Act, 1878. By J. E. DAVIS, Esq., Barrister-at-Law. Post 8vo., 15s. cloth.   1880

*** *The Supplement may be had separately, 2s. 6d. sewed.*

WOOLRYCH ON SEWERS.—Third Edition.

A TREATISE ON THE LAW OF SEWERS, including the Drainage Acts. By HUMPHRY W. WOOLRYCH, Serjeant-at-Law. Third Edition, with considerable Additions and Alterations. 8vo. 12s. cloth.   1864

PLUMPTRE ON THE LAW OF CONTRACTS.

A SUMMARY OF THE PRINCIPLES OF THE LAW OF SIMPLE CONTRACTS. By CLAUDE C. M. PLUMPTRE, of the Middle Temple, Esq., Barrister-at-Law. (Middle Temple Common Law Scholar, Hilary Term, 1877.) Post 8vo. 8s. cloth.
1879

• *A Companion Work to Underhill on Torts.*

" In our last volume we had occasion to mention with approbation two works by Mr. Arthur Underhill, A Summary of the Law of Torts, and a Concise Manual of the Law relating to Trusts and Trustees; the first of these had reached a second edition, and in its preparation the author of the present work was associated with Mr. Underhill. In the preparation of this book Mr. Plumptre has adopted the lines laid down by Mr. Underhill; by means of short rules and sub-rules he presents a summary of the leading principles relating to the law of simple contracts, with the decisions of the Courts by which they are illustrated. Part I. deals with the parties to a simple contract, and treats of those persons exempted from the performance of their contracts by reason of incapacity, such as infants, married women, lunatics, drunkards, convicts and bankrupts. Chapter 4 is devoted to contracts by corporations and by agents, and the following chapter to partners and partnerships generally.

" In Part II. we have the constituent parts of a simple contract, the consent of the parties, the consideration, the promise, contracts illegal at common law and by statute, and fraudulent contracts.

" Part III. gives rules for making a simple contract, and treats of contracts within the 4th and 17th sections of the Statute of Frauds; Statutes of Limitation; the discharge of the obligation imposed by the contract by performance; by mutual agreement; by accord and satisfaction; and by operation of law; oral evidence and written contracts; damages; and contracts made abroad.

" The book contains upwards of one hundred rules, all ably illustrated by cases, and a very full and well-compiled index facilitates reference. It is more particularly addressed to students, but practitioners of both branches of the legal profession will find it a useful and trustworthy guide."
—*Justice of the Peace.*

BARRY'S PRACTICE OF CONVEYANCING.

A TREATISE on the PRACTICE of CONVEYANCING. By W. WHITTAKER BARRY, Esq., of Lincoln's Inn, Barrister-at-Law, late holder of the Studentship of the Inns of Court, and Author of "The Statutory Jurisdiction of the Court of Chancery." 8vo. 18s. cloth.
1865

" This treatise supplies a want which has long been felt. Mr. Barry's work is essentially what it professes to be, a treatise on the practice of conveyancing, in which the theoretical rules of real property law are referred to only for the purpose of elucidating the practice.

The treatise is the production of a person of great merit and still greater promise."—*Solicitors' Journal.*

" The work is clearly and agreeably written, and ably elucidates the subject in hand."—*Justice of the Peace.*

BARRY'S FORMS IN CONVEYANCING.

FORMS and PRECEDENTS in CONVEYANCING; with Introduction and Practical Notes. By W. WHITTAKER BARRY, of Lincoln's Inn, Barrister-at-Law, Author of a "Treatise on the Practice of Conveyancing." 8vo. 21s. cl. 1872

HERTSLET'S TREATIES.

HERTSLET'S TREATIES of Commerce, Navigation, Slave Trade, Post Office Communications, Copyright, &c., at present subsisting between Great Britain and Foreign Powers. Compiled from Authentic Documents by EDWARD HERTSLET, Esq., C.B., Librarian and Keeper of the Papers of the Foreign Office. 14 Vols. 8vo. 18*l.* 19*s.*

** *Vol. I. price 12s., Vol. II. price 12s., Vol. III. price 18s., Vol. IV. price 18s., Vol. V. price 20s., Vol. VI. price 25s., Vol. VII. price 30s., Vol. VIII. price 30s., Vol. IX. price 30s., Vol. X. price 30s., Vol. XI. price 30s., Vol. XII. price 40s., Vol. XIII. price 42s., Vol. XIV. price 42s. cloth, may be had separately to complete sets. Vol. XII. includes an Index of Subjects to the Twelve published Volumes, which Index is also sold separately, price 10s. cloth.*

HERTSLET'S TREATIES ON TRADE AND TARIFFS.

TREATIES AND TARIFFS regulating the Trade between Great Britain and Foreign Nations, and extracts of the Treaties between Foreign Powers, containing "Most Favoured Nation" Clauses applicable to Great Britain in force on the 1st January, 1875. By EDWARD HERTSLET, Esq., C.B., Librarian and Keeper of the Papers, Foreign Office. Part I. (Austria). Royal 8vo. 7*s.* 6*d.* cloth. Part II. (Turkey). 15*s.* cloth. Part III. (Italy). 15*s.* cloth. Part IV. (China). 10*s.* cloth. Part V. (Spain). 1*l.* 1*s.* cloth. Part VI. (Japan). 15*s.* cloth.

INGRAM'S LAW OF COMPENSATION.—Second Edit.

COMPENSATION to LAND and HOUSE OWNERS: being a Treatise on the Law of the Compensation for Interests in Lands, &c. payable by Railway and other Public Companies; with an Appendix of Forms and Statutes. By THOMAS DUNBAR INGRAM, of Lincoln's Inn, Esq., Barrister-at-Law, now Professor of Jurisprudence and Indian Law in the Presidency College, Calcutta. Second Edition. By J. J. ELMES, of the Inner Temple, Esq., Barrister-at-Law. Post 8vo. 12*s.* cloth. · 1869

"Whether for companies taking land or holding it, Mr. Ingram's volume will be a welcome guide. With this in his hand the legal adviser of a company, or of an owner and occupier whose property is taken, and who demands compensation for it, cannot fail to perform his duty rightly."—*Law Times.*

"This work appears to be carefully prepared as regards its matter. This edition is a third larger than the first; it contains twice as many cases, and an enlarged index. It was much called for and doubtless will be found very useful by the practitioner."—*Law Magazine.*

HIGGINS'S DIGEST OF PATENT CASES.

A DIGEST of the REPORTED CASES relating to the Law and Practice of LETTERS PATENT for INVENTIONS, decided from the passing of the Statute of Monopolies to the present time. By CLEMENT HIGGINS, M.A., F.C.S., of the Inner Temple, Barrister-at-Law.   8vo. 10s. cloth, net.   1875

"Mr. Higgins's work will be useful as a work of reference. Upwards of 700 cases are digested; and, besides a table of contents, there is a full index to the subject matter; and that index, which greatly enhances the value of the book, must have cost the author much time, labour and thought."—*Law Journal.*

"'This is essentially,' says Mr. Higgins in his preface, ' a book of reference.' It remains to be added whether the compilation is reliable and exhaustive. It is only fair to say that we think it is; and we will add, that the arrangement of subject matter (chronological under each heading, the date, and double or even treble references being appended

to every decision), and the neat and carefully executed index (which is decidedly above the average) are such as no reader of ' essentially a book of reference' could quarrel with."—*Solicitors' Journal.*

"The very elaborate Digest just completed by Mr. Higgins is worthy of being recognized by the profession as a thoroughly useful book of reference upon the subject. Mr. Higgins's object has been to supply a reliable and exhaustive summary of the reported patent cases decided in English courts of law and equity, and this object he appears to have attained."—*Mining Journal.*

DOWELL'S INCOME TAX LAWS.

THE INCOME TAX LAWS at present in force in the United Kingdom, with practical Notes, Appendices and a copious Index. By STEPHEN DOWELL, M.A., of Lincoln's Inn, Assistant Solicitor of Inland Revenue.   8vo. 12s. 6d. cloth.   1874

"To commissioners and all concerned in the working of the Income Tax Mr. Dowell's book will be of great value."—*Law Journal.*

"For practical purposes the compilation must prove very useful."—*Law Times.*

"We can honestly commend Mr. Dowell's work to our readers as being

well done in every respect."—*Law Magazine.*

"Mr. Dowell's official position eminently fits him for the work he has undertaken, and his history of the Stamp Laws shows how carefully and conscientiously he performs what he undertakes."—*Justice of the Peace.*

DAVIS'S CRIMINAL LAW CONSOLIDATION ACTS.

THE CRIMINAL LAW CONSOLIDATION ACTS, 1861; with an Introduction and practical Notes, illustrated by a copious reference to Cases decided by the Court of Criminal Appeal. Together with Alphabetical Tables of Offences, as well those punishable upon Summary Conviction as upon Indictment, and including the Offences under the New Bankruptcy Act, so arranged as to present at one view the particular Offence, the old or new Statute upon which it is founded, and the Limits of Punishment; and a full Index. By JAMES EDWARD DAVIS, Esq., Barrister-at-Law.   12mo. 10s. cloth.   1861

SHELFORD'S SUCCESSION, PROBATE AND LEGACY DUTIES.—Second Edition.

THE LAW relating to the PROBATE, LEGACY and SUCCESSION DUTIES in ENGLAND, IRELAND and SCOTLAND, including all the Statutes and the Decisions on those Subjects: with Forms and Official Regulations. By LEONARD SHELFORD, Esq., of the Middle Temple, Barrister-at-Law. The Second Edition, with many Alterations and Additions. 12mo. 16s. cloth.   1861

BAYLIS'S LAW OF DOMESTIC SERVANTS. By Monckton.—Fourth Edition.

THE RIGHTS, DUTIES AND RELATIONS OF DOMESTIC SERVANTS AND THEIR MASTERS AND MISTRESSES. With a short Account of Servants' Institutions, &c., and their Advantages. By T. HENRY BAYLIS, M.A., Barrister-at-Law, of the Inner Temple. Fourth Edition, with considerable Additions, by EDWARD P. MONCKTON, Esq., B.A., Barrister-at-Law, of the Inner Temple. Fscap. 8vo. 2s.   1873

SEABORNE'S LAW OF VENDORS & PURCHASERS. Second Edition.

A CONCISE MANUAL of the LAW of VENDORS and PURCHASERS of REAL PROPERTY; with a Supplement, including the Vendor and Purchaser Act, 1874, with Notes. 2nd Edit. By HENRY SEABORNE. Post 8vo. 10s. 6d. cloth. 1879

₊ *This work is designed to furnish Practitioners with an easy means of reference to the Statutory Enactments and Judicial Decisions regulating the Transfer of Real Property, and also to bring these authorities in a compendious shape under the attention of Students.*

" The book before us contains a good deal, especially of practical information as to the course of conveyancing matters in solicitors' offices, which may be useful to students."—*Solicitors' Journal.*

" We will do Mr. Seaborne the justice to say that we believe his work will be of some use to articled and other clerks in solicitors' offices, who have not the opportunity or inclination to refer to the standard works from which his is compiled."—*Law Journal.*

" The value of Mr. Seaborne's book consists in its being the most concise summary ever yet published of one of the most important branches of the law. The student will find this book a useful introduction to a dry and difficult subject."—*Law Examination Journal.*

" Intended to furnish a ready means of access to the enactments and decisions governing that branch of the law."—*The Times.*

" The book will be found of use to the legal practitioner, inasmuch as it will, so far as regards established points of law, be a handier work of reference than the longer treatises we have named."—*Athenæum.*

TOMKINS' INSTITUTES OF ROMAN LAW.

THE INSTITUTES OF ROMAN LAW. Part I., containing the Sources of the Roman Law and its External History till the Decline of the Eastern and Western Empires. By FREDERICK TOMKINS, M.A., D.C.L., Barrister-at-Law, of Lincoln's Inn. Roy. 8vo. 12s. (To be completed in 3 Parts.) 1867

DREWRY'S EQUITY PLEADER.

A CONCISE TREATISE on the Principles of EQUITY PLEADING, with Precedents. By C. STEWART DREWRY, Esq., of the Inner Temple, Barrister-at-Law. 12mo. 6s. boards. 1858

GAIUS' ROMAN LAW.—By Tomkins and Lemon.

(*Dedicated by permission to Lord Chancellor Hatherley.*)

THE COMMENTARIES of GAIUS on the ROMAN LAW: with an English Translation and Annotations. By FREDERICK J. TOMKINS, Esq., M.A., D.C.L., and WILLIAM GEORGE LEMON, Esq., LL.B., Barristers-at-Law, of Lincoln's Inn. 8vo. 27s. extra cloth. 1869

BRANDON'S LAW OF FOREIGN ATTACHMENT.

A TREATISE upon the CUSTOMARY LAW of FOREIGN ATTACHMENT, and the PRACTICE of the MAYOR'S COURT of the CITY OF LONDON therein. With Forms of Procedure. By WOODTHORPE BRANDON, Esq., of the Middle Temple, Barrister-at-Law. 8vo. 14s. cloth. 1861

MOSELEY ON CONTRABAND OF WAR.

WHAT IS CONTRABAND OF WAR AND WHAT IS NOT. A Treatise comprising all the American and English Authorities on the Subject. By JOSEPH MOSELEY, Esq., B.C.L., Barrister-at-Law. Post 8vo. 5s. cloth. 1861

SMITH'S BAR EDUCATION.

A HISTORY of EDUCATION for the ENGLISH BAR, with SUGGESTIONS as to SUBJECTS and METHODS of STUDY. By PHILIP ANSTIE SMITH, Esq., M.A., LL.B., Barrister-at-Law. 8vo. 9s. cloth. 1860

WILLS ON EVIDENCE. Fourth Edition.

AN ESSAY on the PRINCIPLES of CIRCUMSTAN- TIAL EVIDENCE. Illustrated by numerous Cases. By the late WILLIAM WILLS, Esq. Fourth Edition. Edited by his Son, ALFRED WILLS, Esq., Barrister-at-Law. 8vo. 10s. cloth. 1862

LUSHINGTON'S NAVAL PRIZE LAW.

A MANUAL of NAVAL PRIZE LAW. By GODFREY LUSHINGTON, of the Inner Temple, Esq., Barrister-at-Law. Royal 8vo. 10s. 6d. cloth. 1866

ROUSE'S COPYHOLD ENFRANCHISEMENT MANUAL.—Third Edition.

The COPYHOLD ENFRANCHISEMENT MANUAL; enlarged, and treating the subject in the Legal, Practical and Mathematical Points of View: giving numerous Forms, Rules, Tables and Instructions for Calculating the Values of the Lord's Rights; Suggestions to Lords' Stewards, and Copyholders, protective of their several Interests, and to Valuers in performance of their Duties; and including the Act of 1858, and Proceedings in Enfranchisement under it. By ROLLA ROUSE, Esq., of the Middle Temple, Barrister-at-Law. Third Edition, much enlarged. 12mo. 10s. 6d. cloth.　　　　　　　　　　　　　　　1866

" When we consider what favour Mr. Rouse's Practical Man and Practical Conveyancer have found with the profession, we feel sure the legal world will greet with pleasure a new and improved edition of his Copyhold Manual. The third edition of that work is before us. It is a work of great practical value, suitable to lawyers and laymen. We can freely and heartily recommend this volume to the practitioner, the steward and the copyholder."—*Law Magazine.*

HEALES'S HISTORY AND LAW OF PEWS.

THE HISTORY and the LAW of CHURCH SEATS or PEWS. By ALFRED HEALES, F.S.A., Proctor in Doctors' Commons. 2 vols. 8vo. 16s. cloth.　　　　　　　　　1872

"Altogether we can commend Mr. Heales's book as a well conceived and well executed work, which is evidence of the author's industry, talent and learning."—*Law Journal.*

BRABROOK'S WORK ON CO-OPERATION.

THE LAW and PRACTICE of CO-OPERATIVE or INDUSTRIAL and PROVIDENT SOCIETIES; including the Winding-up Clauses, to which are added the Law of France on the same subject, and Remarks on Trades Unions. By EDWARD W. BRABROOK, F.S.A., of Lincoln's Inn, Esq., Barrister-at-Law, Assistant-Registrar of Friendly Societies in England. 6s. cl. 1869

COOMBS' SOLICITORS' BOOKKEEPING.

A MANUAL OF SOLICITORS' BOOKKEEPING: comprising practical exemplifications of a concise and simple plan of Double Entry, with Forms of Account and other Books relating to Bills of Costs, Cash, &c., showing their operation, giving directions for keeping, posting and balancing them, and instructions for drawing costs. Adapted for a large or small, sole or partnership business. By W. B. COOMBS, Law Accountant and Costs Draftsman. 1 vol. 8vo. 10s. 6d. cloth.　　　　1868

*** *The various Account Books described in the above work, the forms of which are copyright, may be had from the Publishers, at the prices stated in the work at page 274.*

WIGRAM ON WILLS.—Fourth Edition.

AN EXAMINATION OF THE RULES OF LAW respecting the Admission of EXTRINSIC EVIDENCE in Aid of the INTERPRETATION of WILLS. By the Right Hon. Sir JAMES WIGRAM, Knt. The Fourth Edition, prepared for the press, with the sanction of the learned Author, by W. KNOX WIGRAM, M.A., of Lincoln's Inn, Esq., Barrister-at-Law. 8vo. 11s. cl. 1858

LAWRENCE'S PARTITION ACTS, 1868 and 1876.

THE COMPULSORY SALE OF REAL ESTATE under the POWERS of the PARTITION ACT, 1868, as Amended by the Partition Act, 1876. By PHILIP HENRY LAWRENCE, of Lincoln's Inn, Esq., Barrister-at-Law. 8vo. 8s. cloth. 1877

"Mr. Lawrence is evidently acquainted with his subject. He explains the state of the law previous to the Statute of 1868, and the means by which under it persons may now maintain a suit. On the sale of land the whole subject is ably treated, and the book contains, amongst other things, a valuable selection of leading cases on the subject."—*Justice of the Peace.*

BUND'S LAW OF SALMON FISHERIES.

THE LAW relating to the SALMON FISHERIES of ENGLAND and WALES, as amended by "The Salmon Fishery Act, 1873;" with the Statutes and Cases. By J. W. WILLIS BUND, M.A., LL.B., of Lincoln's Inn, Barrister-at-Law, Vice-Chairman Severn Fishery Board. Post 8vo. 15s. cl. 1876

"Mr. Bund has done the work excellently well, and nothing further in this way can be desired."—*The Field.* "We have always found his opinion sound, and his explanations clear and lucid."—*Land and Water.*

TROWER'S CHURCH BUILDING LAWS, Continued to 1874.

THE LAW of the BUILDING of CHURCHES, PARSONAGES, and SCHOOLS, and of the Division of Parishes and Places. By CHARLES FRANCIS TROWER, M.A., of the Inner Temple, Esq., Barrister-at-Law, late Fellow of Exeter College, Oxford, and late Secretary of Presentations to Lord Chancellor Westbury. Post 8vo. 9s. cloth. 1874

*** *The Supplement may be had separately, price 1s. sewed.*

BULLEY & BUND'S NEW BANKRUPTCY MANUAL.

A MANUAL OF THE LAW AND PRACTICE OF BANKRUPTCY as Amended and Consolidated by the Statutes of 1869, with an APPENDIX containing the Statutes, Orders and Forms. By JOHN F. BULLEY, B.A., and J. W. WILLIS BUND, M.A., LL.B., Barristers-at-Law. 12mo. 16s. cloth. With a Supplement including the Orders to April, 1870.

*** *The Supplement may be had separately, 1s. sewed.*

OKE'S MAGISTERIAL SYNOPSIS.—Thirteenth Edit.

THE MAGISTERIAL SYNOPSIS : a Practical Guide for Magistrates, their Clerks, Solicitors, and Constables; comprising Summary Convictions and Indictable Offences, with their Penalties, Punishments, Procedure, &c.; *alphabetically and tabularly arranged :* with a Copious Index. *Thirteenth Edition, much enlarged.* By THOMAS W. SAUNDERS, Esq., Metropolitan Police Magistrate. In 2 vols. 8vo. 63s. cloth; 73s. calf.   1881

" Twelve editions in twenty-eight years say more for the practical utility of this work than any number of favourable reviews. Yet we feel bound to accord to the learned Recorder of Bath the praise of having fully maintained in the present edition the well-earned reputation of this useful book."— *Law Magazine.*

" The industrious, capable and painstaking Recorder of Bath (Mr. T. W. Saunders) has edited the twelfth edition of Oke's Magisterial Synopsis. The law administered by magistrates, like almost every other branch of our jurisprudence, goes on growing almost every day of the legal year, and a new edition of such a work as this every few years means no small amount of labour on the part of the editor. We are glad to see that Mr. Saunders has bestowed great care in the revision of the index, which is now a feature in the work."— *Law Times.*

———◆———

OKE'S HANDY BOOK OF THE GAME LAWS.—3rd Ed.

A HANDY BOOK OF THE GAME LAWS; containing the whole Law as to Game, Licences and Certificates, Gun Licences, Poaching Prevention, Trespass, Rabbits, Deer, Dogs, Birds and Poisoned Grain, Sea Birds, Wild Birds, and Wild Fowl, and the Rating of Game throughout the United Kingdom. Systematically arranged, with the Acts, Decisions, Notes and Forms, &c. *Third Edition.* With Supplement to 1881, containing the Wild Birds Protection Act, 1880, and the Ground Game Act, 1880. By J. W. WILLIS BUND, M.A., LL.B., of Lincoln's Inn, Esq., Barrister-at-Law; Vice-Chairman of the Severn Fishery Board. Post 8vo. 16s. cloth.   1881

⁎ *The Supplement may be had separately, 2s. 6d. sewed.*

" A book on the Game Laws, brought up to the present time, and including the recent acts with regard to wild fowl, &c., was much needed, and Mr. Willis Bund has most opportunely supplied the want by bringing out a revised and enlarged edition of the very useful handy book of which the late Mr. Oke was the author."— *The Field.*

" The editorship of the present publication has, we are happy to say, fallen into such able hands as those of Mr. Willis Bund. In conclusion, we would observe that the present edition of the above work will be found by legal men or others who require any reliable information on any subject connected with the game laws, of the greatest practical utility, and that landed proprietors, farmers, and sportsmen will find 'Oke's Game Laws' an invaluable addition to their libraries, and an easy means of enlightening themselves on a subject which closely affects them."— *Land and Water.*

OKE'S MAGISTERIAL FORMULIST.—Sixth Edition.

THE MAGISTERIAL FORMULIST : being a Complete Collection of Forms and Precedents for practical use in all Cases out of Quarter Sessions, and in Parochial Matters, by Magistrates, their Clerks, Attornies and Constables. By GEORGE C. OKE. *Sixth Edition*, enlarged and improved. By THOMAS W. SAUNDERS, Esq., Metropolitan Police Magistrate. In 1 vol. 8vo. 38s. cloth; 43s. calf. 1881

"Mr. Saunders has not been called upon to perform the functions of an annotator merely. He has had to create, just as Mr. Oke created when he wrote his book. This, of course, has necessitated the enlargement and remodelling of the index. No work probably is in more use in the offices of magistrates than 'Oke's Formulist.' That it should be reliable and comprehend recent enactments is of the very first importance. In selecting Mr. Saunders to follow in the steps of Mr. Oke the publishers exercised wise discretion, and we congratulate both author and publishers upon the complete and very excellent manner in which this edition has been prepared and is now presented to the profession."—*Law Times*.

OKE'S LAWS AS TO LICENSING INNS, &c.—2nd Edit.

THE LAWS AS TO LICENSING INNS, &c.; containing the Licensing Acts, 1872 and 1874, and the other Acts in force as to Ale-houses, Beer-houses, Wine and Refreshment-houses, Shops, &c., where Intoxicating Liquors are sold, and Billiard and Occasional Licences. Systematically arranged, with Explanatory Notes, the authorized Forms of Licences, Tables of Offences, Index, &c. By GEORGE C. OKE. *2nd edit.* by W. C. GLEN, Esq., Barrister-at-Law. Post 8vo. 10s. cloth. 1874

OKE'S FISHERY LAWS.—Second Edition by Bund.

THE FISHERY LAWS : A Handy Book of the Fishery Laws : containing the Law as to Fisheries, Private and Public, in the Inland Waters of England and Wales, and the Freshwater Fisheries Preservation Act, 1878. Systematically arranged : with the Acts, Decisions, Notes, and Forms, by GEORGE C. OKE. *Second Edition*, by J. W. WILLIS BUND, M.A., LL.B., of Lincoln's Inn, Barrister-at-Law, Chairman of the Severn Fishery Board. Post 8vo. 5s. cloth. 1878

OKE'S LAW OF TURNPIKE ROADS.—Second Edit.

THE LAW OF TURNPIKE ROADS; comprising the whole of the General Acts now in force, including those of 1861; the Acts as to Union of Trusts, for facilitating Arrangements with their Creditors; as to the interference by Railways with Roads, their Non-repair, and enforcing Contributions from Parishes, &c., practically arranged. With Cases, copious Notes, all the necessary Forms, and an elaborate Index, &c. By GEORGE C. OKE. *Second Edition*. 12mo. 18s. cloth. 1861

CLERKE AND BRETT'S CONVEYANCING AND LAW OF PROPERTY ACT, 1881, &c.—Second Edition.

THE CONVEYANCING AND LAW OF PROPERTY ACT, 1881, together with the Vendor and Purchaser Act, 1874, and the Solicitors' Remuneration Act, 1881. With Notes and an Introduction. By AUBREY ST. JOHN CLERKE, B.A., late Scholar and Student of Trinity College, Dublin, and THOMAS BRETT, LL.B. London University, B.A., late Scholar and Student of Trinity College, Dublin, Exhibitioner in Real Property and Equity, and Holder of the First Certificate of Honour, Michaelmas, 1869 ; both of the Middle Temple, Esquires, Barristers-at-Law. *Second Edition.* Post 8vo. 7s. 6d. cloth.   1882

" The chief objects of this work, the authors state in their preface, are—(1) To point out the various changes which have been introduced by the new Act into the law and practice of conveyancing ; (2) to criticize the provisions of the Act, pointing out difficulties likely to arise, and suggesting means to evade those difficulties ; 3, to render the work as convenient as possible for the purpose of reference, by furnishing the reader with a comprehensive index and a complete table of cases. These objects appear to have been attained. The introductory chapter deals with the effect of the Act in a masterly manner, and shows that the authors are intimately acquainted with the subject in hand. Each section of this important Act is then dealt with fully, and its effect on the existing law explained, great pains being taken to call attention to the clauses which are, and those which are not, of retrospec-tive operation ; and the work concludes with a consideration of the Vendor and Purchaser Act, 1874 (which is, of course, closely connected with the new Act), and the Solicitors' Remuneration Act, 1881. The work is written, no doubt, mainly for the practitioner, but the student who is reading for examination next year will require an accurate knowledge of this Act, and it is very doubtful whether he will be able to meet with a better treatise on it than that contained in the pages being considered."—*Gibson's Final.*

"It is not possible to exaggerate the utility of the work brought out by Messrs. Clerke and Brett. No student or practitioner who desires to be acquainted with the latest phase of real property legislation ought to be without it. The authors are to be congratulated upon the speed with which they have brought out the volume."—*Law Examination Journal.*

THE LAW EXAMINATION JOURNAL.

THE LAW EXAMINATION JOURNAL. Edited by HERBERT NEWMAN MOZLEY, M.A., Fellow of King's College, Cambridge ; and of Lincoln's Inn, Esq., Barrister-at-Law. (Published every Legal Sittings.)

No. 52. Trinity, 1882. CONTENTS:—1. Honors Examination, April, 1882; Questions and Answers. 2. Final Examination, June, 1882; Questions and Answers. 3. Intermediate Examination, June, 1882; Questions and Answers. 4. Digest of Cases. 5. Correspondence and Notices.

Price 1s. each Number, by post 1s. 1d. Nos. 34 & 35 (double number), price 2s., by post 2s. 2d.

** All back numbers, commencing with No. L, may be had.

** Copies of Vol. I., containing Nos. 1 to 14, with full Indexes and Tables of Case Cited, may now be had, price 16s. bound in cloth.
Vol. II., containing Nos. 15 to 28, with Index, price in cloth, 16s.
Vol. III., containing Nos. 29 to 45, price 18s. 6d. cloth.
The Indexes to Vols. II. and III. may be had separately to complete copies for bindings, price 6d. each sewed.

HUNT'S BOUNDARIES, FENCES & FORESHORES.—
Second Edition.

A TREATISE on the LAW relating to BOUNDARIES and FENCES, and to the Rights of Property on the Sea Shore and in the Beds of Public Rivers and other Waters. Second Edition. By ARTHUR JOSEPH HUNT, of the Inner Temple, Esq., Barrister-at-Law. 12mo. 12s. cloth. 1870

"There are few more fertile sources of litigation than those dealt with in Mr. Hunt's valuable book. It is sufficient here to say that the volume ought to have a larger circulation than ordinarily belongs to law books, that it ought to be found in every country gentleman's library, that the cases are brought down to the latest date, and that it is carefully prepared, clearly written and well edited."—*Law Magazine.*

"It speaks well for this book, that it has so soon passed into a second edition. That its utility has been appreciated is shown by its success. Mr. Hunt has availed himself of the opportunity of a second edition to note up all the cases to this time, and to extend considerably some of the chapters, especially that which treats of rights of property on the seashore and the subjects of sea walls and commissions of sewers."—*Law Times.*

"Mr. Hunt chose a good subject for a separate treatise on Boundaries and Fences and Rights to the Seashore, and we are not surprised to find that a second edition of his book has been called for. The present edition contains much new matter. The chapter especially which treats on rights of property on the seashore, which has been greatly extended. Additions have been also made to the chapters relating to the fencing of the property of mine owners and railway companies. All the cases which have been decided since the work first appeared have been introduced in their proper places. Thus it will be seen this new edition has a considerably enhanced value."—*Solicitors' Journal.*

RUEGG'S EMPLOYERS' LIABILITY ACT.

A TREATISE upon the EMPLOYERS' LIABILITY ACT, 1880, with Rules, Forms and Decided Cases. By A. H. RUEGG, of the Middle Temple, Barrister-at-Law. 1 vol. post 8vo. 5s. cloth. 1881

COLLIER'S LAW OF CONTRIBUTORIES.

A TREATISE on the LAW OF CONTRIBUTORIES in the Winding-up of Joint-Stock Companies. By ROBERT COLLIER, of the Inner Temple, Esq., Barrister-at-Law. Post 8vo. 9s. cloth. 1875

"Mr. Collier's general arrangement appears to have been carefully devised, and is probably as neat as the nature of the subject admits of. It is impossible after a perusal of the book to doubt that the author has honestly studied the subject, and has not contented himself with the practice of piecing together head notes from reports."—*Solicitors' Journal.*

"Mr. Collier has not shrunk from pointing out his views as to the reconcilability of apparently conflicting decisions or as to many points on which the law is still unsettled; without making any quotations for the purpose of illustrating the above remarks, we think we are justified in commending this treatise to the favourable consideration of the profession."—*Law Journal.*

THE BAR EXAMINATION JOURNAL.

THE BAR EXAMINATION JOURNAL, containing the Examination Papers on all the subjects, with Answers, set at the General Examination for Call to the Bar. Edited by A. D. TYSSEN, B.C.L., M.A., Sir R. K. WILSON, Bart., M.A., and W. D. EDWARDS, LL.B., Barristers-at-Law. 3s. each, by post 3s. 1d. Nos. 3, 6, 9, 10, 11, 12, 13, 14, 15 and 16, Hil. 1872 to Hil. 1878, both inclusive, may now be had.

₊ *No. 13 is a double number, price 6s., by post 6s. 2d. Nos. 1, 2, 4, 5, 7 and 8 are out of print.*

THE PRELIMINARY EXAMINATION JOURNAL,
And Students' Literary Magazine.

Edited by JAMES ERLE BENHAM, formerly of King's College, London: Author of "The Student's Examination Guide," &c.

Now Complete in Eighteen Numbers, containing all the Questions, with Answers, from 1871 to 1875, and to be had in 1 Vol. 8vo., price 18s. cloth.

Nos. I. to XVIII. may still be had, price 1s. each, by post 1s. 1d.

CUTLER'S CIVIL SERVICE OF INDIA.

ON REPORTING CASES for their PERIODICAL EXAMINATIONS by SELECTED CANDIDATES for the CIVIL SERVICE of INDIA. Being a Lecture delivered on Wednesday, June 12, 1867, at King's College, London. By JOHN CUTLER, B.A., of Lincoln's Inn, Barrister-at-Law, Professor of English Law and Jurisprudence, and Professor of Indian Jurisprudence at King's College, London. 8vo. 1s.

BROWNING'S DIVORCE AND MATRIMONIAL PRACTICE.

THE PRACTICE and PROCEDURE of the COURT for DIVORCE AND MATRIMONIAL CAUSES, including the Acts, Rules, Orders, Copious Notes of Cases and Forms of Practical Proceedings, with Tables of Costs. By W. ERNST BROWNING, Esq., of the Inner Temple, Barrister-at-Law. Post 8vo. 8s. cloth.   1862

PHILLIPS'S LAW OF LUNACY.

THE LAW CONCERNING LUNATICS, IDIOTS, and PERSONS OF UNSOUND MIND. By CHARLES P. PHILLIPS, M.A., of Lincoln's Inn, Esq., Barrister-at-Law, and Commissioner in Lunacy. Post 8vo. 18s. cloth.   1858

UNDERHILL'S "FREEDOM OF LAND."

"FREEDOM OF LAND," AND WHAT IT IMPLIES. By ARTHUR UNDERHILL, LL.D., of Lincoln's Inn, Barrister-at-Law. 8vo. 1s. sewed; by post 1s. 1d.

HOLLAND ON THE FORM OF THE LAW.

ESSAYS upon the FORM of the LAW. By THOMAS ERSKINE HOLLAND, M.A., Fellow of Exeter College, and Chichele Professor of International Law in the University of Oxford, and of Lincoln's Inn, Esq., Barrister-at-Law. 8vo. 7s. 6d. cloth.   1870

WRIGHT ON THE LAW OF CONSPIRACY.

THE LAW OF CRIMINAL CONSPIRACIES AND AGREEMENTS. By R. S. WRIGHT, of the Inner Temple, Barrister-at-Law, Fellow of Oriel Coll., Oxford. 8vo. 4s. cloth.   1873

CHITTY, Jun., PRECEDENTS IN PLEADING.—Third Edition.

CHITTY, JUN., PRECEDENTS in PLEADING; with copious Notes on Practice, Pleading and Evidence, by the late JOSEPH CHITTY, Jun., Esq. Third Edition. By the late TOMPSON CHITTY, Esq., and by LEOFRIC TEMPLE, R. G. WILLIAMS, and CHARLES JEFFERY, Esqrs., Barristers-at-Law. Complete in 1 vol. royal 8vo. 38s. cloth.   1868

LOVESY'S LAW OF MASTERS AND WORKMEN.

The LAW of ARBITRATION between MASTERS and WORKMEN, as founded upon the Councils of Conciliation Act of 1867 (30 & 31 Vict. c. 105), the Master and Workmen Act (5 Geo. 4, c. 96), and other Acts, with an Introduction and Notes. By C. W. LOVESY, Esq., of the Middle Temple, Barrister-at-Law. 12mo. 4s. cloth.   1867

The Doctrine of Continuous Voyages as applied to CONTRABAND of WAR and BLOCKADE, contrasted with the DECLARATION of PARIS of 1856. By SIR TRAVERS TWISS, Q.C., D.C.L., &c., &c., President of the Bremen Conference, 1876. Read before the Association for the Reform and Codification of the Law of Nations at the Antwerp Conference, 1877. 8vo. 2s. 6d. sewed.

Mr. Justice Lush's Common Law Practice. By Dixon.
Third Edition. LUSH'S PRACTICE of the SUPERIOR
COURTS of COMMON LAW at WESTMINSTER, in Actions
and Proceedings over which they have a common Jurisdiction;
with Introductory Treatises respecting Parties to Actions; Attor-
nies and Town Agents, their Qualifications, Rights, Duties,
Privileges and Disabilities; the Mode of Suing, whether in
Person or by Attorney, in Formâ Pauperis, &c. &c. &c.; and
an Appendix, containing the authorized Tables of Costs and
Fees, Forms of Proceedings and Writs of Execution. Third
Edition. By JOSEPH DIXON, of Lincoln's Inn, Esq., Barrister-
at-Law. 2 vols. 8vo. 46s. cloth.   1865

The Law and Facts of the Alabama Case with Reference
to the Geneva Arbitration. By JAMES O'DOWD, Esq., Barrister-
at-Law. 8vo. 2s. sewed.

Gray's Treatise on the Law of Costs in Actions and
other PROCEEDINGS in the Courts of Common Law at
Westminster. By JOHN GRAY, Esq., of the Middle Temple,
Barrister-at-Law. 8vo. 21s. cloth.   1853

Rules and Regulations to be observed in all Causes,
SUITS and PROCEEDINGS instituted in the Consistory Court
of London from and after the 26th June, 1877. By Order of
the Judge. Royal 8vo. 1s. sewed.

Pulling's Practical Compendium of the Law and Usage
of MERCANTILE ACCOUNTS; describing the various Rules
of Law affecting them, the ordinary mode in which they are
entered in Account Books, and the various Forms of Proceeding,
and Rules of Pleading, and Evidence for their Investigation at
Common Law, in Equity, Bankruptcy and Insolvency, or by
Arbitration. With a SUPPLEMENT, containing the Law of
Joint Stock Companies' Accounts, under the Winding-up Acts
of 1848 and 1849. By ALEXANDER PULLING, Esq., of the Inner
Temple, Barrister-at-Law. 12mo. 9s. boards.

Foreshore Rights. Report of Case of Williams v. Nicholson
for removing Shingle from the Foreshore at Withernsea. Heard
31st May, 1870, at Hull. 8vo. 1s. sewed.

Hamel's International Law.—International Law in con-
nexion with Municipal Statutes relating to the Commerce,
Rights and Liabilities of the Subjects of Neutral States pending
Foreign War; considered with reference to the Case of the
"Alexandra," seized under the provisions of the Foreign
Enlistment Act. By FELIX HARGRAVE HAMEL, of the Inner
Temple, Barrister-at-Law. Post 8vo. 3s. sewed.

Keyser on the Law relating to Transactions on the STOCK EXCHANGE. By HENRY KEYSER, Esq., of the Middle Temple, Barrister-at-Law. 12mo. 8s. cloth.

A Memoir of Lord Lyndhurst. By William Sidney GIBSON, Esq., M.A., F.S.A., Barrister-at-Law, of Lincoln's Inn. Second Edition, enlarged. 8vo. 2s. 6d. cloth.

The Laws of Barbados. (By Authority.) Royal 8vo. 21s. cl.

Pearce's History of the Inns of Court and Chancery; with Notices of their Ancient Discipline, Rules, Orders and Customs, Readings, Moots, Masques, Revels and Entertainments, including an account of the Eminent Men of the Four Learned and Honourable Societies—Lincoln's Inn, the Inner Temple, the Middle Temple, and Gray's Inn, &c. By ROBERT R. PEARCE, Esq., Barrister-at-Law. 8vo. 8s. cloth.

A Practical Treatise on the Law of Advowsons. By J. MIREHOUSE, Esq., Barrister-at-Law. 8vo. 14s. boards.

Williams' Introduction to the Principles and Practice of Pleading in the Superior Courts of Law, embracing an Outline of the whole Proceedings in an Action at Law, on Motion and at Judges'Chambers; together with the Rules of Pleading and Practice, and Forms of all the principal Proceedings. By WATKIN WILLIAMS, M.P., of the Inner Temple, Esq., Barrister-at-Law. 8vo. 12s. cloth.

The Lord's Table: its true Rubrical Position. The Purchas Judgment not reliable. The Power of the Laity and Churchwardens to prevent Romanizing. Suggestions to the Laity and Parishes for the due ordering of the Table at Communion Time. The Rubrical Position of the Celebrant. By H. F. NAPPER, Solicitor. 8vo. 1s. sewed.

Deane's Law of Blockade, as contained in the Judgments of Dr. Lushington and the Cases on Blockade decided during 1854. By J. P. DEANE, D.C.L..Advocate in Doctors'Commons. 8vo.10s.cl.

Linklater's Digest of and Index to the New Bankruptcy ACT, and the accompanying Acts of 1869. By JOHN LINKLATER, Solicitor. Second Edition. Imperial 8vo. 3s. 6d. sowed.

Pothier's Treatise on the Contract of Partnership. Translated from the French, with Notes, by O. D. TUDOR, Esq. Barrister-at-Law. 8vo. 5s. cloth.

Norman's Treatise on the Law and Practice relating to LETTERS PATENT for INVENTIONS. By JOHN PAXTON NORMAN, M.A., of the Inner Temple, Barrister-at-Law. Post 8vo. 7s. 6d. cloth.

Francillon's Law Lectures. Second Series. Lectures,
ELEMENTARY and FAMILIAR, on ENGLISH LAW. By
JAMES FRANCILLON, Esq., County Court Judge. First and
Second Series. 8vo. 8s. each, cloth.

Gurney's System of Short Hand, as used by both Houses
of Parliament. Seventeenth Edition, revised and improved.
12mo. 3s. 6d. cloth.
"Gurney's is, we believe, admitted to be the best of the many systems."—*Law Times.*

Gaches' Town Councillors and Burgesses Manual. The
TOWN COUNCILLORS AND BURGESSES MANUAL: a
popular Digest of Municipal and Sanitary Law, with informa-
tion as to Charters of Incorporation, and a useful Collection of
Forms, especially adapted for newly incorporated Boroughs.
By LOUIS GACHES, LL.M., B.A., of the Inner Temple, Esq.,
Barrister-at-Law. Post 8vo. 7s. cloth.

Hunter's Suit in Equity: An Elementary View of the
Proceedings in a Suit in Equity. With an Appendix of Forms.
By S. J. HUNTER, B.A., of Lincoln's Inn, Barrister-at-Law.
Sixth Edition, by G. W. LAWRANCE, M.A., Barrister-at-Law.
Post 8vo. 12s. cloth.

Parkinson's Handy-Book for the Common Law Judges'
CHAMBERS. By GEO. H. PARKINSON, Chamber Clerk to the
Hon. Mr. Justice Byles. 12mo. 7s. cloth.

A Treatise on the Law of Sheriff, with Practical Forms
and Precedents. By RICHARD CLARKE SEWELL, Esq., D.C.L.,
Barrister-at-Law, Fellow of Magdalen College, Oxford. 8vo. 1l. 1s.

Drainage of Land: How to procure Outfalls by New
Drains, or the Improvement of Existing Drains, in the Lands of
an Adjoining Owner, under the powers contained in Part III. of
the Act 24 & 25 Vict. c. 133, 1861; with Explanations of the Provisions, and Suggestions for the Guidance of Landowners, Occu-
piers, Land Agents and Surveyors. By J. WM. WILSON, Solicitor.

Fearne's Chart, Historical and Legigraphical, of Landed
Property in England, from the time of the Saxons to the present
Æra, displaying at one view the Tenures, Modes of Descent and
Power of Alienation of Lands in England at all times during that
Period. On a sheet, coloured, 6s.; on a roller, 8s.

The Ancient Land Settlement of England. A Lecture
delivered at University College, London, October 17th, 1871.
By J. W. WILLIS BUND, M.A., Professor of Constitutional Law
and History. 8vo. 1s. sewed.

Ecclesiastical Law.

The Case of the Rev. G. C. Gorham against the Bishop of Exeter, as heard and determined by the Judicial Committee of the Privy Council on appeal from the Arches Court of Canterbury. By EDWARD F. MOORE, M.A., Barrister-at-Law, Author of Moore's Privy Council Reports. Royal 8vo. 8s. cloth.

Coote's Practice of the Ecclesiastical Courts, with Forms and Tables of Costs. By HENRY CHARLES COOTE, Proctor in Doctors' Commons, &c. One thick vol. 8vo. 28s. boards.

Burder v. Heath. Judgment delivered on November 2, 1861, by the Right Honorable STEPHEN LUSHINGTON, D.C.L., Dean of the Arches. Folio, 1s. sewed.

The Law relating to Ritualism in the United Church of England and Ireland. By F. H. HAMEL, Esq., Barrister-at-Law. 12mo. 1s. sewed.

Archdeacon Hale's Essay on the Union between Church and STATE, and the Establishment by Law of the Protestant Reformed Religion in England, Ireland and Scotland. By W. H. HALE, M.A., Archdeacon of London. 8vo. 1s. sewed.

Judgment of the Privy Council in the Case of Hebbert v. Purchas. Edited by EDWARD Bullock, of the Inner Temple, Barrister-at-Law. Royal 8vo. 2s. 6d.

Judgment delivered by Right Hon. Lord Cairns on behalf of the Judicial Committee of the Privy Council in the Case of Martin v. Mackonochie. Edited by W. ERNST BROWNING, Esq., Barrister-at-Law. Royal 8vo. 1s. 6d. sewed.

Judgment of the Right Hon. Sir Robert J. Phillimore, Official Principal of the Court of Arches, with Cases of Martin v. Mackonochie and Flamank v. Simpson. Edited by WALTER G. F. PHILLIMORE, B.A., of the Middle Temple, &c. Second Edition, royal 8vo. 2s. 6d. sewed.

The Judgment of the Dean of the Arches. also the Judg-ment of the PRIVY COUNCIL, in Liddell (clerk) and Horne and others against Westerton, and Liddell (clerk) and Park and Evans against Beal. Edited by A. F. BAYFORD, LL.D. Royal 8vo. 3s. 6d. sewed.

The Case of Long v. Bishop of Cape Town, embracing the opinions of the Judges of Colonial Court hitherto unpublished, together with the decision of the Privy Council, and Preliminary Observations by the Editor. Royal 8vo. 6s. sewed.

The Law of the Building of Churches, Parsonages and Schools, and of the Division of Parishes and Places—continued to 1874. By CHARLES FRANCIS TROWER, M.A., Barrister-at-Law. Post 8vo. 9s. cloth.

The History and Law of Church Seats or Pews. By A. HEALES, F.S.A., Proctor in Doctors' Commons. 2 vols. 8vo. 16s. cl.

PREPARING FOR PUBLICATION.

Clerke and Brett's Conveyancing Act, 1882, with the Rules, Orders and Fees under the Solicitors' Remuneration Act, 1881. In 1 vol. post 8vo.

Macaskie on Law of Bills of Sale, including the Act of 1882. In 1 vol. post 8vo.

Underhill's The Settled Land Act, 1882. In 1 vol. post 8vo.

Baxter's Corporation Acts. In 1 vol. cr. 8vo.

Baxter's Judicature Acts. Fifth Edition, in 1 vol. post 8vo.

Hertslet's Treaties, Vol. 15. In 1 vol. 8vo.

Law Examination Journal, No. 53, Michaelmas, 1882.

Clifford and Rickards' Referees Reports. Vol. III. Part 2.

Bedford's Preliminary (Solicitors) Questions and Answers. No. 53, for October, 1882.

Imprinted at London,
nvmber Seuen in Flete strete within Temple barre,
whylom the signe of the Hande and starre,
and the Hovse where liued Richard Tottel,
printer by Special patentes of the bokes of the Common lawe
in the seueral reigns of
Kng Edw. VI. and of the qvenes Marye and Elizabeth.

RICHARD ✠ TOTTEL

1553—1882.

www.ingramcontent.com/pod-product-compliance
Lightning Source LLC
Chambersburg PA
CBHW032258280326
41932CB00009B/611